W9-ADR-778

When We Walked Above the Clouds

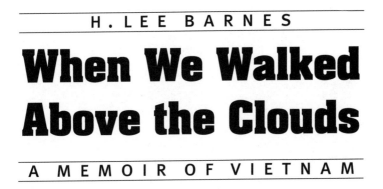

H . LEE BARNES

When We Walked Above the Clouds

A MEMOIR OF VIETNAM

UNIVERSITY OF NEBRASKA PRESS LINCOLN & LONDON

Library of Congress Cataloging-in-Publication Data
Barnes, H. Lee, 1944–
When we walked above the clouds: a memoir of Vietnam /
H. Lee Barnes.
p. cm.
ISBN 978-0-8032-3448-2 (cloth: alk. paper)
1. Barnes, H. Lee, 1944– 2. Vietnam War, 1961–1975—
Personal narratives, American. 3. Vietnam War,
1961–1975—Commando operations—United States.
I. Title.
DS559.5.B375 2011
959.704'38—dc22
[B]   2011011180

Set in Sabon by Bob Reitz.

Dedicated to the memories of John P. Fewell,
Donald "Jake" Jacobsen, Earl "Brownie" Brown,
and Elmer "Joe" Reifschneider. Killed in action, Binh Hoa,
Tra Bong District, Vietnam, January 22, 1966
—*De Oppresso Liber*

PROLOGUE

Forty years later you're sitting across a desk from a psychologist wondering if you'll ever be able to sleep an entire night and if you can find some way to trust people. He asks if nightmares about the war keep you awake. You tell him, as you have before, that you don't have nightmares about it, that you don't have to because whenever your mind is not otherwise occupied, you return to 'Nam and rerun events like disconnected scenes in a trailer from a Hollywood movie—a hundred eighty frames in three seconds and gone. You can't remember names of colleagues you've met at the college or topics covered at the last department meeting or tender words that you once exchanged with a lover, but you can remember with absolute clarity the captain turning a corner in a trench and telling you to shed your gear, that you won't be going. And you can remember the rain, the way it plunged to the ground at a sharp angle, the way it popped on your poncho hood, the way it cut rivulets into the red clay, the way it shriveled the skin on your hands and numbed your fingers. The therapist understands, not because he's experienced it, but because he's heard it from hundreds, it or something similar. Meds help with the anxiety, he tells you. But when you close your eyes you see the beetle, and it's got nothing to do with goddamn anxiety. Nor is it fiction. And that's sad, because fiction is what you best understand; it's what you make bank on, but you can't flip that beetle into fiction and do it the same justice.

He schedules another appointment and leads you to the reception desk where the date for the meeting is logged in a computer and a woman hands you a printout and smiles. She smiles in that accommodating way because she's wondering if you're one of the dangerous ones. She sees them five days a week and needs that smile to help her make it to the weekend. You walk between the rows of chairs where vets, some sad beyond words that define sadness, wait their turns, then you go on your way, carrying with you the secret, and return to that normal world where you keep your secret close to the breast, as you must, for no one outside the therapist or those who were in 'Nam can possibly understand.

In that normal world that's anything but normal, you sit in a classroom occupied by a couple of dozen men and women, colleagues who have never killed or been asked to kill or asked to risk their lives or plucked a leech from their leg or seen a body slammed backward to the ground by a force as powerful as you imagine the hand of God to be. And you hunker under a shell of pretense, pretending it's all fine, pretending that this supposed normal life is normal for you as well.

The fiction I write isn't about me or anything I actually did in Vietnam; still, at lectures and the readings I've given, people draw on their particular assumptions and gather that I base the stories on my experiences. Some ask if I was purging myself, as if writing is some kind of art-as-therapy exercise, as if by turning the war into fiction, I stave off the lions of the past. On those occasions, I want to say, Vietnam is the only thing in my life that isn't fiction. I want to tell the guy that the BMW he drove up in is fiction and the leather jacket he wears with Harley-Davidson written on the back is fiction, as is his thirty-year-old trophy wife. I want to tell him that he's the main character in his own work of fiction, and he's living it, and that is his happy story and it's a pretty pretense. Instead,

I answer that the stories are raw imagination. The past isn't. I leave it at that.

My story is this: Though I served in combat, I did nothing I view as extraordinary, just what the mission demanded. Then I returned, took work here in the World, which was what we called America, and submerged myself in the tedium of daily life, just a faceless veteran among the working stiffs, measuring life as people do—food in, food out; air in, air out. At unpredictable times some memory of the war would pop into my head; then, as quickly as possible, I diverted my thoughts to some pressing matter in the present. Stay busy, I told myself, don't slow down, appreciate the life you've got, and whenever I reflected on Tra Bong, I mostly pictured the men who died. On occasion, I would wonder what happened to those who survived, especially Pablo and Richard, but I never thought to trace them. Leave the past to the past.

With all the narratives that were passed around explaining Vietnam, I became inured to my own experience. We experience the world in color but tend to see ideas in black and white, and Vietnam had become in the popular imagination an idea, on the grand scale a measurement of military and political failure and how future international policies should or would be implemented. It became a line in the sand that divided liberals and conservatives, a point of debate, a metaphor, a tapestry that symbolized loss, and a black well where America's miscalculations were drowned, resuscitated, and drowned all over again. It became the dark half of the narrative that defined my generation, the generation of sex, drugs, and rock and roll. No single story measured up to any of the grand notions it'd become.

My story couldn't measure up to the grander narrative. But the truth is that since returning to the World, I'd lived like a man driving a freeway on two bald tires waiting for one or both to blow out, and that story I'd not written, and had cautiously avoided, was behind it. Being a fiction writer, I probably have a good deal more insight into the characters I create than I have into myself. I knew what happened in Vietnam shaped my attitudes and deeply affected how I viewed others. Maybe shame or the desire to shed guilt is so strong a human impulse that we block out how a particular moment or incident has affected us. Or perhaps time merely bleaches out the color of our memories so we view the past in black and white. The events that shaped us become small ideas that singularly have little meaning.

I was determined to write about anything other than Vietnam. I had other stories to write. But though I was through with it, Vietnam wasn't through with me. In 2000 that history I'd avoided intruded unexpectedly in the form of an online message from Aaron "Gritz" Gritzmacher, who asked if I was the Barnes who'd served with him at Tra Bong. He said that he and others had been looking for me for more than a decade. Later that year four of us who served at Tra Bong reunited, dug through the past, and reconnected, in the process realizing that we had been more than teammates, that we had been comrades in arms, good soldiers who shared an uncommon history—and friends. They suggested I write the story of Tra Bong. I placated them for a time with excuses, until finally Gritz and Pablo exhorted me enough times that five years later I wrote the first tentative lines.

For nearly a year the narrative moved forward but seemed to go nowhere. It just wouldn't take shape. I was about to abandon the project when in a telephone conversation Gritz resurrected a piece of the past that I'd forgotten, something I'd buried in my subconscious. We were recalling a patrol we'd taken into the highlands when he interrupted me and in a few brief words cast what amounted to a killing stone. No,

I insisted, I didn't remember. I wouldn't have suggested *that*. I was a good soldier. Did I really? And then I remembered. We were west of Tra Bong on a two-day walk with Holman in charge. It was night, a few feet separating us, where we lay in an open area surrounded by tall trees. I recalled the sounds of insects and a cold rage filling my chest. Then as the details returned to me, I knew that I had suggested precisely what he claimed I had.

Your colleague across the hall asks how you're doing. It's perfunctory. He doesn't really care because he actually wants to talk about himself. You tell him that if your life was any more boring, it would be his. He laughs and asks where you heard that, thinks you're quoting W. C. Fields or someone famous. But you're not. It's pure you, but he doesn't believe you because he doesn't know you. No one here does. You walk into the classroom and see the anxious faces, the bored faces, the earnest faces. They are young, as you once were, and untouched and untouched and so damned untouched, even the most cynical among them, and so wise in their youth that they all have it all figured out. You wonder, were you that much different? You begin the session with a discussion of Frank O'Connor's "Guests of a Nation." You will lead them in time to understand that he's writing about the terrible master called duty and how acquiescing to it can make a man a stranger unto himself, but first you have to make them see the horror of the event and you have to do it without discussing the dark spot on your own soul.

ACKNOWLEDGMENTS

I wish to express my gratitude to my former teammates Richard Norwood, Aaron Gritzmacher, Pablo Olivarez, Paul Sheppard, Cam Gamble, and Henry Luthy. Though this is a memoir, without them and their contributions, portions of this book would never exist. I extend my thanks also to my friends Mary Sojourner, Bill Brannon, and Deke Castleman, whose keen eyes and criticism were invaluable. Additional thanks go to Lilo Bayati for her support. Last, no book exists without an editor and publisher seeing its worth and championing it through the lengthy process to publication. My thanks go out to Heather Lundine and the staff of the University of Nebraska Press.

When We Walked Above the Clouds

ONE

In midsummer of '63 the outside buzzer to my apartment rang. I'd worked until late at the press preparing layouts for the camera. I lived alone and no one ever came to see me, so I figured it was someone wanting another apartment and mistakenly pushing the button to my buzzer. It had happened before. I lay back. The bell rang again, this time insistently. I awoke and half asleep slipped on jeans and shirt and tottered into the foyer. Mal stood outside the glass door at the end of the hall. He waved and motioned me outside.

Since my moving out the year before I'd rarely seen him or Mother, and neither had ever visited my apartment, or for that matter shown any interest in what or how I was doing, so his showing up was more than just an oddity. It was early afternoon and the temperature in the high nineties. He paced the sidewalk beside their lime-green minibus. Tied under a nylon tarp atop the Volkswagen were bags and boxes packed with household goods. I knew the gypsy ritual from the dozen moves we'd made over the years. He didn't have to state the obvious, but he did.

"We're moving. I start a new job on Monday," he said.

Mother sat in front with George, two years old and squirming about on her lap. I asked where they were moving.

"Las Vegas. We stopped to see if you wanted to come along."

I looked inside. An array of boxes, suitcases, along with Mickey, David, Deborah, and Scooter, the dachshund, pretty well filled up the rear. What remained for me was a two-foot-square space on the floor. Deborah rocked back and forth in the seat, and already the boys were sweating and anxious. Soon enough they would be riotous. Even without them along it would unbearable inside in the un-air-conditioned vw. I felt sorriest for the dog.

"No room," I said.

Mal said, "We thought you could take Mickey and David in your Renault."

"Mickey and David?" I looked at Mother.

She seemed not to care one way or the other. I noticed a front corner of the tarp was held down by a knot that was sure to slip. The tarp would flap until it broke open, and everything on top would spill somewhere on the highway on their godforsaken drive.

Mal said, "And we can pack some of this in your car and . . ."

"We need to retie that," I said, pointing to the tarp.

"I didn't have help." He smiled, the gold crown on his left premolar showing.

"I told you I heard something up there, Mal," Mother said.

I loosened the rope, then he and I lifted off the boxes and suitcases and set them on the concrete. We pulled on opposite sides of the tarp until it was taut, then replaced the load and folded the ends and corners snugly over the package. I ran the rope through the stays and secured it with a triple clove hitch, after which I tugged on the edges from several angles until convinced it would hold.

"You aren't going to go, are you?" Mal said.

Mom said, "He's in college. Thinks he's too good."

"Now, Mother," Mal said. He'd addressed her as "Mother" since Mickey was born.

"That's right, Mom," I said. "I'm in college."

Mother, Mal, and I had a long trail of bad history behind us; still, I shook his hand and wished them good luck. Then I stuck my head inside the driver's window and said good-bye to Mom and the kids. She wouldn't look at me.

As Mal pulled the minibus away from the curb, the full

pathos of their lives struck me for the first time—two weak people who loved but loved inadequately, whose lives would always seem unfulfilled, but who would pretend otherwise. They faced a journey across two deserts in the heat of summer to another strange city where they would eke out a living, Mal broadcasting news from a soundproof room for a pittance, Mom serving food at a restaurant for union wages and tips. I'd been angry at them for a long while. A portion of it dissipated, and something inside me shifted. I felt as if I'd been cut free of a dragline.

I returned to my apartment. Instead of napping, I opened *The Pastures of Heaven* and read the first three stories.

To see me that summer, blond, healthy, tanned, you might think me just another kid, even the kid next door. But I wasn't and never had been. My childhood had been immeasurably unhappy. Its details rekindle the stories of tens of thousands of unhappy stepchildren. Mal was Mom's third husband, the only son of a genteel woman who sent him off to military school, where he was shaped not into the gentleman she'd expected but an angry young man who married young, had a son, divorced, went to war, and became an army officer.

After his leaving the army in Colorado Springs, we traveled the points of the compass in Mal's gypsy quest to find the ideal position as a radio or television announcer, each job proving as disappointing as the last. I don't recall his ever having a friend or anything one would call a social life. I, the boy stepchild, became the target of his bitterness. Confused and insecure, stuck in a shuttle box of humiliation and punishment, I endured abuse the way kids in my circumstance did: I found safety in the virtues of silence and invisibility, learned to never ask for or expect anything, especially privilege.

Confidence is strong magic. It gives power to its possessor. It was a magic denied me at home, where I aspired to being a B-minus boy. Being above just average was nonthreatening, and achieving it took little effort. Mother and Mal, who produced four children from their union, seemed content when I managed at least a B-minus. After all, what could be wrong with being slightly above average? It earned me no rewards, but it brought me no punishment, which I considered a reward.

The one area I had confidence in was fighting. It gave me a place to cast a shadow. No matter where we moved, I encountered bullies determined to humiliate me, the new kid. I didn't take well to bullying. I received enough of that at home. My fuse was short, my hands quick, and I hated bullies. At any sign of a threat, I struck and didn't stop until I'd won or was too exhausted to go on. Even fights I lost or that ended in draws left an impression on my antagonists. None ever wanted a rematch. I wore bruises as a badge of honor.

Tolstoy wrote that "every unhappy family is unhappy in its own way," which applied to mine to the extent that my parents were impulsive and unreasonable, and their views of punishment skirted the grotesque. My older sister reminded me a few years ago of an incident that took place in Butte, Montana, when I was six years old and Mal caught me playing with matches. Claiming it was for my own good, he held my hand over a lit burner on a gas stove. As Mother sat at the kitchen table and watched, he turned up the flame. Though I begged him to let go, he didn't stop until I, in tears, screamed and went limp. I'd blocked out the memory for well over fifty years until Jenny brought it up. Then I remembered it vividly.

Until we were in our teens, neither Jenny nor I knew Mother was an alcoholic, the binge-drinking variety who awoke the morning after with a pounding headache and a rancorous tongue. In rage, she demanded absolute silence in a household with young children, and when she didn't get silence, she lashed out at us with whatever was handy, be it belt or hairbrush or hanger. Other times she was an agitated recovering alcoholic who'd sit for hours cutting and matching cloth to patterns or bent over her sewing machine, tapping her foot to the starter, the whir of its electric motor offering her temporary respite. There were rare periods of grace for her, times when perhaps driven by guilt, she seemed if not joyful, at least generous and spontaneous, giving me money to go to a movie or taking me shopping for school clothes or to a drive-in and treating me to a hamburger.

Mal, on the other hand, wasn't a drinker. His mood, manner, and rules, and especially his enforcement of them, were consistent—no elbows on the table, no laughter or cross conversations at dinner, no running in the house, no joy expressed, ever. He belittled most anything I said or did and enforced silence at meals by rapping me in the head with the knuckle on his middle finger.

Ever since I could remember, debt held a choke hold on the family. Jenny, my older sister, married and moved out when I was fourteen. At the time Mother and Mal both worked, he the night shift as a broadcaster, she as a waitress on the late shift. As eldest, I took on the role of unpaid servant to my little brothers and sister. From that time on until I left home at eighteen, I woke up at dawn or before, cooked breakfast for my younger brothers and Deborah, washed dishes, rode the bus or walked to school, then returned, usually walking home after football or track practice, and prepared dinner. I mowed and weeded the lawn, vacuumed carpets, mopped floors, scrubbed toilets, washed and hung laundry, and performed general household repairs. When George, the youngest, was born, I was relegated to changing and cleaning dirty diapers as well. At night, if not too exhausted, I studied. More often than not, I was too exhausted. A B-minus was just too easy to get and sleep too hard to come by.

I was seventeen before I ever had a girlfriend. She broke

my heart soon after graduation. I liked the way she parted her hair from the top and combed the strands back so they looked like wings. I'd loved her painfully, labeled it love for lack of a word adequate enough to define the feelings. The ache that followed our breakup went deep and stayed there. Afterward I never talked about her with anyone, never even mentioned her name, but I remembered moments vividly, tracing the contours of her face with the back of my fingers as the two of us lay in the pale moonlight on her parents' backyard lawn, her unbuttoning the top buttons of her blouse, loosening her bra strap, and guiding my hand to her breast. Her soft hair shined in the thin moonlight.

Like her hair, her voice was soft, but it grew big and shined when she sang. On occasion I accompanied her to a house downtown where she took voice lessons. I sat in an alcove, thumbing through a *Time* or *Life* and listening to her warm up, trilling scales to the accompaniment of a piano, until she turned loose her gift. The largeness of her coloratura voice reaching a high E-flat belied the soft whispers she sometimes laid on my throat.

Lela — on evenings when we couldn't be together, we parked ourselves on the phone wasting words on nothing important. During melancholy silences we listened to each other's breathing and longed for something more. In the background her mother nagged her to get off the phone. The two of us dragged out good-byes and reluctantly cradled the receivers. The empty line was painful, as painful as the bigger truth: a voice such as hers required someone unlike me. Her talent could allow nothing less, and I was a B-minus student. After graduation we broke up.

At eighteen I bolted from home and got a job. With no money set aside for college, I was on my own, struggling but determined to succeed. The job kept me afloat and paid enough that I could enroll in college. I moved into a studio apartment within walking distance of the campus and completed a semester at Texas Western with a B-minus average. Above average again, my standard as a student and athlete throughout high school. That summer I enrolled for another full load in the fall semester. The printing house paid a only few cents above minimum hourly wage. My paycheck went toward rent, car payment, insurance, tuition, books, and a beer or four after work in Juárez once or twice a week. I had no television, no radio, no clock, no dishes, no phone. I drove an aging Renault Dauphin with a contentious four-banger and a three-speed shifter. After a few months the manager advanced me from making plates for the press to a position as an apprentice layout artist. New job, same pay.

The pressure of full-time work and studies got to me, but it was the nights that found me in Juárez seated on a stool at the El Submarino, a Cruz Blanca in hand, that led to my downfall. Hungover or not, I awoke early in the morning, attended classes, and ground out the assignments, relying on my solid history of being above average to skin out a nominal B-minus and get me through the semester and the next and the next. That was my plan.

All the while a war was smoldering in Southeast Asia, the exotic land I'd first heard of reading *Terry and the Pirates* comics.

TWO

In August my plans hit the skids. It didn't appear I was doing much better in my late teens than I had as a child. Henry Ostuse, the general manager of Sun Publishing, moved me to day-shift work and cut back my hours, the landlord raised the rent from thirty to thirty-six dollars, and the Renault suffered vapor locks. Then I had to replace a fuel pump, that followed by the battery and rear tires. I didn't have enough to pay fall tuition. My friend Randy Villarreal convinced his reluctant father to let me move, rent free, into a room in their house on Magoffin Street, the idea being that it would help me save for tuition and books. I reported my change of status and address to the draft board, hoping that in five months I could register for classes and get my deferment reinstated.

The house on Magoffin was a Victorian-style two-story with a gabled roof built back in a time when the street was home to El Paso's elite. It'd fallen into disrepair and needed paint on the outside walls and plaster on the inside. Mr. Villarreal, a salty World War II veteran and typesetter for the *El Paso Sun*, lived downstairs. On nights off he pursued his hobbies, drinking whiskey and reading books. Randy, Kirit Travidi, a student from India, and I slept upstairs. On the five nights a week Mr. Villarreal prepared pages for the morning edition, Randy, Kirit, and I played chess and argued politics, or took the bridge over to Juárez and exercised being young and stupid. We ate lunch and dinner at Rosa's on the corner west of the house. Rosa prepared homemade Mexican meals, and her attractive daughter Carmina, who was infatuated with Randy, served tables. Occasionally on Mr. Villarreal's nights off, the four of us packed ourselves in my Renault and went to Carlos's Mex-Tex in Juárez for a thick cut of unbled Mexican steak.

I saved a dollar here and there, enough that by October it appeared I would be able to pay for spring tuition and books. Then, the first week in October, the Renault caught fire in the middle of the night. The insurance settlement was enough to pay it off, but I was left afoot.

A week later one of the salesmen who peddled space in the *Sun Shopper*, a paper we published, came in the art department, red faced and screaming at me over a layout he'd ordered. Everyone stopped working and stared. He slammed his fist down on my composition board and demanded to know what I was going to do about his losing an account. He pointed to the sketch of a woman holding a handbag and the cost underneath it. "It's supposed to be sixteen!" he shouted. I told him I had a copy somewhere of the order as it had been originally written up, and it said six dollars. He said he didn't care what I had and that he would have me fired. This was the third time since I'd been working in the art room I'd witnessed him threaten someone. I stood, faced him squarely, and said, "Go fuck yourself." Then I punched out on the time clock.

When I told them what I had done, Randy laughed, Kirit told me I'd made a terrible mistake, but Mr. Villarreal, who'd been distant prior to that, congratulated me and offered to take us all to dinner at the Mex-Tex. Over the meal he confirmed what Randy once told me, that while in the army he'd been awarded a Bronze Star. He didn't elaborate. Something in his matter-of-fact tone said that it was true. Later, across the table in the kitchen into the late hours, he nursed a glass of whiskey and talked about the vagaries of life. He told me he'd come home from the war and married Randy's mother and she'd left him when Randy was a toddler, ran off with another man.

"An Irish woman," he said. "Ran off with another man. She was a tramp."

I recalled my feelings upon hearing that Lela, my high school steady, had taken up with Jay Lofton immediately after our breakup. I said, "I'm sorry."

"Why?"

"Well, I'm just sorry she did that."

"Really? Huh, I'm not."

He left and returned with the latest book he'd been reading and laid it on the table between us. I looked at the title, *To Kill a Mockingbird*. He drank and talked, and I listened to a good but embittered man speak of the disenfranchised, of America as a place of unfairness and restricted opportunities. He claimed the United States had stolen the Southwest from Mexico in an illegal war and confessed to his being a socialist sympathetic to the higher ideals of communism. He asked if hearing that about him bothered me. I lied and said that it didn't.

"What happened to you at work doesn't surprise me," he said. "What surprised me is you standing up the way you did." Even he sensed that I was satisfied to settle for above average.

"It surprised me, too."

"I'll tell you something. I don't love this country like people expect I should, and I only went to war because I had to. My family was in Texas before Americans came, but all I am to America is a wetback, a beaner. Hell, I don't even speak with an accent and . . . Well, here's to you." He lifted his drink and downed a swallow, then poured himself three fingers in the glass and pushed the book toward me. "Read it. Hell, read everything."

Nineteen and I felt good about what I'd done until I started looking for work. The other printing houses in El Paso were small, mostly one- or two-man operations. No one needed help. Then the first week of November my life changed when a letter arrived in the mail.

It was midafternoon, windy, overcast, and chilly. I sat on a bench in San Jacinto Plaza, thinking how much prettier our lives would be if only we could orchestrate them. I held the letter from the draft board. I'd spent five years as an army brat, waking up to a bugle sounding reveille and going to sleep after taps announced the fall of day. I knew what I had to do. I just had to accept it.

A commotion erupted on the sidewalk south of the plaza where a cluster of people scrambled about, popping balloons. On the top floor of the Hotel Del Norte two men and a woman in formal dress dangled bundles of brightly colored balloons out of a window. The clutches of balloons danced in the chill breeze. The crowd on the sidewalk shouted up. A few balloons came down, some bouncing off the outside walls of the hotel. People in the penthouse opened a second window and hollered down to the sidewalk. The three of them held strings tied to balloons. They let go, and the balloons cascaded down.

Other pedestrians rushed to the hotel sidewalk. Some held their hands up and waved dollar bills at those looking down, but when it became apparent most balloons contained no money, the gathering got ugly. People on the sidewalk shouted curses to those above. Those looking down jeered and peppered the others with insults. Then the windows closed.

A few lingered, looking up and cursing, until a police car turned the corner and cruised by. When the gathering dissolved, I wadded up the letter, dumped it in the trash, and walked two blocks to the main post office. Inside, I found the glass door with lettering that read "Army Recruiting Office." I cracked open the door and peered in. The sergeant seated at the desk looked up and smiled.

"Come in."

THREE

Before Mr. Villarreal left for his shift at the newspaper, I thanked him for his kindness. He shook off the thanks, said I had been as much trouble as he'd expected, then took my hand. He said he hoped I didn't get myself killed, but Vietnam was just a small war and was likely to end before I would be sent there. He picked up the brown bag containing his lunch. "If you do go, don't expect anyone to be grateful."

I packed a toothbrush and a change of clothes in my one suitcase, and Randy, Kirit, and I ate at Rosa's for the last time. My friends were asleep when the recruiter drove up to the curb and honked the horn. I'd been waiting downstairs building up a store of adrenaline for the coming ride to the train. I clutched my bag and hurried outside before he honked again. He stood beside the olive-drab sedan, holding open the passenger door. I set the suitcase in the backseat. It was cold, and despite a minor earthquake rumbling in my bowels, the warm air blowing from the heater felt good.

The other inductees, mostly draftees, waited at the train station. We boarded just past one in the morning, our departure timed so Uncle Sam didn't have to pay for feeding us but two meals while en route to Fort Polk. Joaquin, a draftee from El Segundo Barrio, home ground for the notorious El Paso street gangs, took a seat next to me. He adopted me for the trip and talked about how he'd thought about ignoring the draft notice and hiding in Juárez. I slept off and on as the train rumbled east from El Paso across the state, stopping in Midland and Fort Worth and finally in Beaumont, where I stepped off to stretch and urinate. For the first time in my life, I saw whites-only signs at the entrances to the public toilets and above drinking fountains. I was a westerner, where bigotry existed but signs didn't proclaim it. I drank from one of the fountains that said whites only, then from one that said colored to check if the water tasted different and in a small way to defy centuries of ignorance.

A few hours later the train rolled into Leesville, and I knew I was in the army because I and the others were immediately transformed into shit heads as a man in fatigues shouted for us to board the waiting bus. I took a window seat and sat staring dull-eyed at the flat, pine-carpeted land as it lay under a gray sky. Joaquin swung into the seat next to me and tapped a cigarette out of a pack. He placed it between his lips, then held the pack in front of me and offered me one. I thanked him but said I didn't smoke. As Joaquin fished around in his trouser pockets, a sergeant stood at the front of the bus holding onto a pole with one hand. The driver meshed the gears, and the bus jerked to life.

The NCO said, "Okay, shit heads, listen up to ol' Willaford. I'm your boss for a week, then all of you head to a basic training company where the cadre will try and make you soldiers. For one week, if you don't cause me no grief, we'll get along."

Staff Sergeant Willaford was a stubby black man with a round, pleasant face and deep-set eyes. He scanned the bus front to back, nodded a few times as if approving of what he saw. Then Joaquin lit his cigarette and stuck the lighter back in his pocket. Willaford's gaze landed on him. He walked to our seat and looked down at Joaquin. "Who told you to light up?"

Joaquin looked to his left and behind him, then to the front of the bus. He looked everywhere he could, but up. He shrugged and said, "No one."

"Then put it out, shit head."

Joaquin dropped it on the floor of the bus and stubbed it underfoot.

"Not that way. You do not make messes in Uncle Sam's bus. Do you understand?"

Joaquin, who would later assault a training sergeant with a knife and receive a prompt court-martial, bent over and picked up the butt.

"Do all of you understand? You smoke when I say. You shit or piss when I say. You talk when I say. Do you understand?"

We nodded as one.

Willaford shook his head in dismay. "Don't nod at me. When I ask a question, that's the same as telling you it's time to talk. Do you understand?"

As one we answered, "Yes, sir," and were promptly lectured on the protocol of calling officers "sir" and noncoms "sergeant." He walked to the front and took a seat behind the driver.

I heard Fort Polk once described as the only place in America where you can hike over a hill in the midst of a blizzard as sand blows in your face and mosquitoes feed on your blood. Everything I saw outside the window—the flatness of the landscape, the clusters of stocky pine, the black slush at the edge of the road from a recent snow—confirmed the description. No wonder Willaford seemed angry. He'd been assigned to Fort Polk.

That week would have been the same story all soldiers experience in the early phases of indoctrination, but it took a strange turn on November 22 when the president was assassinated in Dallas. Willaford marched us to the temporary billets and told us we were restricted to quarters. A gloom fell over the barracks as Fort Polk was placed on lockdown. We spent the next two days in a state of sadness and anticipation as rumors dominated the barracks. We were at war with Russia. Troops were on the way to invade Cuba. The communist Chinese were behind the plot because of America's involvement in Southeast Asia.

Then the lockdown was lifted, and the details of events following the assassination turned even more surreal. We were informed that the man who'd killed Kennedy had been arrested and was himself killed while in custody. Enemies were everywhere, outside and within our borders.

We were shipped to Golf Company. Upon our arrival, the cadre mustered us in the center of the company compound. First Sergeant Spencer mounted the steps leading to the back of the mess hall and told us to stand at ease. He was a Kentucky Colonel type, square jawed, with a gaze that drilled its way into a soldier's head.

"Welcome to Golf Company, you sorry sacks of civilian shit. I wanna make certain you know that this is not your mommy's house. If you don't like it here, I could care less. If you don't like the army, I could care less. If you want out, I could care less. But the only way you'll get out is with an undesirable or dishonorable discharge, which means you'll become an even sorrier sack of civilian shit when you go home. And no one will have any respect for you. The rest of you, we'll make into soldiers somehow. Do I make myself clear?"

"Yes, sergeant!" we shouted.

"I can't hear you, ladies," he said. "Sound off like you got balls."

We shouted ourselves hoarse before he finally heard us. He offered up a few more words of encouragement, telling us that he and his cadre intended to kick our "asses into shape" and make us into men, despite our obvious lack of male genitalia. Then he turned us over to the callous mothering of half a dozen snarly NCOs under whose screaming instructions we would begin shedding a little of our civilian selves each day.

Our commanding officer was Captain Anderson, a recent graduate of Ranger training and a mustang who'd served in the Eighty-second and the Eleventh Airbornes as an enlisted man. The captain often joined our morning runs and led us in cadence, shouting, "Just three things I wanna be, airborne, Ranger, infantry!" I'd enlisted to go airborne, primarily for the jump pay, and the captain on those runs gave me a taste of what was ahead.

My introduction to the captain came the day after I served my first tour on KP. A former airman named Blassingame who boasted of himself as the "Steel Man from the Steel Town" went berserk when I dumped some trash from the dining hall in the kitchen trash can. He was at the sink scrubbing a pot when he wheeled about and shouted that I had my own trash can. He grabbed my shirt and pulled at my collar. I told him to let go and pushed his hand away. I didn't want to fight and told him so. We'd been warned about fighting during indoctrination. Truth was I was scared, not of him, but consequences I might face under the Code of Conduct for fighting.

He doubled his hand into a fist and caught me below the cheekbone. As I landed, I broke my fall with my hands and gazed up from the floor. He stood, fists clenched, daring me to get up. He didn't know my history with bullies. Before he realized it, I was on my feet, tossing punches as he backpedaled toward the sink. Others on duty pulled us apart.

In the morning Sergeant Spencer summoned me to the commander's office, where the captain reprimanded me. The captain warned that he would be keeping an eye on me, and in an odd twist he gave Blassingame a position as acting platoon leader in charge of Second Platoon, the barracks next to the one my platoon occupied. He saw in Blassingame a man of intimidating size with prior military service who would scare the hell out of us recruits and keep us in line. I saw another bully getting by without punishment.

Midway through the cycle, the sergeants mustered us at midmorning on the company grounds. First Sergeant Spencer arrived a few minutes later and told us to take a seat. With him was a sergeant first class, dressed in starched fatigues with razor creases in his trousers and sleeves, on his head a green beret and on his chest jump wings. He eyed us as if searching out the ones who had potential. He couldn't weigh more than 140 pounds, but something in the way he carried himself hinted that his 140-pound frame housed a stud of a soldier.

"Gentlemen," he said in a carefully inflected, slow southern accent, "I'm Sgt. Jimmy Easter, and I'm here to tell you about an opportunity to serve with the finest unit in the military. If you're the kind who likes a challenge, take a look at what your sergeants are passing around. It's not for everyone. And we don't want everyone, just the best among you."

The cadre passed out literature that described a unit that specialized in unconventional warfare, each soldier an expert in one combat specialty while skilled in at least two others. I looked at the glossy-colored pictures of men paddling an inflated raft in swamp water, others rappelling down cliffs, a few parachuting in a cloudless sky. He gave us a twenty-minute pitch about the elite unit and asked if we had any questions and if any of us thought we could make the grade. I liked the idea of being one among the best. I was done with being above average. Equally important was the answer to another question. I raised my hand.

"Do men in Special Forces pull KP?"

"No."

His reply was the kind of white lie parents tell children to placate them, but that lie, his pitch, and the pictures in the brochure determined my decision. I signed my name to a form, and that afternoon some fifty of us, from my company and others, including my buddy Batterham from New Orleans, took a battery of written tests that would be the first step toward earning a green beret. Of those who took the tests, I was the only one in the room whose scores qualified him to go on to the next phase. One out of fifty was just the start. Ahead were innumerable tests. Being average and above average wouldn't suffice. I was determined to earn that beret.

As we progressed through training, I excelled at all of the phases and gained more and more confidence as the cycle neared the end. The final proficiency test was a physical training course. The captain wanted his company to score the highest in the training battalion. The cadre drilled us relentlessly. I finished first in the mile run and the forty-yard crawl and scored second-highest overall in the company. Had it not been for points lost on the grenade throw, I would have scored highest. That second-place finish contributed in small measure to Golf Company's recording the best overall score in the training cycle within the battalion. It gained me a reluctant "congratulations" from the company commander, who remembered me only as the brawler he had dressed down in his office.

FOUR

A sergeant who'd served a tour in Okinawa once said that when you flunk hell, you're assigned to Fort Bragg. Combined with Fayetteville, service there motivated more than a few to volunteer for 'Nam. When there was no rain, the air was one part oxygen, five parts dust, and when it rained, the air was reduced to four parts dust, one part mud. The place was acres of rolling hills, green parade fields, barracks and buildings painted baby-shit yellow, firing ranges, and stunted pine trees that dropped cones winter, spring, and fall. It was home of miserable weather, the Eighty-second Airborne,

airborne spit and polish and propaganda, and, of course, my elite unit.

I arrived at Fort Bragg and Special Forces (SF) Training Group. I was a newly hatched bring-it-on gung-ho paratrooper on fire to become a Sneaky Pete. I was ready to get on with the task of making the world a safer place for democracy and the set of ideals that constituted America's mythos. I anticipated months of paddling up swampy rivers, rappelling down steep cliffs, and dropping earthward from silent heights. Unfortunately, the good Sergeant Easter neglected to mention that specialized training such as rappelling and sky diving came much later, if ever. In the interim between training cycles trainees performed normal army duties. My first week at Bragg I caught KP twice and guard duty once, a pattern that would repeat itself off and on for the next eight months.

The trainees were largely white and from middle- and lower-middle-class families. Among us were a scattering of blacks and Hispanics, probably fewer than ten divided among three training companies. A handful were draftees. A good number had attended college one or more years. A couple were graduates. Of those in the barracks when I arrived, a half dozen or so were destined to wash out.

The first stage of training was a weeklong course in methods of instruction. We learned how to speak in front of an audience, use props, perform demonstrations of skills, and organize drills. All of this was in preparation for the unit's functions as advisers to armies in foreign countries or as trainers and leaders of guerrilla forces in one of the world's "hot spots." The cadre administered a battery of tests to determine what field of expertise best suited each man. I spent an hour listening to code through earphones and learned that I had no ear for differentiating dits from dots or desire to do it. My preference would have been to be a weapons man, but those slots in Training Group were reserved for those who were already NCOs. My options were becoming a medic or demo man. The army paid an additional fifty-five dollars a month to blow up things—nothing extra for stitching up wounds. Hand me that detonator.

A team demo man was required to be a combination soldier, laborer, mathematician, and garage chemist. Course work in the classroom focused on formulas, mathematical calculations, and laws of physics. *Stress*, *sheer*, and *momentum* became common in our vocabulary. We performed work with electrical currents and chemicals that deflagrated. How, the instructor asked, do potassium chlorate and sugar react with sulfuric acid? Can battery acid be substituted? We made Molotov cocktails and improvised grenades and trip devices and booby traps and tinkered with timing devices, delay trips, pressure firing devices, anything that would initiate detonation or deflagration. We cut timber and nailed planks, dug footers, squared a foundation, and built a structure that could house a squad of men. We mixed concrete in precise measure, calculating slump factors and curing time. We poured footings and abutments. We learned a dozen uses of rope, from makeshift bridges to pulley hoists to the deadly Malayan swinging gate. We spread concertina wire and raised double apron fences, dug postholes, and filled sandbags. We mapped out minefields and laid mines, then dug them up. We shouted "Fire in the hole!" and plugged our ears, then watched in awe as the flash bang of a pound of c-4 scattered dirt and rock. We felt the earth rumble. We stared with odd delight as the shoulders of an ever-blackening cloud billowed upward several stories high. We trained no fewer than ten hours a day, and at the end of nine weeks, those of us who'd passed all the written tests and performed at least competently in the construction phases rode to Camp McCall and for a week put it all to work in a field exercise under the hawkish gazes of our mentors.

On August 2, in the midst of our training, the cadre called us into formation and announced that American ships had been attacked off the coast of North Vietnam. What had been a war limited to an "advisory" role on America's part was about to change. Two days after the alleged attack, the U.S. Senate at the urging of Lyndon Johnson passed the Gulf of Tonkin Resolution, a pronouncement that fell just short of a declaration of war. All of us trainees knew that the resolution was a word game. The small war Mr. Villarreal had all but dismissed was about to become a real war.

At McCall we lived in a crude encampment and slept on the ground. As the NCOs who'd trained us constantly evaluated our performance, we fortified the place, pulled guard at night, patrolled, crossed swampland in a rainstorm, constructed a bailey bridge. We slipped through a guerrilla ambush and set a blasting cap on the outside curve of a railroad track as we would if ever required to derail a train. All the while we were on guard against a guerrilla force of trainees and cadre whose job it was to make us fail as a group or individually.

The ride back to Bragg seemed longer than the ride out had been, and the beer at the EM Club seemed the coldest we'd ever had. The final evaluation deciding who passed wasn't — and couldn't be — objective. Who would or wouldn't earn in full the beret was reduced to one final factor: who among us wouldn't those sergeants want beside them on an operation in the jungles of Vietnam? Instead of sharing a beer with the class, two among the dozen who'd started with us packed their duffel bags that evening. They had performed above average, which amounted to failure. They received orders to a conventional airborne unit, transfers that would come swiftly. The rest of us earned a short rest and a future reward—twelve weeks in northern Virginia, a thirty-minute drive from Washington DC, where, word had it, women outnumbered men four to one. We returned to our former roles, pulling KP and guard duty as we awaited the final phases of our training and orders to Fort Belvoir for the next cycle of advance combat engineer and demolition training.

Branch Training, as this phase of Training Group was known, began in late October and culminated on an overcast December day after a blizzard had swept through Appalachia. Some fifty or sixty of us wearing fatigues and loaded with full equipment parachuted onto a fallow field in the Pisgah National Forest. Once on the ground, we lined up on the frozen earth near a farmer's fence. The cadre randomly separated us into six- and twelve-man teams to conduct counterinsurgency operations against a group of volunteers acting in the capacity of a guerrilla force who could wear civilian clothing, drive civilian cars or trucks, and hide wherever they wished.

We would spend the next four days shivering, humping mountain woods, and trying to ferret out the enemy. Training sergeants would only monitor our performance. We were on our own. The cadre provided us maps and told us where we were to rendezvous on the fourth day for the final stage of the fieldwork. Each twelve- and six-man team was given a different route to the designated point. Then we formed up in our bands and trod into the wood line.

Our goal was to locate and destroy or capture any guerrillas while we ourselves avoided ambushes and booby traps. I was in a six-man team that consisted of a radioman, one weapons sergeant, another demo man, and two medics. We trudged through the snow-laden woods in a daytime temperature that hovered at twenty degrees. The irony of conducting our final training operation in near-Arctic conditions wasn't lost on us.

Though we saw tracks in the woods, we encountered no

guerrillas. We kept on the move all day. By nightfall the temperature closed in on zero. We camped for the night on a precipice so attackers could approach us from only one side. We packed a skimpy supply of rations and were otherwise dependent on what the land provided. We ate cold C rations, then using poncho halves improvised shelter from the wind. We rotated one-hour guard shifts until dawn. Though painful to crawl out of a warm sleeping bag into the freezing air, we did it without complaint. Any lapse on our part, any lack of discipline, any failure in duty might be witnessed, and if it were considered a serious breach, whether an act or omission, any one or all of us could wash out.

In the morning we stumbled upon a field of turnips and used bayonets to dig up our breakfast and lunch. We took no more than needed and broke the thin film of ice at a creek and washed them. After eating, we followed the route outlined on our map. As we might in combat, we stopped civilians to gather intelligence and asked if they'd encountered any guerrillas. The locals were used to the training exercises, and some took sides, providing food and hiding places for the guerrillas or giving assistance to the counterinsurgents. The first two men we encountered merely laughed when asked about guerrillas, telling us they'd seen a few bears but no monkeys. The second men were loading hay on a pickup. They were a friendly duo who happily drove us to our first objective, where we hid in the woods and ate a second turnip.

That night we found an empty barn and heated Cs over a Sterno can. The ham and lima beans combined with the raw turnips bent me over with cramps. We were somewhat sheltered from the cold that night, but the turnips took their toll on me and sleep was hard coming. In the morning, avoiding roads and highways, we proceeded to the next checkpoint without being ambushed.

On the morning of the fourth day at the designated time

we converged with the rest of the trainees. Though we'd never engaged a guerrilla group, our trek had otherwise satisfied the cadre. We loaded up on deuce-and-a-half transport trucks and drove to an isolated canyon where we completed our training. It consisted of rappelling down cliffs, then crossing the rapids fifteen feet below using a three-rope bridge, a two-rope bridge, and finally a one-rope bridge. We lost two to the water. They came out of it shivering, but both eagerly lined up again.

Tired, but in good spirits, we mounted deuce-and-a-halves and drove back to Fort Bragg. As the trucks rumbled over the back road, we hunkered beneath our ponchos and kept warm as best we could. To a man, all of us were glad it was over, and though no one said as much, we were hopeful in equal measure that if we saw combat, it would be in a jungle or even a desert, anywhere but in the Great Smokey Range or any part of Appalachia—and never in snow.

FIVE

No more Georgetown coeds and making out with one in the bathroom as her roommates played Beetles songs and got wasted on Portuguese rosé. No more puking in fountains. No lazy holiday afternoons walking through the Smithsonian. In April, after three months, party time ended and hup-to-it time began anew. Weekends in Washington DC had taken some starch out of military life, but in no time Fort Bragg put it back in. Like the others from Training Group who'd earned the full flash that went on their berets, I expected orders for deployment to 'Nam. Instead, along with a promotion to Specialist 4 I was assigned to E Company of the Seventh Special Forces Group where I was among the lowest-ranking soldiers in the unit—Peon Barnes reporting as ordered.

All of Smoke Bomb Hill, the center of Special Forces, was a termite mound of officers and senior noncoms. Wherever I turned in the area of E Company of the Seventh, a captain or a lieutenant was waiting for a salute. I soon returned to the old routine of KP, guard duty, and mowing the lawn in front of the Special Warfare Center Headquarters. Two days into my new assignment I was wearing starched fatigues and spit-shined boots and pushing a manual lawn mower as troops in a deuce-and-a-half from the Eighty-second hooted at me. The next day it was KP. Then the next week I reported to Pappy Riggs at the Special Forces Museum, where I swept and mopped floors and carried out garbage as the aging master sergeant entertained me with stories about men he'd fought beside in the First Special Service Force in World War II.

During a Fayetteville outing, one of my new barracks mates suggested that a possible way out of KP was to find a special-duty assignment playing a sport. In high school I'd played football and run track and had swum competitively one summer for a team in Sunnyside, Washington. Surely, the army had some sport I could compete in. The last week in April I took the bus to the Special Services Gym nearest the fort command center and knocked on the door of the NCO in charge. The staff sergeant invited me in and asked what I wanted. He was a black man in his forties whose nose and face suggested he'd spent some time in the ring and had forgotten to hold his gloves up. I told him I wanted to play a sport. He asked what I was good at doing.

"I can run."

"So can a horse. And you ain't got four legs."

"I swim."

"So do fish. Can you box?" he asked, sizing me up.

"Yeah, I could do that."

"Are you any good?"

I told him I couldn't say one way or the other, but I was willing to try it.

"Why would you wanna box?"

"To get out of KP."

"Okay, I'd say that's motivation enough."

The sergeant gave me a skeptical look and judged by my blond hair and fair skin that I would fail. Nonetheless, he walked me into the gym and held a heavy bag as I punched it; then he gloved me up and sent me in the ring with a rangy black kid with ropelike arms. My opponent and I danced around on the mat and threw a few punches at each other, mostly missing the target. He had long arms and a quick jab. I took a few on the forehead and arms, then I fired off a couple of shots. Neither affected him.

Sensing he had an advantage in skill, the black kid circled to my right and closed the gap. I ducked his next punch, then landed an uppercut right to his midsection and left hook that drove him to the ropes. When he caught his breath, he complained that I'd hit him below the belt and came off the ropes throwing haymakers at my head. The NCO stepped in and separated us.

"You're pretty raw, but I see some potential. Come see me in May. You train and we'll see. First, I gotta find out if you Sneaky Pete boys can get special duty."

The next day I was in the barracks, seated on my foot-locker. A sergeant first class hurried through the bay and said, "Get your full TO equipment and get out on the parade field." Assuming that it was a drill to measure our response time, we packed everything and headed to the field, where some seventy to eighty were gathered. The sergeant major called for a formation by team. As he lined us up for roll call, Captain Anderson, our team leader, informed us we were deploying to the Dominican Republic, where civil war had broken out. A war was welcome news. No KP. No broken nose.

We were issued weapons and ammunition, and within the hour we loaded ourselves and our theater-of-operations equipment in deuce-and-a-halves and were ferried to Pope AFB. After receiving a hastily dispensed batch of inoculations, we boarded the next waiting C-130, strapped our seat belts, and flew south without a designated mission. Already fleet marines had landed, secured the embassy in Santa Domingo, and evacuated Americans and foreigners from other delegations. By the time we were airborne, C Company of the 506th of the Eighty-second Airborne had breached the Duarte Bridge and was engaging factions of forces called Constitionalistas.

After a quick stop to refuel at an air base outside Orlando, Florida, our plane descended through a lightly clouded sky and landed a little past dawn. Upon deplaning, we heard distant gunfire and occasional blasts from recoilless rifles. Our captain told us to lock and load before we climbed aboard a troop truck to our bivouac area near the airport.

The battle to secure a corridor between the warring factions progressed in spurts, with C Company spearheading the building-to-building combat. They plunged steadily forward but took intense fire and some wounded and dead in the process. The Eighty-second was tactically well suited for the block-by-block fighting going on in the city. With no specific mission as yet, we were held back. Fighting continued for two days, and for two days we waited. Whatever our purpose, the army was in no hurry to commit us to it. So we ate rations and drank warm beer from quart-size bottles labeled El Presidente that we'd bought from a kid no older than thirteen.

C Company was still carving out the corridor as we mounted a deuce-and-a-half, sandbagged from front to rear. The driver, a PFC from the Eighty-second, pulled the truck to a stop about a quarter of a mile from the Duarte Bridge, the only passage into Santo Domingo. He told us to get ready, that he would take a running start, then gun the engine once we were on the bridge. He'd made the trip several times a day and advised us to keep our heads down. "They got two fifties over to the other side of the bay, but I'll get you Sneaky Petes there."

Halfway across the bridge the unmistakable *ka-chunk*, *ka-chunk* of a .50 caliber sounded across the bay. We didn't have to hear it to know we were under fire. Projectiles the size of a man's forefinger whizzed overhead. Fortunately, the closest the shooter came was hitting the bridge wall and a single ricochet that pinged harmlessly off the tailgate of the truck. The driver delivered us safely to the far side of the bridge and as we climbed down said, "Sure wouldn't wanna be one'a you guys."

We were ferried by jeeps a mile or so into the corridor. Air wafting in from the rebel sector smelled of bodies in various stages of decay. The gunfire — sometimes sporadic, sometimes intense — told us nothing was yet settled. We secured the top floor and roof of an empty tenant building that overlooked the rebel sector. And waited. A SEAL team showed up that evening. They toted two M-14s with Starlight Scopes, the military's latest wonder toy that rendered objects clear at night without the use of infrared. They were green-lighted to pull the trigger on any armed rebels. Our job was to provide security for their mission, which was to test the scope in combat. When the SEALs weren't picking off rebel shooters, they did calisthenics. We found their enthusiasm for exercise generally entertaining.

On our third day in the city a P-51 Mustang, a vintage World War II fighter flown by a Dominican, made several failed efforts at strafing the radio station Voz Dominicana from an altitude of about two thousand feet. Early in the struggle the rebels had seized the station to broadcast propaganda in an effort to gain support from the populace.

Electrical power to the sector had been cut off, but the rebels used a generator bunkered with sandbags. We watched the pilot's feeble runs. Sandbagged in atop the roof and armed with two .50-caliber machine guns, the rebels staved off each dive. It was obvious the pilot was too concerned with saving his airplane and himself to accomplish the task. Gutless pilots aside, both General Wessen y Wessen, commander of Dominican forces, and the CIA wanted the broadcasts silenced. Someone had to destroy the generator or transmitting tower.

That next afternoon our entire detachment gathered in an open field by a roadway where demo men and a few light weapons men were culled out of the teams. Separated from the others, we waited in a line as a man in a wrinkled short-sleeve shirt and gabardine trousers and our B-Team major conferred a few yards away. Two men in civilian clothing arrived in a truck and called us to the tailgate, where they passed down 9mm Swedish submachine guns—without serial numbers.

That night the radio station went silent, and one of our own, Jesse Flores, was wounded and flown to Walter Reed for surgery.

In a few days the battle to secure Santo Domingo was all but over. The shooting petered off once the Eighty-second secured the corridor separating the opposing sides. People feared exposing themselves to gunfire, so the bodies remained unclaimed. The stench wafted up. In daylight we could see human remains sprawled out along sidewalks and in the narrow back streets. The number of American dead had grown to thirteen, and some two hundred were wounded. Any accurate count of Dominicans killed was impossible, as many bodies in the rebel sector were dumped into the river and washed out to sea. The estimates peaked at near two thousand. The army called it an expedition and didn't recognize it as a war, but the dead and wounded told a different tale.

As fighting fizzled, troops from nations representing the Organization of American States entered the city. Soldiers from Brazil and Honduras rolled across the bridge first and patrolled the streets in trucks and armored personnel carriers with machine guns mounted on top. After our days in the hotel doing little more than watching the SEALS do pushups or occasionally snipe at rebels, we were moved to a hotel near the beach, fed hot meals, and given free rein to walk the wall on the boulevard paralleling the shore. When nightfall descended, women appeared out of the shadows on the ocean side of the seawall and strolled the walkways where for fair barter, they offered soldiers pleasure beneath palm trees on the sandy slope above the beach.

A few days later we were bivouacked outside the city in an area we dubbed Tarantula Heights because it was infested with large hairy spiders. It was on a slope perhaps three miles from Santo Domingo. We found ways to stave off boredom. Rain had driven spiders from their lairs. They were everywhere, along with centipedes and black scorpions, crawling over web gear and backpacks, nesting in our boots. Bullock found an empty ammo box. We put a huge spider with brilliant orange striping in the container, then caught a scorpion about its size and introduced it into the box. The timid creatures retreated to opposite corners and tried to climb to freedom. That was unsatisfactory. I snapped the lid down and shook the box. When I opened it, the scorpion lay mangled in a corner. I freed the victorious spider, which seemed none the worse for what it had gone through.

Light fighting continued in the city. We sat idle. To keep our parachute pay active we jumped into a makeshift landing zone in a cane field. We slept in jungle hammocks, mosquitoes buzzing our nets, the distant isolated gunshot a reminder of where we were. A few at a time, we took R & R in San Juan. When my turn came I roomed at the Caribbean Hilton and partied in clubs downtown. Exhausted after three days with no more than five hours sleep, I climbed into my hammock and slept the better part of a day and night, even as a tropical storm raged down.

Finally, we were pulled out of Tarantula Heights and given a mission we were trained for. My team was transported to a drop-off point at the foot of the Cordillera Central. For the next few weeks, we trudged over the mountain range near the border of Haiti, our mission to interdict gun smugglers if we sighted any and to gather intelligence on communist activity—though no one told us what signs to look for in distinguishing communists from noncommunists in a country where everyone pretty much looked alike.

After being issued maps, we broke up in three- or four-man units and began humping back trails up and over peak after peak. The mountain region was dense with tropical vegetation. Rivers and streams crisscrossed the land. Farmers eked out a livelihood harvesting mangos and bananas and cultivating rice and coffee beans on mountain slopes. Where our patrol converged on a farm or a hamlet we interrogated the people in broken Spanish, asking, "*Hay communistas in la aldea?*" Though familiar with communism as a word, they had no sense of the ideologies driving world politics. Most villages had no electricity. The populace had limited communication with the larger world and seemed little affected by the civil war. Here, politics was the next meal, the next rain, the next harvest. Wherever we arrived, they welcomed us and invited us warmly into their huts, fed us from their scant store of beans and rice. They delighted in the ritual boiling of their unique coffee bean into a thick espresso sweetened with cane sugar. During a rainstorm one night some local cops in a village invited us to sleep on bunks in the jail. We uncovered no communists or encountered any hostiles, no rebels or gunrunners, no Cubans or Russians crossing the border. If any among our units did, the news of it would never reach the media.

All but spent, we ended the mission and left the mountains. Captain Anderson finagled us a short R & R at a beach resort on the eastern tip of the island. The rippling inlet was warm, and we waded out to the protective reef in water no deeper than our waists. At lunch waiters served fresh coconut and banana and mango and iced tea. After a second swim, we drank cold beer on a veranda overlooking the sea. That evening we dined on shrimp and Spanish rice and black beans, gathered around Charley Vessels, the team's senior demo man, and read the latest *Stars and Stripes*, the military newspaper that featured month-old news. The operation in the Dom Rep had pushed Vietnam from the headlines to the middle pages. On the front page were photos of marines looking out from behind sandbags as they protected the American Embassy. The article made little mention of the Eighty-second and said nothing about our unit or the airlift that brought us here.

"Guess the marines did it all," someone said.

"Yep, and without the help of the Girl Scouts," Charley said. "Imagine that."

And we laughed as one.

The Dominican military had performed poorly during the coup and the battle that ensued. E Company, as part of a nation-building task force, was now tasked to retrain the army. I returned to barracks. Ahead lay weeks of training in preparation for a six-month tour in the Dom Rep, so before the instruction began, I took a week's leave and flew to Las Vegas.

It was late July, Mojave Desert hot. I'd not seen my family in two years since their move from El Paso, and Mom and Mal seemed uneasy to have me home but determined nonetheless to show me a good time. They dragged me in my summer khaki uniform from the Strip to Fremont Street through club after club, each more crowded, more smoky, and noisier than the previous. Mother and Mal played slots. I watched. People unfamiliar with my unit stared at my uniform and beret. Others, who likely knew of the unit because of the release of Barry Sadler's song that elevated us to near–folk legend status, smiled as they might at a neighbor's ugly kid. Even in the land of celebrities, I felt conspicuous, a public oddity.

At home, where the television blared constantly, I was an intruder, relegated to sleeping on the living room couch. My brothers and Deborah were indifferent to me, except in the morning, when they found me on the couch where they intended to park themselves and watch cartoons. George, a baby of two when I'd last seen him, had developed a foghorn voice and an annoying snarl, Deborah still lived to throw tantrums, and Mickey and David, when not held immobile by the spell of the boob tube, were adolescents high on sugar and at the peak of their destructive stage. Nothing that could be taken apart was safe.

By the third day, I was anxious to return to my unit. At the end of the week, I hurriedly packed my belongings and said good-bye to the kids, who grunted a response but didn't divert their gaze from the TV. Mother had to work a shift at the Flamingo as a hostess, so Mal drove me to the airport. On the way there he talked more than I recalled his ever having talked, chatter about his job as news gatherer, the boys doing poorly in school, Scooter the dachshund biting a neighbor. At the gate he finally got to the point he'd been working up to. They were "strapped at the moment." He wanted to know if I could cash some savings bonds I was setting aside that I intended to use later for college. I asked how much.

"Three hundred?"

I told him I'd send a money order. He shook my hand and said they were pleased I would be returning to the Dominican Republic instead of going to Vietnam.

Mission training began soon after I returned to Bragg. Most of our time was spent in a classroom at the Seventh studying the topography, history, and culture of the island or at the Special Warfare Center, learning basic Spanish. The struggle in the country was over and a peace established between the opposing factions. Both former leaders, Juan Bosch and Joaquin Balaguer, had returned to the country, and an election was planned. It would be a stable country soon. Returning there didn't inspire much enthusiasm in me.

I settled into a routine. Evenings, after chow, I lifted weights for an hour, then ran the perimeter of Smoke Bomb Hill, a track of roughly three miles. I read voraciously, whatever books I could get hold of, my preference novels. After lights out, I carted whatever I was reading to the latrine, sat on the commode, and read. On weekends if we didn't take the Vomit Comet into Fayetteville, the barracks rats would buy two or three six-packs, sit on our footlockers, and trade stories. One got orders to 'Nam. That weekend we threw a party in the bay and stacked empty cans on one end of the aisle. When the last drop was drained from the last can, we placed it atop the others, and he ran in stockinged feet and slid into the pile. Some, I among them, envied him.

The small conflict Mr. Villarreal had alluded to was becoming a major war. Despite the arrival of marines in I Corps, our unit still bore the brunt of combat. The Fifth SF Group that once occupied the westernmost portion of Smoke Bomb Hill was moved en masse and became the unit tackling all Special Forces missions in Vietnam, including Special Operations. Tours, once six-month temporary-duty assignments, were now a full year.

A mystique was beginning to build around our unit. We became the early poster boys for the war. Barry Saddler's "Ballad of the Green Berets" had hit the top twenty on the chart. Then with millions of viewers watching him he sang it in uniform on *The Ed Sullivan Show*. The year before that Capt. Roger Donlon, A-Team leader, had been awarded the Medal of Honor, making him the war's first recipient of America's highest medal. About the same time *The Green Berets* was published. It became a best-seller. Even among us stories of desperate fights floated into discussions and became incorporated into the mystique about our organization. In particular the story of Hector Camacho's harrowing escape from his Vietcong captors in Cambodia and his four hundred–mile trek through the jungle eluding capture while living off the land inspired even hardened veterans. To a man, we saw Vietnam as *our* war.

As each trooper in the barracks or others I knew received orders for 'Nam, I felt a growing sense of unease. What would it be like?

Troopers were needed to replace the natural turnover and

mounting casualties. On a near-daily basis troops from the Seventh and the Sixth Special Forces Group were ordered to premission training in preparation for their joining the Fifth in Vietnam. Among them was Captain Anderson. Meanwhile, I sat in a classroom, learning more than I needed to know about the defunct Trujillo regime.

A couple of weeks into our training a sergeant told a cluster of smokers outside the classroom that he'd been on a mission to Cambodia before the war expanded. He figured the Dom Rep would be "a bit of paradise" and went over imagined benefits such as being housed in a villa somewhere near the beach. While training Dominican soldiers in weapons and small-unit tactics, we would live a kingly life, with servants to do the laundry and clean rooms, food aplenty, time for lying out on the beach, and "Don't forget the booze and women."

What sounded good to his audience struck an opposite chord in me. Later, as I sat in the classroom, pencil in hand, taking notes, I felt as if I were again taking the easy route, cruising by at an above-average pace. I could complete the six months and return to Bragg for a few more while awaiting an honorable discharge and then go attend college. Easy enough. But except for one brief moment in the Dom Rep, I hadn't been tested, and now I was returning. And to what? Lie on a beach and work on my tan? Or I could volunteer for 'Nam and earn my beret in the fullest sense. My mind wouldn't let the argument rest. The months of training, the anticipation of action, the boiling energy in my veins, all seemed squandered on something less worthy if I returned to the Dom Rep.

That night, I pitched about in my bunk. It was humid and the heat in the topside bay stifling. Sometime around midnight I got up, slipped on my fatigues, and went outside, where I sat on the top stair of the stoop to the barracks. I listened to crickets chirp. Duty in the Dom Rep would be reasonably risk free and no strain—beaches, no KP. I remembered the excursion to the resort, two days living like lords—pictured the streams in the mountains and the pleasant island people. They would be rebuilding their country. Maybe I could do them some good. Maybe. I thought about the effort I'd put into the sixty-pound rucksack race on Activation Day, the pain of the run and no one quitting, Pace, a kid from the Sixth SF Group, staggering across the finish and passing out, me finishing second by two yards and at day's end seeing blood in my urine and never going on sick call.

The charge of quarters came by and asked if anything was wrong. I said I was fine, that I'd gotten up to piss and couldn't go to sleep. Even as I mounted the steps to the top bay, I was sure I didn't want six months in paradise. I didn't fully understood the kind of high-principled insanity I shared with Pace and the others who ran the race that day, but I knew it was behind what I had to do next.

I checked into a dive hotel near the bus station in Washington DC. That night I tossed and turned on a worn mattress, adjusted and readjusted a flat pillow, and knotted myself up in sheets. Around two o'clock someone rattled the doorknob. Beneath the base of the door, I saw a shadow move about and growled out a warning. Whoever it was staggered off. His lumbering footfalls faded down the hallway, followed shortly by a dull thud, then silence.

At dawn I awoke with perhaps two hours' sleep. I rolled out of the rack, slipped on a T-shirt and trousers, then grabbed my shaving kit. From a hook beside the door, I snatched up the towel the desk clerk had handed me the previous night. I locked the door and walked down a narrow hallway that reeked of human sweat and cheap perfume and of even cheaper booze. I stepped over the splayed-out legs of an unconscious drunk. After showering and shaving, I again stepped over the drunk. His eyelids flickered as he gazed up and tried to focus, then he rolled over and curled himself into a fetal position on the hardwood floor.

Back in the nine-by-nine room I sat on the bed and shined my boots and brass. I dressed myself at a leisurely pace, then stood in front of a warped mirror and studied my reflection. I brushed lint off my sleeve, slipped on my beret, and pressed a deep crease behind the crest. True or false, my identity had become tied up with the image of the young man in the mirror wearing a beret. I knew him, yet he was a stranger to me, someone about to do something that would seem foolish to most everyone.

I gathered my gear, checked out of the hotel, and walked to the bus terminal, where I stored my overnight bag in a locker. My appointment wasn't until 1530 hours, so I walked the wet sidewalks alongside office workers and civil servants bound to work. A little past eleven I stumbled upon a theater that featured an early matinee. I bought a ticket and napped in a seat until an usher aimed a flashlight in my eyes. He said someone had complained and that I had to stay awake or leave. I tried but couldn't keep my eyes open. I pulled myself out of the seat and left. While I'd napped inside, a downpour had come and gone.

I passed the Capitol and the White House and the Department of Justice building and banks and brokerage firms and furniture stores and art galleries, past the America that puts a soldier in uniform and forgets him. As my boots swallowed up block after block, I thought about my last visit with my family and my childhood before Mother married Mal. A waitress, she'd moved from job to job and man to man, dragging my sister and me along—Jenny, a checkerboard game, and I bound in whatever direction Mother's impulse aimed the car. Our life had been one of sharing a sandwich in the backseat for dinner, often going to sleep hungry, or sitting restlessly awake and watching moon-shadowed communities drift by. Everything was decided for us. Now, I wore a uniform, a grown man capable of independent decisions.

It began to sprinkle. The water-filmed streets and sidewalks reflected the tall buildings. Car tires sluiced over the wet pavement. Clouds pinched out all evidence of sunlight. Dusk or dawn or high noon, all seemed the same here as the weather boxed in the city. I ducked into a coffee shop, where I downed a couple of cups of java and watched the gloom outside the window. It was nearly 1400 hours when the rain lifted and I stepped outside. I gazed at the towering buildings against the gray backdrop. In that world that excluded me and my ilk, I wondered, are they happy? Do they worry less? Do they worry more? Pedestrians toting umbrellas hurried by. A few glanced my way. Some pretended they didn't see me at all. A man in uniform. A soldier. Probably needs a leash.

I rode a bus over the Potomac to Arlington and the Pentagon. Across the street was the National Cemetery. I gazed at row upon row of white tombstones, where dead from the nation's wars lay interred. Death was a distant and unfathomable occurrence, not a matter I usually dwelled on, but the overcast day and grave markers spoke to me. I could turn away and spend my remaining enlistment training Dominicans, drinking rum, and swimming in the Caribbean. Despite the graves or because of them, my mind was made up.

It took a half hour to track down the office of the man I was told to see. Rain had milked away the shine on my boots, and the ironed pleats were gone from my trousers. In a hall outside his office I waited and watched a clock. At 1529 hours I stood obtrusively in the threshold until his not noticing me made me self-conscious. His general appearance surprised me—a nondescript Ivy Leaguer or corporate-executive type. A desk jockey in army green, he wasn't one of us, not Special Forces, not even airborne, and in this palace of generals, a mere major too low on the ladder to merit his own secretary.

Holding my beret in my left hand, I saluted. He informed me no one salutes in the Pentagon and asked who I was. I gave him name, rank, and serial number, which, despite the fact that I had an appointment, he asked me to repeat. He jotted down the information and, before I could explain my purpose, told me to stand at ease and state exactly what I wanted, cautioning me that if I came to get relief from being assigned to 'Nam, I could just forget that.

"Sir, I have orders to go back to the Dominican Republic."

"What's wrong with that?"

"Sir, I don't want to go."

"Well, son, we have . . ."

"Sir, I want to *volunteer* for Vietnam."

He looked at me as if I'd suddenly shrunk or grown in his estimation, hard to tell which. "Why?"

I couldn't explain my desire to go without explaining the shadow over my shoulder. How could I explain the longing I'd experienced as Mother drove past a sleeping town or the anxiety that enveloped me as I registered at each new school, where I would sit silent and unobtrusive and settle for being above average? It seemed clear to me. I had to go to 'Nam. It was the only war I would ever have, the looking glass through which I could know myself.

"Just do, sir. Can you do it?"

"Now, you look smart enough. Why wouldn't you want to go to the Caribbean? Blue water, beaches. No shooting. Hell, I wouldn't mind it. Do you think this is great duty?"

"No, sir. I don't, but . . ." Thinking the beret, the symbol of what I was or imagined myself to be, was explanation enough, I held it out for him to see. "Sir, I have to go to 'Nam. That's all."

"I've got paperwork to finish up," he said.

It wasn't what I wanted to hear, "Yes, sir." I saluted.

Instead of returning my salute, he stood, leaned over the desk, and offered his hand to shake. "I get one or two of you in here a week. They all want the same thing." He scratched something down on a pad and handed it to me. "She'll take care of it. Now get lost and good luck."

I saw Billye Alexander, the name he'd written down. I gave her my name and serial number and left assured my request would come through. I went to a bar to celebrate that unknown and uncertain future. An hour later, still sober, I left the bar, and as the door closed, I heard a refrain, Elvis's melancholy proclamation of love's illusion. Now and then, I thought, there *are* all different kinds of fools. I found a vacancy in a somewhat better hotel, one I could barely afford, and slept well for the first time in days.

SEVEN

Two weeks following the Activation Day celebrations the C-Team sergeant major called me into headquarters and said my orders had come. I was to report for premission training at the Special Warfare Center that day and an assignment to a new A-Team. For purposes of meals, billeting, and pay, I would remain housed in E Company. I was assigned to Special Forces Team A7/03 and reported to join my new A-Team for training indoctrination that morning.

As Vietnam escalated, the demand for skilled advisers increased, and the initial Special Forces' mission of infiltrating behind enemy lines to train, equip, and lead insurgents shifted to the role of training troops in counterinsurgency. The A-Team was the basic unit tasked to perform that mission. Our training at the Special Warfare Center was aimed at that mission. The twelve-man teams consisted of two officers and ten enlisted men, mostly noncommissioned officers. Generally, a captain led the team assisted by an executive officer with the rank of lieutenant. A master sergeant, the senior noncom, oversaw operations. Next in line was a sergeant first class, responsible for intelligence gathering. A fully complemented team consisted of those and two weapons sergeants, two medics, two radio operators, and two demo men. In theory, all of the enlisted ranks could perform at least two more of the specialties.

As the sergeant in charge read the manifest, we gathered into teams, shook hands with our new teammates, and took seats to hear the training cadre tell us what we already knew. Vietnam was our future. The training would prepare us for it. But the gathering served a purpose beyond detailing the training and mission ahead. Men sized up the members they would be deployed with. To function within a team, each man had to fit. Competence wasn't enough, and passage to 'Nam on A-Team wasn't guaranteed. If one couldn't do the job, if one couldn't adapt and get along, if one was too weak or too slow, or if even a hint of quitting surfaced in him, he would wash out. His team would see to it. We could tolerate nose pickers and farters, even the loquacious and boastful. There would be no room for whiners, quitters, or cowards.

Most enlisted men in the room came from working-class backgrounds. A few were reared in metropolitan cities, but most came from towns in West Virginia, or Kentucky, or Alabama, or Ohio. There had been no daddy money in households, no scholarships following graduation. Choices were limited to physical labor for low wages or donning a uniform for even lower pay. The outfit wasn't a good career field for those who had their eyes on stars. Generals rose out of the ranks of the conventional army, primarily combat arms units, so officers in our unit understood serving in the unit wasn't an elevator to the top. Each had his own reason for wearing a beret, but in common they had the same basic motivations as the enlisted men they commanded. They were dedicated, wanted to serve with the best, and wanted to be challenged.

It wasn't going to be easy for me to assimilate into the team. I was the kid. Six among us had served tours in Vietnam. Captain Fewell, Lieutenant Morris, Sgt. Cam Gamble, Sgt. Pablo Olivarez, and Rich Norwood had not and were considered green. I'd been to the Dom Rep, but despite the shooting and casualties, it didn't count. In any case, it was a far cry from combat in 'Nam.

Norwood, the junior medic destined to the job of camp sanitation, was closest to my age. A blue-eyed Californian and married, he had surfer good looks, a gymnast's physique, and chiseled features, but he was shy to the point of aloofness. That first day he struck a chord with Brownie, the senior medic. They would remain inseparable during the entire training cycle. Brownie, a family man with two children, had an enigmatic smile and a relaxed, unpretentious manner. He was glib-tongued and his sense of humor wry. Sheppard, the small weapons man, and Hausenfauk, the senior radio operator, were the least friendly. Cam Gamble, a likable but nervous chatterer, was the junior commo man. His awe-shucks ways made him seem like a character on the stage of the Grand Ole Opry. Though they didn't truly resemble one another, Gamble and Hausenfauk were so much alike in manner, it seemed they could exchange faces or body parts and be unchanged. I imagined them experiencing dreams and nightmares in Morse code.

Pablo Olivarez, an affable Hispanic Texan, was built like a canvas heavy bag. His role on the team as assistant intel sergeant was improvised to replace a slot reserved for a senior demo man. He laughed often and easily. Three years my senior, he was still considered a kid and subjected to a great deal of teasing, especially from J. V. Sgt. 1st Class J. V. Carroll, a squat man with dark caterpillar-like eyebrows, was our intel sergeant. At age sixteen, he'd fought in the infantry in World War II and later in Korea. He'd been a weapons man at Boan Mi Thuit when a Montagnard insurrection broke out in camp and spent two days as a captive when the team house was surrounded. He had a fondness for whiskey and an abrasive sense of humor. Sober, his tongue was sharp and ruthless; drunk, it was dull and nasty.

Jacobsen, a staff sergeant and heavy-weapons specialist, was the team's thumb to its fingers. He could time a car's engine by ear, fire a mortar by sight alone, and talk a bartender into a free round of drinks on the house. If something needed to be done swiftly and discretely, bypassing paperwork and chain of command, Jake was the man to do it. He was a full-bellied bull of a man, the kind you had no doubt you wanted beside you in a foxhole or in a dense jungle.

Herman Fisher, our team sergeant, had seen combat in both 'Nam and Korea. A lanky forty year old with a steady gaze and a pipe perpetually clamped in his teeth, whether lit or not, he had a rugged New Englander whaler profile. Something about the contemplative way he listened to others before talking himself assured us we were in safe hands. Lt. Ray Morris, the team's xo, had fair skin, reddish blond hair, and sun-reddened cheeks. He warmly welcomed me to the team, asking where I was from, what unit I'd been with, and when I'd completed Training Group. He was what we termed "a soldier's officer," and despite his boyish looks, he was a tough, experienced vet who'd come up through the ranks.

John Fewell, our captain and leader, had a Wheaties-box clean-cut face, boundless enthusiasm, and an energy that could be exhausting to others. He put considerable effort into encouraging us as a team and getting to know us as individuals. To a man we respected him for that, but in short time, it became obvious he would need a strong lieutenant to advise him and a level-headed top sergeant to curb his exuberance. Fortunately, we had Morris and Fisher.

I was the exception in most every way — youngest, single, living in the barracks, the kid who frequented bars in Fayetteville and would three weeks later show up on a Monday morning with two black eyes and ten stitches on the crown of my head.

We addressed the officers as "sir" but often used last names or shortened nicknames when talking to or about one another. Sheppard was never Paul, just Shep or Sheppard. Brown was that or Brownie. Norwood was occasionally Rich, but never Richard. Gamble was always Cam to his face and Gamble when otherwise referring to him. Jacobsen was Jake. In Hausenfauk's case, we used his first name or called him House because his last name presented a bit of a challenge. Olivarez was usually Pablo, but I took to calling him Pablito or Primo, which means "cousin." Carroll was J. V. or Pappy, while Herman Fisher was called "Top" for "top sergeant." Everyone called me Barnes.

Gradually we became acquainted, but there remained among us a tacit understanding that ensured a degree of separation. We were tight-lipped about anything of an intimate nature, and any references to personal history or feelings were vague. Dark humor pervaded our jokes. Doubt or fear never entered a conversation, nor did any mention of death. These unspoken terms dictated how we could interact. They functioned in a way that was equally subtle. Among us some might die, and whereas the loss of a teammate hit hard, the death of a friend would hit harder. Grief would not be allowed as a distraction.

Nonetheless, and perhaps because we abided by the

unspoken rules, we became close-knit. Most personal information shared was mere veneer. The captain had a family. Lieutenant Morris was married. Jake built stock cars and raced them on dirt tracks. Pablo's wife was named Connie; they had two kids. Norwood was a newlywed. Brownie had a wife and family. Sheppard liked his fatigues tailored. J. V. preferred Jack Daniels to Jim Beam, but drank either. I offered nothing about myself. No one asked because no one was interested. What was of interest to us was how each performed in the field. Every man's life might well depend on what the one next to him did in a given moment. Though disparate souls from all corners of the map tossed together by a set of orders, we shared a commitment to our mission. Ours was not the romantic stuff of patriotic songs or saluting with rapiers or wearing capes and hats with plumes. We weren't the Hollywood version of anything, and neither was our mission; it was the stuff of sweat and work combined with the likelihood of some of us shedding blood.

So the grind went — up at dawn and train into dark, boots dirty, fatigues wet. I cleaned and polished boots, laid them aside, and set out laundered fatigues for the next day. Slept. Got up. Shaved. Ate. Trained again. Got my boots and fatigues dirty. Repeated the cycle. We either marched or ran most everywhere — firing ranges, classrooms, drop zones. Running, sweat, more running, the airborne shuffle.

Hi, yo, airborne, airborne, all the way, every day. Sound off! One, two! Sound off! Three, four! Can't hear you! Are you pussies? No, sir!

We were ferried in deuce-and-a-halves to Pope Air Force Base and flew around in c-2s for two hours for our last Stateside pay jump.

"Stand up. Hook up. Check static line. Check equipment. Shuffle to the door. Stand in the door. Go."

I left the plane. My umbilical cord, the static line, pulled and separated, and I floated above the earth, seeing it from the angels' view, miles of plowed farmland framed by roads. Trees in rows. Trees in clumps. A winding stream. I loved this, and Uncle Sam paid me to do it. Sweet Jesus, envy this blue-eyed boy child.

I'd failed to secure the helmet strap to my chin. It flew off and arced away from me. I watched it fall gracefully ground-ward, a beautiful sight I knew I'd catch hell for. And I did. A sergeant major greeted me with the trophy in hand. He told me to put on the steel pot and take a little run. He'd tell me when to stop.

We were required to learn Vietnamese. We sat in Language Lab with earphones. I imagined it the most painful language in the world to learn. It was not the *en-cantar-al-vuelve* Spanish that sang in the ear or the *non-sibi-sed-omnibus* Latin I'd dreaded in high school. Despite the intonations and stops, I couldn't make discrete distinctions. Too many sounds were similar. *Phut, phuc. Toc lam, sau lam. Sin loi, chung toi.* Six meanings alone for the syllable *ma*, depending on the intonation. My mind couldn't separate and recognize sounds, much less decipher words. I would never grasp the rudiments, much less speak as they did. *Sin loi*, boy. Translation: too bad about that.

The command thought we should understand the Vietnam-ese peoples and their culture and provided lectures to that end.

Honest, men really hold hands?

Yes.

Fine, Sarge, but no man's holdin' mine.

If you are offered a *blut*, eat it. It's an honor.

It's a rotten egg, Sarge.

Not true, son. It's a nearly developed embryo inside an egg. It's considered a delicacy there and may be a century old.

Sounds fucking great. I'll take two.

Gentlemen, they eat dog, too, and monkey. I know Fido or Cheetah are not your idea of barbecue, but get used to the idea.

Any of them cannibals?

Only cannibals I ever met were in Hayes Street in Fayetteville. Next question? Okay, then. Moving along. The Montagnard—call 'em Yards. They're good soldiers, when trained. Warrior tribes, kinda like Indians. No, not Hindus. The other kind. Indians, Comanche. Good people.

Do they eat *bluts*?

Next stupid question.

Saturday night on the Smoke Bomb Hill parade field I played football, a wild contact game, five on each side. It was autumn and the season for it. I teamed up with two black kids from a signal company with the Eighty-second Airborne, one all bone, the other all gristle. We won the first game, split up teams, and went again, split up again, and played a third time. There was no Vietnam, no army, no army chow, no training. I floated down field, feinted right, cut left, and hauled in a pass over my shoulder. As I raced to the end zone, I left behind every concern. I could smell the grass and nearby pines and damp earth. This, I could do forever, I thought. I wanted this small joy to drift on and on in perpetuity. But it was only a small moment in passing.

Instructors—they stood in front of the class, the wisdom of bad days in their eyes. They taught us what we already knew, that a country was more than a map. The cautionary stuff that has nothing to do with battle.

Disease is the second enemy. Water is the killer. Schistosome, microscopic wormy parasites, get in your bloodstream and enter your intestine and eat away your guts. Don't drink the water. Don't swim in it. The Vietnamese shit where-fucking-ever, boy, in the water, the rice paddies you'll be crossing, all of them a breeding ground for cholera. Purify water; boil it; use every pill Uncle Sam provides.

Malaria's carried by the female anopheles mosquito. She needs your blood to feed her eggs—a little mosquito sperm, add blood, and boom, you get the next generation of blood-suckers. Malaria can kill you. Mostly it makes you miserable, and Uncle Sam won't have any use for you, so hard-dicked or not, it's medicaled out into civilian life. Dig? Take the pills the medics dispense, horse-size tablets, and swallow the motherfuckers like they're Italian meatballs.

When it's standing at attention, put a raincoat on your soldier. Any sweet thing you dip your dick in might be the one that brings tears to your eyes when you whiz. They got VD over there that's so resistant, it'll still be with you when your grandchildren are in retirement homes.

Do you understand?

Yes, Sarge.

Throw away what you learned in school about the history of war. It doesn't matter that the Greeks conquered civilizations under Alexander, that tactical Western warfare began with Rome and reached its pinnacle when Caesar's legions conquered Gaul and the British Isles, or that the English defeated a hugely superior French force at Crécy by employing the long bow. The Vietminh, Charlie's predecessors, would have turned back the Greeks, Caesar's legions, and the English, archers and all. Uncle Ho and his hosts hid in rain forest and backwater villages and ambushed the Japanese and later defeated the French. We wouldn't be facing inept coffee bean–growing Dominicans who'd never before fired a rifle. We'd be operating in Charlie's playground. Learn his rules. Learn his ways.

These men, our mentors, had been there. The soles of their boots had trod the steep central highlands and sunk into the deep red clay of Vietnam. These men went. They saw. They survived. Think beyond what we say. Be "strac" — military for "steadfast." Be tough. Stay vigilant. Charlie is ahead. Charlie is tough. Charlie is hard-core. Sucker's been fighting for decades. Think Charlie. Better still, think like Charlie thinks.

Firing range, midmorning, temperature cool. Autumn had at last set in. I gripped the .50 caliber. It slapped against my palms as it throbbed to life, a heartbeat matching my own. No thrill like it, I thought, or at least none better.

Then I took a quick refresher course in explosives, my specialty. Oh, yeah, baby, yeah. Twisting the detonator was like taking the joy stick on a fighter jet at full throttle and swallowing air as five GS compressed the chest. The blast was better than a dozen big .50s. I watched a plume of smoke funnel upward and dissipate like a spirit summoned back to the ether. I imagined Fermi watching his dark but brilliant child flare up like the sun and then mushroom. Had he wondered what terrible havoc he had unleashed?

Weapons were familiar tools to all of us, but Sheppard was the authority. He'd taken every advanced course on weaponry offered at the Special Warfare Center. He'd taught weapons and tactics. He knew rifles, carbines, assault weapons, submachine guns, automatic pistols from most nations, mortars. Jacobsen knew the weapons that reached out and said hello over treetops and mountains, across long stretches of ground. I knew the skill I'd most need would be weapons. I could fire a rifle as well as any, but I had little training in mortars or recoilless rifles. So I hung around Jacobsen and listened.

Though at first Jake had mostly ignored me, sometime after my blackened-eyes incident he'd noticed my fascination with the mechanics of weapons. While my stepfather had thought the best use of a screwdriver was breaking up ice for a daiquiri, I used them as a kid to disassemble and reassemble anything that was held together by screws. Jake understood.

I prepared to lob a mortar round downrange. Jake hovered over me as I cut increments, the packets of propellant that deflagrate in the tube and send the round in flight. I showed him my work, waited for approval. He nodded. He was a man of machines and speed. But what he really knew was mortars. One was as familiar to him as the curve of his wife's hip. If he said it was right, it was.

I pulled the pin, set the fins inside the lip of the tube, let go, and plugged my ears. The white phosphorus round we knew as Willy Pete or just WP burst into fragments of color that were like a southwestern sunset, neither pink nor orange, but some color in between. Its smoke was ashen, not white or gray, and the explosion wasn't exactly an explosion. The round flared and spread a fiery bacteria. Once the phosphorus touches flesh, it becomes a chemical tick that burrows through tissue until it reaches bone. But for an instant when it lands and bursts, it's about the most beautiful deadly sight in the world. This one was even prettier, because it landed right on target.

The range sergeant nodded and said, "Next."

I climbed out of the pit. "Top that," Jake said to the two men who jumped into the pit to take their turn. I would later in life hear from a heroin user that two addicts would recognize each other in the stands of a crowded stadium. That's true of tinkerers. True of men like Jake and I. He grinned and slapped my shoulder. Grinning back, I knew I had a friend.

"Some of you," the sergeant first class said, "may opt to carry another weapon into the bush. Personally, I prefer an AK-47, but then it ain't army issue, 'less you join the commie army."

"So join up," some wisecracker said.

"Tried. Wouldn't have me. Sumbitches claimed my accent was too thick."

I laughed along with the others, then took my place on the range and started laying lead on pop-ups, black silhouettes, each of them Charlie. Someday soon, I thought.

The 5.56mm M-16. Plastic stocks, techno gun. Bangs like a toy, little recoil. You can tell it's Mattel, it's swell. The slug was another matter entirely. Evil. Its velocity, after spiraling out of five lands and grooves, was nothing short of amazing. Brought smoke, as we would say. In the open, barring high wind, it was effective up to two hundred meters, deadly at anything less. The projectile tumbled after penetration, found a pathway, be it fat, sinew, or bone, and tore through its target. Its shock waves liquefied organ tissue. Heart, lung, kidney, spleen, liver made mush.

But its velocity was so fast that a twig could alter its trajectory.

In a jungle thick with leaf, branch, and trunk were a million pockets of deflection every square mile. Men disguised as bushes, twig men, awaited us. Obscured behind green clumps and dense shadows, they settled in to ambush us. Charlie, come out and play, I thought. Pop up in the open like a silhouette target where this deadly toy I hold can do its deadly wonder. But Charlie wasn't so stupid. He hid where the copper-coated lead missile was readily deflected.

Tactics. Immediate action saves your life. Charge into the sound the first burst you hear. Sound is your guide. Go, go. Overrun the kill zone.

The L-ambush? Where's the firepower concentrated?

There, Sarge.

Good, that's right.

Wake up. Smell the gunpowder.

First aid for a sucking chest wound. Act fast. Do you administer morphine? Shock. What do you do? Elevate the legs. He ain't fainted. It's real shock.

They got snakes. Cobras don't much bother anyone. It's the little green ones, about a foot long, thick as your middle finger. Two-step death. Keep an eye out.

What do you do if you're bit, Sarge?

Sit down, bend as far forward as you can, place your lips to your butt cheeks, and kiss your ass good-bye.

In case of nerve gas, what do you do?

Atropine.

Do they have nerve gas, Sarge?

No gas. Just nerve. Little guys, but all nerve. Can't shoot for shit, but by damn they got them mortars down pat, put an HE (high-explosive) round right there on your top fatigue button at half a mile.

We broke from training early Friday. I hit Hayes Street, Fayetteville, the Brass Rail Bar, where paratroopers and the Fayette Cong congregated. I had a beer. Had another. Placed a quarter on the rail to buy a rack on the pool table. The guy holding the table was good, a local, a real fuck-you-for-a-buck hustler who preyed on drunk soldiers. Said, two a game. I nodded. He broke and shot one in a corner pocket, muffed the next intentionally. My rack now. Easy on the stroke. I ran the rack, dropped the eight ball. Double or nothing, he said. Sure. Two racks later, I was up sixteen bucks and he was calling for another double-up.

He'd been holding back, sandbagging piece of work

that he was. Shaking my head, I said enough, did so with a smirk that let him know my IQ was more than 85. I turned and stacked the cue stick. When I turned back, he waylaid me—the thick end of his stick on my skullcap.

My legs buckled. I fell to one knee, yet managed somehow to deflect a second blow with my forearm. The hustler dropped the cue, grabbed the bills off the rail, and hoofed it for the back door. Barely aware of following him, I stumbled into the alley, too late and too disoriented to give chase. Somehow, I wove my way to Bragg Boulevard, where two paratroopers from the Eighty-second pulled to the curb in a GTO and coaxed me inside the car. They cannonballed it straight to a dispensary on post.

"Won't feel it," the medic said.

"I won't?" I asked.

"Oh, you'll feel it, but I won't." He chuckled as he dug the needle into my skin.

As I stood in formation on Monday, the captain told Herman Fisher that we had better get to 'Nam pretty soon because "Barnes might not survive another trip to Fayetteville."

Booby traps. The Malayan swinging gate, wooden spikes on a limb. You *will* be shish kebab. Skewered, screwed, not just dead, but dead-dead. Get it? The snare. The bouncing Betty. Remember them. They *will* kill you. Death traps. Can you recognize them in time?

Disarm that grenade. Replace the pin. Good luck, dumb fuck. You just blew up your own shit.

Camouflage, an action or disguise meant to conceal or deceive. Can you spot the enemy? Don't deceive yourself. He's always within, somewhere close and watching.

Sarge, if that's the case, why don't we just blow the shit out of them all?

'Cause in the case of some, we're there to win their hearts

and minds. This is about instillin' fucking democracy, boy. We blow the shit out of the ones don't see things our way. The others get democracy.

Now, look for the entrance to the tunnels, *all of them*. Charlie will snuff your shit. If you think it's a bush, you're dead. Don't live in doubt. Don't wait for it to move.

He knew, truly knew, this guy with a beret on his head and a map in his mind to the graves of all the doubters. I listened up, listened well.

Eight weeks later, the hard work done, we were ready. Congratulations, you got what you asked for. No graduation ceremony. No diploma. Your official orders to 'Nam will serve as your sheepskin. Instead of crossing a stage, you'll cross the ocean and the international date line.

I couldn't wait for 'Nam. It was nuts. I could die there. But I didn't picture myself dead, and I didn't want to be a hero. Being a fool was a tough-enough burden to tote around. And I *wanted* to live. It came down to one thing. I couldn't live the rest of my life knowing that I didn't go. I was ready, but it was days before Christmas 1965, and first I had to take a leave that I had no desire to take. I had nowhere to go but to Las Vegas and visit my family.

Enjoy Christmas, the captain told us. But by January 2, be ready to fly. Sing, hallelujah, hallelujah!

At the beginning of our training, I didn't know what entertained the others, what brought them joy or what their personal ambitions were. And I didn't know any of that at the end of our training, either, but in our preparing for war, what I learned was each of them was dependable and honorable and they would do whatever was required. That was what made us a team.

EIGHT

New Year's, my last night at Bragg, the barracks rats bought a case of beer, stacked the empties at the far end of the bay, ready for one of us to take a slide down the aisle.

Say, who's got the fucking church key?

There's a beer left?

A bleary eye cast a look my way. You fuckin' A, dead man. It's mine.

We laughed at that. We hooted at anything anyone said. We told every joke we could remember, told some same-old lies. We laughed at them, too. We laughed when the stack of empties clattered over the floor whenever someone smashed into them, then stacked them up again. Somewhere around midnight, the beer supply and ourselves exhausted, we crawled into our bunks. I stared at the springs supporting the mattress on the upper bunk. About time, I thought, as minutes ticked toward that coming midnight when any hour, even high noon, might be witching hour. Forget nothing, boy. Every piece of your training will fit somewhere in that crossword puzzle, and there will still be blanks and no letters to fill them in with. Vietnam, the enigma, check it on the map one more time. It's the last good look you'll ever get of it.

The morning of January 2 was inhospitable, humid, cold, breezy, what soldiers called "Fort Bragg miserable." I paced in a circle outside the shadows of the pine trees lining the edge of the airstrip at Pope Air Force Base. Nearby, Pablo and Norwood grabbed what sunlight was available. We were dressed in jungle fatigues and boots, garb too thin to ward off the cold. I stuffed my hands in my pockets and stomped my feet. At least, I thought, over there my fingers won't be numb. It seemed since enlisting, I'd continually been subjected to extremes, cold or hot. Never mild.

Upwind, those who smoked lit up. J. V. fired a Camel and used the cigarette as a pointer to emphasize what he was saying. Whatever he said raised laughter among the others. I halfway wished I smoked to help pass the wait. Congregate with them, socialize.

There was the gray haze overhead and the cloud of my own misgivings. I'd begun to second-guess my decision, wondered if the others did. The longer the delay, the more doubt whittled away at me. The Dom Rep was now at peace, a struggling democracy reassembling its society. They played baseball, revered Joe DiMaggio and Mickey Mantle. I could have enjoyed an easy six months and drawn per-diem pay, tanning myself on beaches and watching kids hitting a ball with a bat. And there were women, sensuous, dark-eyed, brown-skinned women.

And still I was anxious to blow the scene, cut out, get gone. I looked from plane to ground to nearest man, stomped my feet again and shivered, only seconds later to repeat these actions. I spit on the frost-laced pine needles just to break up the routine.

This was the captain's first full command, and a near fervor for the job glistened in his eyes. He drifted from man to man, appealing for patience. Eventually, he sidled up beside me and told me to relax. It was January. The pine trees sparkling with frost told of it, and we were dressed in baggy cotton fatigues meant for tropics. Relax was not in the cards.

He pointed to my head, asked again if I was all right.

Was I all right atop my head or *in* it? I removed my beret to show the stitches were gone. Only a thin line of scab remained, and hair was already growing over it.

He grinned as if to suggest it could have been worse. "You'll be doing a different kind of fighting from now on," he said in an agreeable way.

"Yes, sir."

I thought, should I say I didn't fight for fun, that I wasn't wild, that it just appeared that way? Tell him that ever since I could remember, a hell dog's been chasing my tail? Tell him I was a weed, scolded, battered, demeaned, and handed responsibilities beyond my years? That I had too keen a sense of justice and once took on two bullies who'd hectored another boy on the school bus, did so because if not me, no one else would, not the bus driver, not Ralph Lino, a football teammate who also witnessed the bullying? It was justice at the cost of a broken nose and black eyes. No, I didn't tell him any of it. We were men and didn't talk about such matters.

"I'll be fine, sir," I said.

He smiled again. I returned the smile and watched him walk away.

A moment later the C-130's turbos sputtered and coughed to life. The exhausts poured a plume of black smoke under the wings. Time to blow this hole. Turn on the heater in that shiny bird. The exhaust smoke turned white, and the loadmaster gave the signal. We gathered up our rucksacks and weapons and clamored up the tailgate and into the belly of the plane. It was one of the few times I'd boarded a military plane without wearing a parachute. I felt a little naked as I strapped in, our destination a three-day trip away, every butt-sore mile of it suffered on a nylon seat in the cramped bay of a cigar-shaped aluminum fuselage. But the plane had a heater, a good one.

NINE

Clark Air Force Base. An hour's refueling time. The Philippines, roughly the same latitude as our destination. After departing San Francisco and hopping the Pacific, fuel stops in Hawaii, Guam, and here, we were exhausted and hungry. We ate in an NCO club, the last air-conditioned room we would experience for a long time. We hadn't showered for three days, all of us smelling gamy. With their expressions of disgust, those sitting close by confirmed that fact. When word arrived that the plane was fueled, we strolled to the tarmac—slightly more refreshed. To a man, we had no desire to reboard the aircraft.

"It's a quick hop," the pilot announced over the intercom.

Inside the belly of the plane, we separated as had become customary by rank or age. The captain and Lieutenant Morris sat near the front by the pilot's cabin. Brown and Hausenfauk took seats where they could. As soon as we were airborne, J. V., Jake, Sheppard, and Fisher found space on the other side of the crate, where they broke out a deck of cards and smoked and recycled old stories. Much of the cargo bay was filled by the eight-by-ten-by-six-foot crate that stored our equipment, so we had no room to stretch our legs. The nylon seats burned our butts.

I looked out the porthole as the plane gained altitude, saw wispy clouds and endless blue water. Ten thousand feet above the ocean was a monotonous view. I opened *Travels with Charlie* and read. In what seemed a few minutes later, the aircraft began a descent. Norwood said something. He pointed downward. I looked through the mingy porthole. The ocean was blue and everywhere. Then I caught a glimpse of what he was pointing out—the edge of Vietnam. I pressed my cheek to the porthole, looked inland, and saw spots of afternoon sun reflected off the surfaces of rice paddies where the lowlands merged with emerald-green foothills. Seeing it stirred something unexpected, not excitement exactly, but a feeling akin to a stepchild's anticipation as Christmas neared, hope mingled with a fear that disappointment was inevitable.

The plane veered left and the engines slowed.

There it was in clear view. At Bragg I'd read whatever was available about Vietnam, especially its recent history with war. I knew more about it than any country in the world other than my own. Annamese kings ruled from the ancient Citadel in Hue. French introduced rubber trees from Africa and built impressive plantations. As allies of America, Giap and Uncle Ho polished their guerrilla tactics fighting the Japanese, then took on the French, who lost the battle at Diem Bien Phu by overestimating themselves and underestimating the enemy. After fighting the French from 1946 to 1954, the Vietminh, as they were called, took a two-year hiatus. In 1956 they renewed the cycle of war, now as the Vietcong. We called them Victor Charlie, applying the military phonetic alphabet, and shortened that to Charlie. Three weeks before his own death, John F. Kennedy approved a coup that led to the assassination of South Vietnam's president, Ngo Dinh Diem. Facts. History.

Our plane touched down in Nha Trang in the Land without Plumbing. The tailgate dropped, and the expansive heat that defined Vietnam thrust itself into the aircraft. No reporters or cameras awaited us, as was the case when the marines, the first conventional troops, landed months before on a beach near Marble Mountain. No hero's welcome. No photo op. Just a hundred and ten degrees of Vietnamese air.

We clambered down the tailgate. I stretched. Around was the inexhaustible enterprise of war — army vehicles, crates, mortars, guard towers, fuel drums, food rations strapped on palettes, men and machinery moving with an urgency and energy that belied the oppressive humidity and heat. To the far west palm trees grew before a distant diorama of forested peaks and deep-blue sky.

Breathing was labor. Sweat poured from my forehead and armpits. I'd left frosty winter air to swelter here. I wondered now if I'd ever again feel cool. The air smelled of tar, diesel, solvents, urine, and a stench like that I'd smelled coming from the rebel sector of Santo Domingo, where bodies lay for days, some in distorted angles on doorsteps where they'd been dragged, others on sidewalks, discarded like last night's trash. Even when an ocean breeze blew in from the opposite direction, we could smell bodies blocks away. Now nearby on the apron lay body bags in a neat line, a row of postcards from Vietnam, bagged, tagged, and ready to load.

An officer and master sergeant from the Special Forces Operational Base (SFOB), the command center for all our operations, pulled up in a jeep. A deuce-and-a-half followed. It parked behind the jeep, engine idling. Behind the first truck another stopped. The master sergeant stayed with the jeep, but the officer, whose rank I couldn't determine, motioned Captain Fewell, Lieutenant Morris, and Sergeant Fisher aside. He pointed to the west and then to the north as they talked. The rest of us stood on the hot tarmac, sweating.

J. V. farted and said, "Been holdin' back."

"Could'a held back a bit longer." Jake stepped a few feet away.

Cam Gamble and I also moved and planted ourselves beside the first truck, where we waited as a forklift operator loaded our cargo. Once the first truck was full, the captain directed us to mount the second. He and the lieutenant then climbed into the jeep. I tossed my gear over the tailgate and scrambled up. I stood and held onto the cattle rail, determined to take advantage of whatever breeze came along. The driver ground the gears, and the truck jerked to life.

Near the exit gate I caught my first glimpse of Vietnamese culture. A huge net sank under the weight of a six-foot stack of fish suspended over a metal vat. *Nuc maum*, oil from rotting fish, was the seasoning of choice here. If offered, eat it but hold your nose.

We drove to the Special Forces Operational Base. Twenty-five years of near-continuous warfare had left its mark on Nha Trang. Everything seemed in a state of decomposition. The truck bounded over potholes and ruts, rarely missing one. It was dry, and dust from the red clay winnowed into the air. Open sewers ferried human excrement to the sea. The stench and frantic banter of vendor and client squabbling at vegetable stands, the teeming streets, and rampant squalor reminded me of scenes from Graham Greene novels. At guard posts on street corners, diminutive soldiers and policemen armed with carbines or M-1 Garands nearly as tall as they themselves flagged us along. Broadsides hung above villas with white-stuccoed walls, arched entries, and rusted tin roofs. It was the land of *Terry and the Pirates*, a comic strip I'd never grasped until this moment, and it was populated by people I'd come to fight for, though I didn't understand what that meant in the sense that fighting a war comes at a terrible price for all.

At the SFOB we exchanged American currency for an equal amount of military scrip and Vietnamese dong. The transaction came with a warning that we were not to use the scrip off post or engage in trading American green or in any kind of black marketing. Pending assignment to a camp, we were billeted in transient barracks. The captain and lieutenant were assigned officers' quarters; the rest of us grabbed open cots and tossed our gear down in the enlisted bay in a wood-framed barracks with slat siding, the bottom four feet walled in by sandbags.

It was too hot, the place too foreign and too exotic at the

moment to consider sleep. I left the others and wandered the pathways that connected the slat-board compound. I wanted something cold—iced tea, lemonade, air-conditioning, a bath in ice. Along the way I noted guard towers, sandbagged foxholes deep and wide enough to accommodate two. The perimeter fence was double-apron, barbed wire a dozen feet high, prisonlike walls meant to keep the inmates safe. Far beyond the placid palms and sun-glazed paddies, an exchange of gunfire cracked, a few stiff bursts, then a scattering, then nothing.

I stumbled upon the cavernous wooden structure that served as the NCO Club. A steeply pitched galvanized roof in an early stage of rust topped it. Inside the air was heavy with cigarette smoke and the smell of beer. I gradually adjusted to the dim light. The place seemed left intentionally unfinished, as if sending a message to its occupants: abandon if need be; nothing here is permanent or worth saving. Narrow shafts of sunlight filtered in through pinholes in the ceiling. Sun-bronzed troopers wearing faded uniforms lined the bar. A few tables were empty. I went to the bar, and though no one paid me attention, I was self-conscious about my winter-pale skin and fatigues with a fresh Stateside shine. I smelled an odor nearby, fecund and wild. Then I saw the source, a twelve-foot boa with a head the size of a small dog's, lying on the concrete floor looped around a table leg, its blunted nose resting atop its coiled body.

"Harmless," a sergeant said as he passed by.

I bought a Budweiser and threaded my way across the room to a table a discreet distance from the snake. Five men played poker at the adjacent table. One slapped his cards down faceup and raked in the pot. The others nodded disinterestedly and anted up. I sipped beer until fatigue from the journey finally overcame me. I swallowed the remaining contents in a single gulp and stood to leave when a voice called my name from behind. I glanced over my shoulder and glimpsed a familiar face. I hadn't seen Batterham since basic training, a nice guy, a bit slow in the think chambers. In New Orleans before being drafted, he'd been an amateur featherweight. The layers of scar tissue on his brow spoke volumes about his defensive skill in the ring. I couldn't remember his first name, and it occurred that maybe I never knew it. The green beret and sergeant stripes on his sleeves surprised me, as he'd taken the test at Fort Polk alongside me and flunked it.

"Batterham," I said.

He turned a chair backward and straddled it, extended a hand. He smelled of beer. I shook his hand and sat back down. Thinner now than I recalled, he looked older than his twenty-four or twenty-five years. I was curious, being that he didn't qualify for Special Forces training, how he ended up in my unit.

I pointed to his beret. "How'd you get that?"

"Lemme buy a drink." He offered an intoxicated smile, left, and returned with two bottles of Ba Muy Ba, a Vietnamese beer called Rat Poison with "33" on the label. He set one before me and held his up, label facing me. "Means thirty-three fuckin' ways to die."

I took a swallow. "Terrible."

"Compared to Tiger Beer, this stuff's fuckin' champagne."

"So tell me, how'd you end up one of us?"

He explained that after completing communications school, he earned his jump wings and was assigned to the 101st Airborne. His specialty as a radio operator being a critical skill for Special Forces, he was transferred to my unit upon arrival in country. That was five months ago.

"Boom, transferred in. No fuckin' orders. Didn't have to put up with the bullshit."

I felt a little resentment. After all, the others and I in the unit had spent a year or more in training. "I thought you were a draftee?"

"Reenlisted. Regular army now."

"Crazy," I said. What I really thought was absurd.

"Look around. Crazy's the only thing that makes sense."

He drank and chattered away the next two hours, his tongue getting thicker as the night wore on. He told of how the month before, he was ambushed in the highlands. Pinned down by automatic fire, some of the South Vietnamese soldiers refused to return fire. Others squatted down behind a wall of boulders and ate rice balls as bullets whizzed overhead.

"Slopes're either scared or useless," he warned. "You'll find out."

I sat and nursed beer until Batterham was too wasted to talk coherently. I yawned and said that I was on Stateside time and hadn't had a good sleep for the better part of three days. I was going to cave up for the night and suggested he do likewise.

It was still hot outside. A machine gun rattled in the distance, a three-shot burst followed by the distinct pop and whistle of a mortar. Seconds later the round exploded at some farther point. Batterham squinted at me through his bleary eyes. I looked above his head and noticed the Southern Cross. I was not just in another country, but in the torrid zone, 12 degrees and 15 minutes north latitude, a mere thousand-mile hop to the equator.

Batterham wobbled alongside on the wooden pathways. Twice I stopped him before he fell. The second time he gazed up as if trying to recognize me. He asked what I wanted.

"Nothing," I said. "Come on."

Halfway to the billets, he insisted on going into Nha Trang to find some mattress material and get laid. He turned toward the wrong gate, the one leading west, where the gunfire originated. He took a few steps and collapsed.

I helped him to his feet. "You're not going anywhere but bed. I'll get you back to your bunk," I said.

"Fuck you." He took a swing at me and backed away.

I watched him turn to leave. He dropped again, and this time he passed out. I couldn't leave him like that. I lifted him to his feet and hoisted him onto my shoulder. He was shockingly light, about 120 pounds at best. I started out for the billets, but on the way his beret came off and landed at my feet. I bent down, picked it up, and headed off again. He came to, kicking and cursing, and demanded I put him down. I set him on his feet. He threw a lame jab, followed it with a hook and a right cross, all missing their mark. I tossed his beret at his feet, backed away, and left him throwing jabs at the air and cursing the empty space in front of him.

As I entered the billets, gunfire erupted somewhere to the west, too far away to disturb anyone's sleep. I found my cot, removed my boots, and let the day fade off.

We had nothing to do but get acclimated. Still, we'd come to meet Charlie and were impatient to get on with the mission. Until word came of our assignment, the captain asked us to stay together as a team as much as possible. I broke away from the group and spent the morning at the beach charging into breakers and later sat on the sand and watched fishing boats bobble on the South China Sea. In the early evening, I hung with a few of the others. We dined overlooking the shore on a tiled veranda at a restaurant where French plantation owners and Legionnaires once enjoyed the profligacies of colonial privilege.

Near dusk, mosquitoes swarmed in to feed on our Stateside blood. They were ubiquitous, tenacious. Though we swatted and killed a few, nothing discouraged them, an introduction of sorts to the futility of body count as a winning strategy here. J. V., who claimed authority in most matters from impregnation to degeneration, assured me that I would adjust to the insects. I just needed to store up enough whiskey in my blood to discourage them.

"Yes, sir, Jim Beam." He downed his shot, closed his eyes, and inhaled a mouthful of cigarette smoke as if doing so were an act of transubstantiation.

I took most of what he said with a grain of salt. He was forty, oldest among the team. Ancient by my standards. I kept up my guard around him. He was a cat that rubbed itself on your leg, then scratched your hand when you reached to pet it, but he knew soldiering, and despite the layering of bullshit, he was a good man. He ordered another shot, asked if I was old enough to drink. I shook my head, picked up my iced tea, and sipped on it. Ice was a prize and the feel of the cold glass in my hand a miracle.

As darkness descended, the *côs* came out, lovely and lively, dressed in colorful silk *au dais* and white pajamas bottoms. Their shiny hair bound in pencil-thin ponytails, they flitted from table to table, little kites in a crosswind. They smelled of flower and spice, jasmine or hyacinth or cinnamon. In daylight they glided down streets on bicycles, their silk garb whispering with the rise and fall of the pedals until the sound dissolved like a sinking wind. In daylight whispers that slipped away on two wheels, but under a darkening sky they turned into brazen capitalists, skilled hustlers of indeterminate age, sixteen or perhaps thirty, chittering pidgin, accosting soldiers to buy them drinks and soliciting what we wanted most—sex.

Some glanced away demurely, feigning innocence. Some flashed a gold-capped smile to lure a trick. Others giggled. Lub you, too handsome you, they said. Beaucoup boom-boom, they promised. What say you? they asked. They giggled. Shrewd dollies, each bold as a carnival barker, callous as an inquisitor, conniving as a mortgage broker. They honed their craft to an art.

One landed on my lap and wrapped her arms around my neck. "Buy me whiskey, GI."

I shook my head.

She touched my blond hair and winked. "Lub you, GI. Much boom-boom. *Ngàn dong.*"

"A thousand piasters? Never met a slope knew how to fuck," J. V. said. "Offer five."

She sprang off my lap and aimed a scolding finger at him. "I no likey you, *sau lam.* You talk dirty me." She sneered and wiggled off to another table.

He laughed and sucked on his cigarette.

In the midst of the low rumble, waiters scurried about serving beer and whiskey. It was as if life here had a fever, as if everyone was desperate to live everything at once. Little of it seemed real in the sense I understood reality. I saw what brought adventurers and merchants to these shores long ago. The French molded this illusion so they could trifle their lives away drinking chartreuse and cognac with their exotic mistresses in paradise. Now, we'd come with our new opera at Uncle Sam's behest to fight a proxy war with the Soviets because we couldn't fight the real one without destroying the world. What was left to us was the skeleton of an illusion, the remains of what once existed here, before the land was torn by war.

Story ran amok. The air hummed with tales of boonies, things gone bad, acts of courage that in another sphere would be considered insane, some sad, respectful talk of friends who'd been killed. Other tales were cautionary, stories of fatal lapses made in the boonies, words spoken in awe about the devastation wrought by 120mm mortars that fired rounds capable of penetrating four feet of reinforced concrete and sandbag. A-101 Khe Sanh, the camp destined to one day become synonymous with all that was right and all that was wrong about the American effort in Vietnam, had taken a heavy bombardment from the big mortars.

Nearby a circle of NCOs tossed bills into the middle of their table. They nodded and began to count aloud. On the count of three each unzipped his fly. A *cô* crawled underneath the white linen table cloth. A moment passed. The soldiers exchanged questioning glances until one raised his hand and said, "Me." He reached to the center of the table. He cupped the money and leaned back.

"Zipper roulette," J. V. explained.

Beneath the table, she was busy earning a share of the pooled money.

In the Dominican Republic a grizzled lifer said, "Wherever Americans go, they turn the women into whores." Perhaps.

I listened to the singsong voices and thought of Lela and the miles between us and the time that had passed. I felt homesick and realized that I'd been homesick all my life for a home that I'd never had. Somewhere, certainly, I thought, some Frenchman who'd made Vietnam his home was bemoaning the loss of this wanton lifestyle that we'd inherited. Then I heard machine guns in the distance and was reminded that somewhere Charlie was missing nothing.

I went with one who smelled strongly of perfume. I didn't know who'd arranged it. She came and said, "You come me. You too handsome." Perhaps it was the forthrightness of her approach or the way she took my hand or a desire to rid myself of the feeling of homesickness. Or I just wanted to get laid.

Her head barely reached my chest. She was perhaps twenty and pretty in a featureless sort of way. She led me to a walled villa two blocks away. We entered a downstairs room where the air was dank and smelled faintly of urine. Light filtered through shutters, enough to distinguish only shadow and shape. She flipped on a lamp and got right to it, set the price at five hundred piasters, no shyness, no pretense. Money was foreplay, a three-dollar exchange for succor from what waited beyond the walls of the veranda and the boundaries of illusion. I peeled off five bills that she stuffed in her rubber-banded bankroll, and then she turned off the lamp.

The foreplay consisted of my removing my holstered .45, which I placed within reach as she slipped out of her silk garments. She helped me out of my fatigues, closed the mosquito net, and tucked the hem underneath the edges of the shallow mattress. I peeled back the foil wrapper containing a condom. She pulled me on top her on the hard cot. Nothing suggested love or even intimacy, and it didn't take long. It was commerce.

She threw back the delicate mosquito net and rose off the cot. In the corner was a covered hole that served as a toilet. She lifted the lid and squatted. I could barely see her looking at me in the shadows as she peed. I sat on the edge of the cot, my feet flat on the cool tiles, and listened to the splash. From afar muffled rifle and machine-gun fire popped sporadically.

She massaged me until I nodded off. Later I gathered my clothes from the floor, dressed, and snapped on my .45. I checked my money and found it untouched. I reached the SFOB before curfew, stumbled into the darkened bay, and stripped to my skivvies. I slid under the net and sweated and sweated as mosquitoes buzzed frantically. You too far from home, GI. Too far.

TEN

We flew a C-2, a wasp-shaped twin-engine plane, up the coast and over the lowlands and the infamous Highway 1, where the Vietminh took the French to school more than once. The Vietnamese wasted no patch of fertile land. A quilt work of rice paddies spanned from shoreline to foothill. Every inch not bombed out was cultivated and green and shimmering. It seemed a land drawn from myth, fecund as the ancient womb that cradled man, except that this was neither Eden nor the east of it.

We deplaned at the air base in Da Nang, boarded a waiting deuce-and-a-half, and rode to C-1, the command compound at the north end of the airstrip. The operations command center for Special Forces I Corps was a wonder of pioneer construction, two rows of slat buildings and twelve-man tents planted on loose sand. The smell of brine wafted in from the nearby bay.

The captain told us not to get comfortable. We would be here a day, perhaps two. We tossed our gear in the temporary billets. Pablo and I passed time outside the club playing Ping-Pong. The rest occupied themselves in some other manner. That afternoon, Captain Fewell pulled me aside and told me that the team might be separated. The sergeant major wanted to assign me to A Shau, the second-northernmost camp, a spit and a half from the Laotian border.

"They need a demo man."

A Shau meant nothing to me, just another far-flung camp in a valley with an exotic name. Dozens were spread in strategic hamlets over the country from south of the demilitarized zone to Delta Region. For several years those manning them had borne the brunt of combat. That had changed. The insurgents didn't care to take on a well-equipped infantry, so now that conventional forces of Americans were conducting offensive operations, the camps had become strategic targets for Charlie's hit-and-run tactics. I said that I preferred staying with the team mostly out of a sense of loyalty. He said he appreciated that but couldn't promise anything. The final decision wasn't his. I couldn't then comprehend the full significance behind what he said next, or what, in time, it would mean to me.

"I would like to keep you on the team."

That afternoon Team A7/03 was disbanded. Lt. Raymond Morris, the executive officer, and Ray Hausenfauk, the radio operator, were headed to Ba To, and Herman Fisher was assigned to Khe Sanh. The captain, J. V. Carroll, Paul Sheppard, Earl Brown, Rich Norwood, Cam Gamble, Pablo Olivarez, and Donald Jacobsen would fly out in the morning for Camp A-107 at Tra Bong, a hundred kilometers south of Da Nang, and relieve a detachment of Australians.

No decision had been rendered on my status. I wondered who decided the selection and how and concluded only that it was done the military way, which, like the weather, was uniformly unpredictable. Those going elsewhere offered brief good-byes, sans sentiment, and flew out. Losing them was a kick in the guts. Fisher's calm demeanor and wise advice had been a mainstay for us enlisted during training, and Lieutenant Morris was a solid thinker not given to following impulse. We would miss their contribution, but at the time we couldn't know how much and how soon.

It was nearly evening before the captain informed me that I too was heading to Tra Bong.

In the morning Jake commandeered a half-ton truck and then informed me that I was taking a ride. I climbed into the bed and settled onto a bench behind him and Brownie.

Before he started the engine, Jake glanced back and said that the C-Team had wanted to send me to A Shau.

"I argued to keep you."

I thanked Jake.

He said, "Don't. No camp here can be mistaken for paradise."

He'd served a six-month tour here and knew. Brownie, who'd also done a hitch here, nodded in agreement. Jake handed him a map, told Brown to navigate, then started the engine.

For a half hour the truck jostled over the gutted blacktop and dusty roads of Da Nang. Vietnamese police or soldiers at bridges motioned the truck to a stop and peered over the tailgate. They looked about officiously at the empty truck bed before signaling us on. I wondered what they were looking for. Did they think we were smuggling Uncle Ho into the country?

Jake pulled to a stop at a sprawling compound ringed by wire fences. The marine MP guarding the gate motioned the truck through. A PX sat on a towering hill of dusty red clay in the middle of a field of more dusty red clay. We entered a huge bargain basement under a tin roof.

Marines and soldiers lined up at sales counters to buy Rolex watches and Akai recorders. They ordered cars from government-contracted vendors, domestic and foreign, and they bought Japanese motorcycles, purchased all of it tax free at discounted prices. The vehicles would await them Stateside, assuming they reached home. Buy-buy-buy, consumerism combined with good old optimism, the American equation in spades.

Jake passed me a shopping list and told me to get going, that the team didn't have all day. Brownie already had his list in hand. We gathered up bottles of whiskey, cartons of cigarettes, a Japanese tape player with speakers, and a Zeiss Ikon

35mm camera. Jake pulled the truck up to a loading ramp, and Brownie and I along with some Vietnamese dockworkers loaded the goods on the truck bed, along with six cases of Schlitz.

I rode in the back and listened to the wind and the engine and the rattling of the truck as Jake and Brownie talked and smoked. The next stop was a naval base. I watched over the truck as Jake and Brownie toted two bottles each of whiskey down a wooden sidewalk and disappeared inside a Quonset hut. Ten minutes passed before they returned. Jake pointed out a loading ramp and told me to back the truck up to it. Two sailors in fatigues emerged from the Quonset. Under the supervision of a petty officer, they dollied a dozen cardboard crates out of the hut and onto the bed of the truck. I helped stack the goods. When the last containers were loaded, a ten-day supply of food—eggs, potatoes, two dozen steaks in dry ice—lay beside the cases of Schlitz.

Jake's Buddha belly jiggled as he and Brownie laughed again at some joke that passed between them. Seemingly satisfied, Jake settled in the front seat and lit a cigarette. I wondered what the penalty was for black marketing. I gave it some thought and concluded there was none provided you didn't get caught. They were still laughing as we pulled away. Though I didn't know it, it was the laughter of the ghosts of my future. But at the moment they were flesh, as I was, the three of us scofflaws off to war with our plunder of meat and eggs and bread.

ELEVEN

The Caribou zipped over the coastal floodplain a couple of miles inland, nine of us packed inside along with a half-dozen pallets, nine footlockers, and crates containing food and weapons. The tailgate was down. Already temperatures at ground level exceeded a hundred degrees; a mile above cool air flowed into the craft. I lay near the edge of the ramp and watched the plane progress. The shadow of the aircraft skated across the shimmering ground. It seemed the plane was stationary and the land was slipping away.

To the right the forests of the Annamese Cordillera appeared purple in the morning sun. Below rice paddies scotched in berm stretched southward mile upon mile. Villages linked by a system of foot-worn roads and trails dotted the countryside, paradise except for the devastation—a bridge tossed aside like a bad poker hand; roads scored with bomb craters the size of swimming pools; charred skeletons of huts and a demolished church, its charred rafters a haunting message that Charlie rejected the religion as well as the presence of Westerners.

The plane veered west and turned up the mouth of a valley of backcountry unchanged for centuries—quaint hamlets, shimmering paddies, green hedgerows, and tall palms. To the north the Song Tra Bong wound lazily though the valley and the floodplain like a well-fed snake. A couple miles up the throat of the valley, the plane took automatic fire from a weapon hidden somewhere in the forested slopes. A few green tracers trailed groundward just short of the craft. Norwood's jaw knotted, relaxed, and knotted again. His serious blue eyes and expression conveyed what I felt: we were at the mercy of bad shooting, but even a bad shot got lucky on occasion.

We flew over Camp Starlite, a marine battery. Two of its 155mm howitzers on treads pointed to the west, where we were headed. The other big guns aimed toward Ha Tanh, the next camp to the south. The loadmaster tapped my shoulder and shouted for me to take a seat. The pilot dropped the flaps, and the plane shifted. I strapped in as we passed over a string of tranquil-appearing hamlets ringed by rice paddies. Near one of those seven weeks before, two Australians, two Vietnamese, and four or more vc died in a firefight.

Farther on the pilot dipped the wings and eased the craft into a soft glide. I glimpsed my camp for the first time. Shaped like a huge footprint, the heel pointing east, ball and toes aiming west, Tra Bong was encased in a triple row of wire and divided into three distinct compounds. Trenches connected the bunkers in each. The gun ports of the sand-bagged caverns gazed out at the perimeter like half-buried skulls of one-eyed creatures. The camp's defenders, some shirtless, some in full tiger stripes, some barefoot, stood atop the bunkers and waved. The Caribou tracked to the right of a landing strip that appeared far too short to accommodate it.

A jeep and a three-quarter ton waited on the apron, where a plume of purple smoke drifted northwesterly. The plane banked sharply and struggled with a crosswind as it crabbed its way to the ground. The instant the landing gear touched down, the pilot reversed props. We rattled over steel skid plates, and when we finally came to a stop, the plane's nose hung over the sheer edge of an embankment that dropped some twenty feet.

The pilot wasted no time in turning the Caribou back through a wall of red dust. He feathered the props, ready to leave in an instant should the need arise. An airstrip in the boonies was not to be confused with a parking lot. I shouldered my gear, clutched my rifle, and waited for the tailgate to drop. I asked the crew chief if all the landings were like that.

"Just most of them." He lowered the ramp.

The jeep and truck pulled to a stop under the tail wings. An Aussie officer swung down from his seat in the jeep and stood with his feet planted shoulder-width apart. Two other round-eyes in jungle fatigues and a half-dozen Vietnamese circled the truck.

A shirtless American waited at the bottom of the tailgate with a cigarette dangling from his lips. He was thin, his chest sunken, face long and narrow, nose protuberant and riddled with broken blood vessels. As we deplaned, he extended a hand to each of us. When my turn came, he furrowed his brow and introduced himself as Fox, Doug, Master Sergeant. He wobbled slightly and pointed to his bare arm, as if to indicate his rank. The smell of whiskey orbited him.

"Call me Top or Doug," he said in a voice rough as asphalt. He squinted into the cargo bay. "Any beer in there? Been on water a week now." When he saw the cases of Schlitz stacked on a pallet, a near-lewd smile formed in the corners of his mouth.

Norwood and I exchanged apprehensive looks.

The Aussie commander was about business first. He didn't bother with introductions or handshakes. Instead, he hustled Captain Fewell aside. Without delay the captains mounted the jeep with Sergeant Fox in the driver's seat. I wondered if it might not be preferable for someone more sober to take the wheel. Fox punched the accelerator. The jeep tires spewed dust. I asked J. V. if it was always this dusty.

His face in a knot, J. V. lit up a Camel and ran his tongue over his lips. "Come monsoon, you'll be wantin' some dust."

We began unloading equipment. The air smelled of dung and dust and fecundity. The sun was high. Even in the shade of the tail section, the heat bored into us. As soon as the belly of the craft was emptied, the loadmaster signaled with a thumb, and the pilot throttled the engines. A fierce gust from the props stirred even more dust.

Jacobsen and Sheppard left with the driver of the truck, a sergeant who went by Joe, but whose name was Elmer Reifschneider—tall and slim with a wry smile. Scheduled to rotate out of camp in three weeks and return home, he should have been packing to leave the next day but instead was ordered to remain and assist us with the transition.

The plane raced to the end of the strip, dipped from view for a heart-stopping instant, then rose again, barely clearing treetops as it passed over Tra Bong. It flew east, gaining altitude. There, I thought, goes the only way out. I watched until it was a memory on the horizon, then looked around at this place where I would spend at least the next six months—or die, a possibility now worth considering.

Mountains rose steeply on three sides to peaks in excess of four thousand feet. Except on the most vertical cliffs, the slopes were covered with vine tangles. Under the jungle canopy was a complex ecosystem that had existed for millennia—home to birds, monkeys, snakes, tigers, elephants, and exotic insects—a briar patch where Charlie himself hid and a free range for American bombers to drop their arsenal. The wild things shared the forest with the Co, a tribe of small-game hunters and slash- and-burn farmers. The mountains, part of a geological formation of peaks and valleys that form the Tra Bong Sheer, emerged from volcanic upheavals millions of years before the first Annamese migrated south from ancient Cathay. The formidable mountains and fertile valleys run east to the coast and create a boundary between the Kham Duc and Ngoc Linh formations that originate in the Indonesia archipelago.

None among us knew or needed to know the geological or anthropological history of Tra Bong. What was crucial was the practical information of the terrain and the people. What we knew with certainty was the populace was divided into friendlies and hostiles. Until the shooting started, and even after the fact, it wasn't always possible to distinguish between them. Charlie was the boy herding buffalo or the woman fanning herself with her straw hat. Trust the American beside you. Be wary of all else.

The truck returned with Montagnard laborers, who helped load equipment. Reifschneider ferried Brownie and Norwood and a load of equipment to the camp. An hour or so later, he returned for Pablo, the remaining equipment, and me. As the three-quarter ton bounded over the rutted road from the airstrip, I got a passing glimpse of the village. Mothers nursed babies; men and women hoed the fields; boys herded water buffalo; a Buddhist monk stepped aside and bowed respectfully. Children waved. The teeth on the elderly who smiled were stained black from chewing betel nut. Still water glistened on the paddies. It seemed everything with roots was a shade of green, from pale emerald to deep highland, a seemingly pastoral setting complicated only by the presence of war.

Except for the stench, the oppressive heat, and dust roiling up from the roadbed, the valley could have been a setting for a fairy tale. I reminded myself that two Aussies recently died here. Remember that and why you are here. Another kind of story lurked in this place, not one that precisely pitted good and evil, but a narrative with its own sinister twists. As the last turn in the road neared, the camp came into view. I looked at Pablo, who sat beside Reifschneider. The near-perpetual smile common to his face was gone, and his jaw was clenched.

I shouldered my gear and jumped down from the truck as the Aussie commander and Captain Fewell rounded the road and headed for the perimeter. The Australian officer paused and pointed out a feature in the surrounding landscape. Tall and erect, he filled the air with self-importance. They turned the bend and disappeared from view. I pulled open the screen door and entered the team house. The Australians gathered at the table stopped talking to look up, and then returned to their conversation.

Fox introduced us to the interpreters, Pham, who went by Johnny or John, and Henry, whose actual name was Tuan or Nguyen or something similar. He said it so fast it was hard to catch. Fox briefed us on the house rules, the beer kitty, where to mark our names on the acetate board, that rations were purchased from a team fund and we were to contribute forty dollars in scrip each month. He spoke in a gruff tone, his vocal chords sounding like machinery gone to rust. Even through the detectable slur and the rheumy-eyed gaze, I sensed a keen mind at work appraising us.

He assigned Norwood and me to the same bunker, the first on the north side of the trench that connected all the bunkers and the mortar pits. Our new home faced the river and was barely large enough to accommodate us, the bunks, and our lockers. It was dank and smelled of mildew, something else I'd have to adjust to. At most, I had eleven months to do it in. Claiming the first bunk on the left, I tossed my rucksack down beside it and looked out the machine-gun port. We had a riverside view and the mountains as a backdrop. I figured I could see the field of fire if I stood on my toes. Norwood, three inches shorter at five feet nine inches, hadn't a prayer of seeing much but mountain and sky. It wouldn't do if we had to use the weapon. I figured the base of the wall was a good place for my footlocker.

I toted my locker from the team house to the bunker, set it beneath the machine gun, and arranged my gear. Then I sat and looked around.

Norwood came in, laid his gear at the entrance, and took a whiff of moldy air. "Well," he said — *well* being a word usually prefacing an understatement from him, "we're here for a while." His way of saying get used to it.

The next morning just past dawn a Marine Force Recon unit back from a three-day operation waded across the river. The six of them lumbered into camp and headed straight to the team house. When I entered, they were seated at the table eating C rations. I recognized one from jump school. Back then Bucholz was huge, around six feet two and 240 pounds. He'd shrunk to about 190.

"Small world," I said.

"Yeah."

In jump school the marines had stayed pretty much to themselves, but I was assigned in their jump stick, so I got to know a couple. He and I went outside to talk. I asked about the marines whose names I remembered, where they were, if he ever saw them. It had been a year and nine months since we'd earned our jump wings. He told me a few had been discharged already, but most were in 'Nam, spread among different units. This was his seventh month in country, and he'd spent a good deal of it in the boonies. That experience came with stories, one of a squad mate who, when cornered in the mountains by the vc, smiled and lifted his rifle overhead as if in surrender, then did a backflip off the cliff.

"They were so amazed, they didn't go after him," Bucholz said, smiling to himself. "Guy made it out on a broken leg."

I hoped I would never be that desperate. I asked what had been on my mind when I saw them wade across the river: "What'd you guys find out there?"

"Didn't see any Charlies, but the signs were there." He grinned and asked how I got such a plush assignment.

"What do you mean?"

"'Cause you're in the shit hole of Vietnam."

In November the camp defenders and the local Vietcong slipped into a tacit understanding, not exactly a cease-fire but something similar, mostly on the part of the camp commander, who wasn't inspired to wage operations in the area where two Aussies had been killed. Cooperation had soured under the watch of Captain Fazikas, our captain's predecessor. Our team was directed to reestablish relations with the Vietnamese and run operations with the intent of racking up a little body count. Change of command came swiftly. Some Aussies flew out on the craft we came in on. The rest, with the exceptions of Misters Green and Whitten, left midmorning on another flight. The two remaining behind were meant to reinforce the team and keep on hand some familiar with the area. The Aussies' departure seemed to cheer my new team sergeant. As soon as the last of them was airborne, Fox put a mark by his name on the beer roster, grabbed a cold one from the fridge, and put the church key to work. He spent the rest of the day getting familiar with his new team, squinting at them through bleary eyes and smiling.

Pablo and I walked the camp and got a first look at the Montagnard and Vietnamese we would be fighting alongside. They were a ragtag lot of reserve volunteers. Rather than being conscripted into the regular army, they opted for two-year duty in their own district as part of a Civilian Irregular Defense Group Strike Force. We referred to them simply as strikers.

Neglect was everywhere — poorly maintained weapons, wire in need of repair. An expanse of seven-foot-tall elephant grass spread from the wire to the river; rolls of unused concertina sat rusting; cement had hardened inside a bag; bindled sandbags rotted; boxes of ammunition had mold. Bunkers could withstand an 81mm mortar but nothing more powerful. Here and there claymore mines tilted skyward or tipped forward, rendering them useless. The tin storage shed contained stacks of M-1s and carbines, some in Cosmoline, BARs, and an A-4 machine gun, all stored alongside explosives. A single mortar round would wipe out the entire reserve arsenal.

I stood atop the camp's mantel and wondered how a camp built so recently by navy Seabees had fallen into such a state of neglect and why the location was selected—and whose myopic eyes conceived the design. It had no escape route built into it. Nor was there any fixing that. If we were hit by a hard-core unit of any size or by North Vietnamese, Tra Bong would be Custer at the Little Big Horn, the Japanese at Guadalcanal, a clay mound of anonymous dead.

Good or bad, it was now ours to suffer.

The captain sidled up beside me and asked if I had any opinions.

I pointed to a galvanized shed that served as the armory. "That's useless, except as a registration point for vc mortars." I pointed in the direction of the outermost perimeter facing the river. "And the elephant grass growing over there . . ."

He looked.

". . . can hide a platoon."

He asked what I thought needed attention first.

"Everything," I said.

That afternoon I was given a stack of requisition forms and instructions to start ordering ordnance and construction supplies. I'd never seen the forms before, never had to requisition anything, and I wasn't certain exactly what all was needed. I sat down at the table in the team house and started by making a list of things I was certain we needed for construction—more wire, cement, and rebar. J. V. drifted out of the back room he'd adopted as the intel center and told me to write up a list of office supplies. After him came Brownie and the captain with their requests. Jacobsen needed solvent for cleaning weapons. The list grew.

As I started transferring the list to the forms, I wondered

what the men who'd returned to the Dom Rep were doing at that moment. Swimming in warm water? Romancing some beauty? I filled out the first form slowly and, halfway through, made an error. I wadded it up and tossed it into the wastebasket. Fortunately, the container was close enough that I could shoot baskets with my mistakes. I spent much of the afternoon improving my shooting technique.

TWELVE

Fox motioned me out of the team house. As I stepped outside, I looked at him, a man of forty, lifer lines that made him look even older—too much whiskey, not enough soda, hardly a poster boy for Special Forces. He aimed a bony finger at the water trailer and told me to go on a water run. I had no idea what a water run was. Vietnam had its own vocabulary, and the camp had its.

"Follow me," he said, his words sliding together.

We walked to the three-quarter ton, where he instructed me to lift the trailer and set it on the hitch after he backed up. He climbed in the driver's seat, started the engine, and looked over his shoulder. "You ready?" he asked and looked in the side mirror.

I nodded. He told me to let him know when the hitch was over the knob, then backed up, two inches too far for me to seat it. "Won't go on, Top," I said. "Pull forward a little."

He hit the accelerator. The truck lurched forward, and the ball joint connected with the hitch. I barely managed to get my hand away in time to avoid smashing a finger or worse. The truck pulled the trailer forward a half foot and came to rest. I secured the hitch with the cotter pin as Fox stepped down from the truck. He pointed to Reifschneider, who waited in the jeep.

"When Olivarez gets here, follow Joe," he said.

I pointed to my hand. "Top, I could have lost a finger."

"Count 'em," he said, walking away. "If you got ten, you're okay."

I climbed into the driver's seat. Brownie swung aboard the jeep next to Reifschneider. Four strikers clamored up behind me, and then Pablo, wearing a steel pot and flak jacket and packing an M-16, a grenade launcher, and a .45 on his hip, emerged from the trench.

As he settled into the passenger seat, I said, "Who you expect out there, John Wayne, a division or a full army?"

"Just drive," he said.

I shrugged and pressed the accelerator.

We followed a cloud of red dust left by the jeep ahead. At the turn to the village a *bà* packing firewood shed her load, rolled up her pant leg, and squatted alongside the road to urinate. The strikers hooted at her.

Nearing the village, we hit a blockade, three water buffalo, and a boy with a switch. The jeeps stopped and I pulled the truck behind it. The boy snapped the lead buffalo in the flanks, but the animal was on its own time and didn't budge. The kid smiled meekly and tried his luck on the next buffalo with the same results. Pablo muttered and, weapon at the ready, stepped down.

Reifschneider tried honking, but the beasts merely turned their heads and stared at the jeep. The boy turned his attention to the lead buffalo, shouting and bringing the switch down on its rump. The beast snorted, lowered its head, waddled down the ditch and up the berm, and sloshed into the rice paddy. The other two followed.

Pablo, wet from armpit to waist, swung into his seat.

"Hot enough in that?" I asked, meaning his armored vest.

"You're not funny, Barnes."

Our caravan proceeded as before, the jeep stirring up dust,

the empty tank rattling. From under frond-shaded stands, villagers tracked our progress with amused disinterest. Youngsters waved. We passed the district chief's compound and the airport. The road inclined and then curved north and canted into a rocky washbasin where the Song Tra Bong formed a water boundary that separated the Montagnard hamlet from Vietnamese village. When I stopped the truck, the strikers piled out of the back. They squatted in the nearest shade and lit cigarettes, seeming as if interested in anything but protecting us.

I turned the truck in a half circle and backed up, but it took three attempts before I was able to position the trailer so I could back it into the shallows. Pablo posted himself beside the truck in the shade of a tree. Brownie brought along a box of chlorine and chemical tablets to make the water potable. I lifted the pump from the truck bed and attached the hose. After about a dozen yanks on the cord, the Briggs and Stratton engine sputtered to life.

As Reifschneider called out directions, I waded into the water with the running end of the hose in hand and primed the opening. Water swirled around my calves and filled my boots. It was refreshing. River water gushed into the tank.

"Got it under control?" Brownie asked.

I nodded and the jeep drove off.

Across the river some Co had gathered at the bank. Heavy-breasted women, nipples swollen from feeding infant after infant, stood beside their young. They were unabashed in their nakedness and flashed their betel-nut blackened teeth as they grinned at our efforts. Some girls, more modestly clothed, clustered close together, while young males, naked or wearing only loincloths, ventured to the water's edge. Downstream a boy stood on the bank and sent a stream of urine into the river. And they shit in it, I thought. What armament do we have to combat that?

Pablo looked at the boy, then at me. There was no need for comment; his expression of disgust said everything. We were seeing the Vietnam we'd only imagined in premission training. I looked at the Song Tra Bong, rusty and tepid, and thought, it's the only water we've got. Besides the human waste, it was infested with parasites that could grind through human organs. While foreign to us, Montagnard had been pissing in rivers for centuries. Now they lived on the verge of losing their way of life, suffering under a yoke of persecution from the Saigon government and Vietcong alike. Who were we to judge them, uninvited as we were, wary and watchful, strangers quick to condemn, foreigners here for war—again?

We filled the tank, wasted no time loading the hose and pump, then hustled back through the village to the rings of wire and fields of fire that stood as our best illusion of safety.

In the BAR and M-4 machine gun, the headspace determines the rate of fire of the weapon on full auto. Timing is adjusted by pressing the tip of a round into a slot in the timing ring at the breach and turning the mechanism either clockwise or counterclockwise. In military jargon, checking headspace may also mean ascertaining whether a man thinks clearly.

Fox stood beside me in the mortar pit and squinted, one eye drooping, both red. He gave me a listen-up-dumb-shit look, but he didn't talk, just stared with a bland gaze the way my mother did when she suspected I'd done something wrong. When possible, I'd avoided him those first days, managed to by staying busy, which wasn't hard, given the sad condition of the camp. He kept looking at me fixedly. I felt I had to speak up.

"You okay?" I asked, and to set him aback said, "You look pretty tawdry."

"Tawdry. Now, just what the fuck does that mean?"

"Nothing really."

"Then don't be a flannel mouth."

A what? A flannel mouth? Fox came from the streets of Philly, where he learned a hot dog on a stick constitutes a meal, a wise guy's a man with connections, and no one trusts a flannel mouth. In time, I figured he meant don't be tricky, don't be clever, speak clearly what's on your mind. Whatever one was, it didn't sound like something I cared to be.

He began drilling me, question after question about the mortar. "How many clicks? How many increments do you cut? Just what the fuck do you know?"

I knew nothing about him, except I figured in his condition he couldn't make it beyond the base of one of the mountains surrounding us. But he was the tester, and it wasn't up to him to prove himself, especially to me. I had to prove myself, starting now. I studied the face of the mountain across the river, all of it dense foliage and stone cliffs. I spotted a cluster of tall boulders at the foot of the mountain, ideal cover for someone to direct mortar rounds into the camp.

I pointed them out. "There, that one."

His eyes narrowed on the potential target.

"We should have that zeroed," I said. "A mortar there could take out the team house."

I took the acetate-covered map and grease pencil in hand and began applying everything Jake had tutored me in. I consulted the map, calculated distance, moved a sighting stake to mark the azimuth, then lined the bipod with the stake. I fixed the sight, leveled the mortar, and chose a white phosphorous from the magazine. I cut increments, pulled the pin, and said, "One hanging." I dropped the round home and plugged my ears.

A flash was followed by a dull pop. Then a puff of white smoke rose. I'd landed short, slightly to the left. I adjusted the angle of the tube, realigned the sight on the stake, and repeated the firing process. The second round hit target center.

"Close enough," he said, as close to a compliment as he would ever come.

He lifted the poncho that covered the magazine, where the rounds were organized by type—Willy Pete, high explosive, illumination. He peered in, then looked me in the eyes and asked if I could build a bunker and a watchtower.

This was the Alamo. One last stand. No way out. We all knew that. With no escape possible, the best choice for us was to make overrunning the camp so costly in casualties that Charlie wouldn't attempt it. The last holdouts would die in that bunker, but Charlie would be stacked four high outside the gun ports. I said, "I've been thinking about something like that."

He looked about as if he hadn't heard. I waited without speaking.

"Where?"

I motioned at the corrugated shed that the Aussies used as an armory. "There. I'd tear down the shed and use the metal to laminate the concrete and reinforce the roof and walls."

He looked at me through his slitted eyes.

"Walls need to be about four feet thick, reinforced, two stories, twelve feet deep. Two-story bunker, one aboveground, sandbagged. Firing ports, all four directions."

"Okay. And the tower, where?"

"On top of the bunker. Eight-foot tower," I said. "See the whole valley."

He looked at the formation where I'd placed the round. "You got lucky on that shot."

I looked at the hill and said, "We can place claymores outside. And . . ." When I looked back, he was staring at the tin shack. "I can rig the team house, so that if we're overrun . . ."

He looked at me askance and said, "Don't be a flannel mouth."

"Top," I said, my tone respectful, "this place is held together by splints."

"We get hit, this is your post. Work on some more registration points."

I was selected. I don't know who made the decision, the captain or Brownie. No matter, someone decided I needed a little cross-training in first aid, and not just first aid but treating the ill. And Norwood was picked to train me to help on sick call.

We stood under the canopy of an open tent. As a line of malingerers waited in the sun, he showed me first how to start a drip line, which he said I wouldn't be doing that day but should know how to do nonetheless. He picked up a syringe from a tray and demonstrated injecting sterile water through the rubber diaphragm into a bottle of powder. He shook the mixture and drew it out with the same syringe. I took a turn at it, aspirated properly, flicked the syringe, and pressed the air out with the plunger as he had. He seemed satisfied.

He told me to pay attention to where he wiped the alcohol swab and warned me about the sciatic nerve. I watched as he gave the first man in line a shot in the buttocks. For what, I didn't know. The next sick man was mine. He stepped up. Norwood watched as, step by step, I administered the shot. Perfect. He didn't feel a thing. I withdrew the needle and wiped the injection site with a swab. Norwood seemed proud, perhaps of my small accomplishment, but more likely of his success at teaching someone as thickheaded as I was.

One at a time, Norwood examined them, listened to ailments rendered through the interpreter. I stood by, a syringe at the ready. Between the two of us, we treated three more patients and gave two shots. I gained confidence. Bring 'em on, I thought, your tired, your weary, your sick. Dr. Barnes at your service, the best medical help in all of 'Nam a step away. What's troubling you? Too much boom-boom? A little gonorrhea? Yes, we have a quick fix for that. Next patient, please. Don't be shy. We're all professionals here. Top grade.

Norwood sent the next striker my way with instructions to give him antibiotics for his clap. I prepped as instructed. The man dropped his trousers.

"Too much fucky?" I smiled.

I swabbed the injection site and jabbed him in the buttocks. Bull's-eye, a perfect hit. But then his eyes promptly rolled up in their sockets, and he tilted forward, passed out. As he and I lifted the patient to a stretcher, Norwood, a bit testy, reminded me about the sciatic nerve. I shrugged. It wasn't as if we'd get sued for malpractice.

First time I saw it, I was amazed it had gone unclaimed, an orphan from the Korean War. The army had replaced the 57 with a shoulder-fired 75mm recoilless rifle, but this was the original, a genuine M-18, affectionately called a reckless, all of its component parts intact and plenty of rounds. It struck a chord in me, an instrument built with a practical purpose behind it. A soldier can understand and appreciate function and beauty as well as watchmakers, race car drivers, and roulette dealers. I liked its heft, forty-five pounds, unloaded. Its five feet of steel balanced nicely on my shoulder, and it tucked in just right when I placed my eye on the scope.

It had been neglected, needed cleaning, bore sighting, and its throat blocks adjusted. I stored its ammo in the mortar pit and took the gun to my bunker. I cleaned it until the inside of the barrel shined, then took it to the top of the mound, mounted it on a tripod, and tossed a poncho on the ground. I tied intersecting strings in the notches at the lip of the barrel and pulled the crosshairs taut, then abstracted the firing pin from the breach block, closed the breach, and lined up the barrel with a granite rock on the mountainside across the river, a distance of roughly five hundred meters. I lay on the poncho, adjusted the crosshair on the target, and tightened the scope's set screw.

After replacing the firing pin, I loaded a high explosive in the breach and locked the block. It was going to be loud, raise dust, and spray a ten-foot tail of fire from the breach. When it announced itself, the recoil lifted the barrel up a couple of inches, and the tripod cut a foot-long slash in the clay. The throat blocks were too closed. I adjusted the throat blocks with a tool, opening them a smidgen to release more gas. There was no precise formula. It was like setting the fuel-air ratio on a Holly carb by ear. No manual can be as exact.

I fired it again. Almost right. I gave the top block a sixteenth of an inch more exhaust. When the time came to use it, it had to be precise. Once the breach cooled sufficiently, I fed it another shell and hoisted it to my shoulder. The barrel wobbled. I bent my knees, let the muzzle settle, and closed my left eye. As I did, I realized a recoilless was a right-handed man's weapon, exclusively. And I was right-handed. This time, it was a deadly line of poetry.

THIRTEEN

The camp was infested with rats. The fourth day in camp one bit J. V. Norwood had to treat him with injections under his abdominal skin. Although not subjected to needles in the belly, we were all affected by being in country, which meant sweating off at least five pounds each and occupying the latrine almost nonstop. We had a two-seater. Often both were busy.

Treated or otherwise, the water as soon as round-eyes were exposed to it turned their guts into a mill for diarrhea. There was no way to combat it. The bacteria causing the sickness thrived despite pharmaceuticals and chemicals. Give me a bowel! the bugs demanded. The sole treatment for the malady was a near-useless chalky liquid that left the mouth tasting as if you'd eaten dirt.

J. V., already out of sorts from the shots, was hit harder than anyone else. There was no point in drinking water, he claimed, if the chemicals provided to purify it didn't work. He used that reasoning to justify his drinking only beer. Like the others, I purged my guts, twice, three times, sometimes four or more a day. Farting became a risky proposition, and it seemed as if I was losing not just liquid but intestine an inch each time and a bit of stomach and a few blood vessels. Combined with the fluid lost from our sweating, we were all dehydrated. Like J. V., some others drank beer to stave off the runs. I tried. It rendered me worse than before. Coke and orange soda had a similar effect. I craved pure water over ice, fantasized about it.

I asked Brownie if there were something besides bismuth I could take. He said a broad-spectrum antibiotic would treat it, but it would return. Smiling, he said enigmatically, "Drink a lot of liquids."

"Isn't that what causes it?"

"Yeah," he said, his smile fading away.

I took it philosophically. Our diarrhea benefited niches in the biosphere, especially flies that fattened up in the latrine and dive-bombed us, bluebottles and bloated black ones. The latrine became a giant petri dish where bacteria begat bacteria and flies begat flies. I viewed diarrhea, along with the incessant heat, rats the size of house cats, and little green snakes that shut down a man's nervous system in seconds, as nature's way of keeping me from getting too attached to the neighborhood. As if those weren't enough to discourage my buying property here, there was the war and the village women with their betel nut–blackened teeth.

Half dehydrated, I took my list of details out into the heat, but kept the latrine in sight, in case. I set out to check and adjust all the claymores in camp. Before I finished the perimeter of the main compound, I doubled over in pain. Then when the pain passed, butt cheeks tightened, I hurried to the latrine, hoping that I didn't explode along the way and that one of the holes was free.

An hour later the cramps returned, and I tripped again to the latrine.

After a week the symptoms lessened.

What a luxury potable water was. I'd always taken it for granted, along with music on a radio and a hamburger cooked medium rare. I wondered if Charlie suffered the in-countries. I hoped so. Something had to level the situation a bit, something small he couldn't avoid such as bacteria, instead of something big such as bombs, which he seemed to avoid rather well.

FOURTEEN

Bacon was frying. The team was down to one day of bacon. Then we'd be on Spam. As I neared the entrance, I heard J. V. busying himself outside the team house. Ever since he started on rabies shots, he'd been on a tear, and though he wasn't supposed to drink, he did. His moods depended on a few variables, on how hard the in-countries hit him, what and how much he drank the previous night, and if his back or hemorrhoids were acting up. The absence or presence of any of these ailments might leave him pleased with the entire planet or ready to cut a throat. I usually avoided him until midday, and if possible until evening.

Second and last watch last night, and I was feeling both now. I rested the shotgun on my shoulder, came up from behind as he was bent over sifting coffee grounds. He wheeled around and aimed the strainer at me. "Gawdamn. You're gonna get yourself shot. And not by no damn vc." He furrowed his brow, ladled coffee into an aluminum cup, wrapped the cup in a rag, and handed it over. "Here. It'll wake you up if it don't kill you. Slopes hit the supply tent again?"

On my first watch I'd surprised two strikers who'd crawled under the wall of the supply tent to steal rations. Steaks, eggs, potatoes, and carrots, the best the navy had to offer, perished fast out here, so we binged for a few days and then resorted to eating Spam or C rations. We needed what was in the tent. The strikers hit the wire and managed to squeeze under before I could grab either of them. One left a strip of cloth from his uniform on the barbs. Mr. Whitten, who relieved me my first watch, asked why I hadn't shot the "buggers" and said he would have.

"Slopes 'ud steal us blind if they could. Don't trust none since Boan Mi Thuit," J. V. said, referring to when his team had been caught in the middle of a scrape between the Vietnamese and the Yards. He obviously wanted to tell the story again, but my silence didn't encourage it.

The captain had ordered the team to dispense with terms such as *slopes* and *gooks,* but J. V. wasn't about to discard the diction of a lifetime. He explained in unequaled fashion that he'd "fought the Japs, and they were gooks. And then the North Koreans and the gawdamn Chinese, and by damn they were slopes as well." He added that he'd been promoted through the ranks to sergeant first class and had served in 'Nam twice before and no one had corrected his language.

The coffee was too hot to drink. I set it aside. He forked some strips onto a waiting plate. His pans sizzled. He went about his task deftly, fork and spoon in one hand to turn potatoes, salt and pepper in the other to season them. He had standards. It was critical the potatoes come out charred and hard as poker chips and soaked in grease. Some in camp credited J. V.'s cooking as the source of our diarrhea.

His face darkened. "Somethin' wrong with my coffee?"

"Hot." I picked up the cup and blew on it.

"'Spose to be hot. It's coffee, by gawd." He felt compelled to pursue the issue. "What's the point in cold coffee? Why don't you just put some of your mother's milk in it? Damn bunch'a pussies. You'd rather hear a fat boy fart than a pretty girl sing."

I nodded to placate him. He turned his back and farted.

"Say the slopes'd grow potatoes 'stead'a rice." He faced me and curled his brow. "There'd be no damn war."

All I could do was humor him. "You may have something there, Pap."

He went on to explain how the Russians used potatoes to make vodka, which he claimed was *serious* liquor, and that didn't make them much different from Americans, though we, meaning him, preferred rye and sour mash. He said that it was similar thinking. He looked over a shoulder, gauging my attention before he continued. I took a quick sip and set the cup back down right away.

"Slopes waste all that rice makin' wine," he said. "Ain't enough to feed the sumbitches. They got no bidness wastin' good rice on bad licker."

He said that the war was really about rice, North suffering a shortage and South having an abundance. He drew an analogy with the American Civil War's being over cotton, which he insisted was the true cause. I feigned interest and sipped the coffee. It was now cool enough.

He was putting the last eggs and potatoes on the fire when Brownie sauntered in, cup in hand. J. V. asked if he found anything in the rat traps. Norwood set traps at night. First thing in the morning either he or Brownie checked them. Since J. V.'s rat bite, Norwood had declared a private war on them, and whenever he snared one, he doused it with gasoline and lit it on fire. As reserved as he was about most things, he took relish in hearing their dying hiss.

"Empty." Brownie frowned. "One took the crackers without springing the trap. I'm using Spam tomorrow."

"It ain't the crackers. You put them traps in the wrong place." J. V. told Brownie that the rats near his bunker were "diggin' straight to China."

"J. V., we're on the other side of the world," Brownie said. "They're digging their way to South America, which, if we had any sense, we'd be doing ourselves." He put down the hot cup and blew on his fingertips.

"You mean, we'd dig our way to the U.S. of A."

They passed the next few exchanges arguing whether Vietnam was opposite the United States. Brownie thought he had J. V. pinned down when he said that Vietnam sat at entirely the wrong latitude.

J. V. said digging to China was only an expression. "No matter, racket from them rats keeps me awake. And you got them traps in the wrong spots."

Brownie blew on his cup, then winked at me and said, "Smart rats."

I figured it was time to change the subject. "J. V. has a theory we're fighting because the Vietnamese use too much rice making wine."

"Very apocryphal," Brownie said.

"Don't be usin' words you don't know what they mean," J. V. muttered and went back to turning potatoes and eggs.

"Actually," I said, "the rats would end up somewhere in the Caribbean."

"What?" J. V. said.

"If a rat dug its way, you know straight and perpendicular with the plane of the land. *Straight* being the key word." I looked at Brownie, who turned away to conceal a smirk.

J. V. forked the food on three plates and set one before me. "Next time you can just fix your own breakfast."

I looked at my charred poker-chip potatoes and greasy pig and picked up a fork.

At midmorning a supply plane flew up the valley. I motioned old Ong Dao, who supervised the Montagnard laborers, to take a break from digging and lead the workers to the truck. Then I recruited Ralph Whitten to accompany me to the strip; others were on patrol or grinding away in the heat at one task or another. The other Aussie, William Green, had asked to be called Bill; Whitten preferred being addressed as Mister. Although slotted as an intelligence specialist, his primary contribution to the camp consisted of putting holes in a dartboard that hung in the team house. He set his darts aside and reluctantly agreed.

It was an intrusion on his day, which consisted largely of passing time in the shade of the team house, shirt off, drinking beer, while tossing darts at the board and snide remarks in the air. He held everything in contempt, starting with the Vietnamese, whom he mistrusted to an absurd degree. He seemed to bear a subtle but perceptible resentment toward Reifschneider as well. I had no idea what the source of the antagonism was, but sensed it in Mr. Whitten's tone when Reifschneider left the room and the Aussie said, "Thought he was to be gone by now."

Old Man Dao sat in the back, smoking his long-stemmed pipe and stroking his wispy gray goatee. He knew little about construction, never turned a shovel or lifted a bucket, but without his presence, construction would come to a standstill. He squatted near whatever project was in progress, watched the laborers, and after taking his share from the payroll distributed money. He understood fully the privilege his control allowed him, but didn't flaunt it.

From the beginning, Pablo maintained Dao was actually vc, basing his opinion on the fact that the old man seemed more interested in the goings-on around camp than the projects he was hired to supervise. Neither Pablo's nor anyone's opinion weighed much when it came to Ong Dao. He was part of an entrenched system, invaluable to the higher-ups. Already he'd wheedled his way into J. V.'s favor, a source of supposed intelligence, though J. V. didn't say as much. Still, Pablo insisted that Dao was doing double duty, spying for us and Charlie.

The heat was as dogged as a process server. Mr. Whitten mumbled as he approached. His face was red. His hairy red chest glistened. He didn't sweat; he leaked. His most notable characteristic was grouchiness, a lot of grunting and growling. Today, he was disgruntled over having to ride to the airstrip, probably dreading it might lead to something resembling labor. He looked in the bed of the truck and sneered. "Sneaky shirt lifter," he muttered, meaning Ong Dao, whom he detested, perhaps because he and the old man shared at least one characteristic—their impunity from labor.

He swung onto his seat, said, "Well, what're we waitin' for, young Barnes?"

The laborers loaded the incoming supplies: sacks of cement for the bunker, two fifty-five-gallon drums of gasoline, and chemicals to mix defoliant. I supervised the loading. Mr. Whitten supervised his suntan. When we returned to camp, Mr. Whitten walked straight from the truck to the team house, leaving me and the laborers to unload the truck.

I got to the next task and pumped JP-4, jet fuel, into the canister. The instructions warned that the defoliant was toxic and advised wearing rubber gloves and a face mask as precautions. None were supplied with the chemicals. Nor were any lying around camp. I unsealed the container, mixed the contents according to the instructions, capped the spray canister, pumped the handle, and marched into the elephant grass. The blades sliced fine cuts on my arms, wounds that burned intensely from the salt in my sweat.

The instructions said spray the stems and earth around the roots. I aimed the nozzle and pulled the trigger. The task took up the remainder of the day. I sprayed and inhaled poison. Mr. Whitten tossed darts. At dusk I filled a canvas bag with water for a shower and hung it. Mr. Whitten strolled up and asked that I save some water for him. I didn't.

The air was unusually thick and the day still. It seemed I could reach out and cup the humidity in my hands. Scattered clouds raced far overhead, but there was little ground wind in the valley. The Song Tra Bong lolled its way eastward. As the Vietnamese in camp took a siesta, I slipped off my shirt and repaired broken wires, twisting and tightening splices, first with the handle of the wire cutters and then with one of the stakes I fashioned for that purpose, tedious, the kind of work done almost unconsciously. Sweat trickled off my forehead, down my throat, and back on my neck. My trousers were soaked in it. That week I'd developed an insufferable itch from ringworm. It was the bane of soldiers over here. Norwood told me to use foot powder to relieve the itch. At night I sprinkled powder on it and scratched the irritation all the same because the itching kept me awake. Scratching it gave me relief and was oddly pleasurable. I scratched until it bled, then scratched some more.

I caught sight of a girl squatting on the river's bank, pant legs rolled up. She rinsed a cloth in the shallows and wiped her forehead. I wondered, why here? Why now? What was she doing out in the heat of the day? She stood, placed her straw hat on her head, and waded into the water. Air-conditioning, I figured, Tra Bong style.

Lost in work, I passed two hours almost unaware of time. Then, while splicing two strands, I pricked a finger on a barb and drew blood. I licked my finger, sucked the blood away. I was again aware of the heat, of the burning sweat in the wound. I wiped the blood on my trousers and tested the last strand. It held. I cussed the sky and blamed Lela for my situation. If not for her, I might have taken a different course, stayed in college. None of it was likely true, but blame doesn't require truth, just a target.

I sized up the rest of the day. Work, play cards perhaps. Someone would shake me awake in the dark of night for guard duty. I sipped from my canteen, wiped sweat from my forehead, and looked east. Paddies stretched from the outer fringe of the camp about another four hundred meters to a stand of thatched huts. Foot-length stalks jutted up from the mirrored surfaces—rice in its perpetual cycle of growth to harvest to growth again. Vagrant clouds slipping inland reflected off the surface of the paddies. I hoped the clouds would come soon. Anything but the sun.

A shadow crossed the ground and halted in front of me. Jacobsen asked if I needed help. Red-neck big, Jake was a doer and didn't wait for an answer, just kneeled down on his own accord and threaded a patch through the tip of a cleaning rod. He picked up a barrel, held it toward the light, and peered into it with one eye. "Could grow vegetables in here," he said and ran the patch through the breach. He dangled the results under my nose.

"Filthy," I said.

He hummed "A Hard Day's Night," off-key to everyone in the world but himself, and inserted a fresh patch in the eye of the rod. He dipped the patch in the solvent and rammed it through the barrel. Satisfied the barrel was clean, he ran another patch through to dry it, set the weapon aside, and picked up another.

His fingers on the carbine were as sure as a flutist's, never a hurried or missed note. He couldn't be idle. He probably tinkered with some gizmo or another in his sleep. On the first day in camp, he started the engine of the three-quarter-ton truck, lifted the hood, and reset the carburetor and timing by ear. Then, within the hour, he turned his attention to the generator, which fed electricity to the camp.

"Here," he said. "Take this." A bolt. "And this." A trigger housing. "And this." A spring. He watched me assemble the parts and play the action. "Is it good now?"

I nodded. "Yes, good."

He smiled and picked up another rifle to clean. "Hope the storm cools things off. 'Course, it's gonna slow down business."

A strange word, I thought, *business*. War as business. But it was. Far from danger, someone was getting rich. That was the real business of war, but for Jake and me the business of war was the labor we were performing.

The smell of grilled meat wafted over from the strikers' compound. Somewhere, I thought, back in the World someone *was* making money off the war; someone else was enjoying a hamburger with a Coke so cold that water condensed on the glass.

"Smells like hamburger," I said.

I thought again of Lela, a girl no longer, now a woman of twenty. I recalled her sitting across from me at the Red Rooster Drive-In, a french fry dangling from her fingers. Were I to write her, what would I describe? Could I give life to what I saw here? The work? The land? The people? Would she care? Would she write back? I shook off the idea. Weapons, work, those were me now.

Jake grunted and set the last barrel down. "Well, I got stuff to do."

I thanked him and reassembled the carbine, tested the bolt, then looked to the east. Clouds were already swallowing the sun.

FIFTEEN

J. V. handed over a map and told me to hold it open. He was interested in "this," he said, pointing to a swath of jungle northwest of Tra Bong. We knew that the mountains and valleys of Tra Bong Sheer were part of an important infiltration and supply route for the enemy. J. V. said, as he pointed out the areas, that Charlie was all over the place, but didn't say much more. It was G2. He meant secret shit, not for my eyes.

The last few days he'd spent a great deal of time in the operations room, tacking pins on a map of Tra Bong District, red, yellow, green, blue, and white pins, finely printed numbers taped to them. Some, in clusters surrounding Tra Bong, represented by their numbers a huge enemy force. He spoke vaguely of battalions, regiments, divisions—hard-core Vietcong and North Vietnamese, scary stuff provided it was not based on bogus information. Sometimes he sounded paranoid. Who could say? Maybe we were surrounded.

"They're somewhere in here," he said, tapping his finger on the map.

I was ambivalent if not skeptical. I wasn't alone in doubting. J. V. might be right, but his drinking undermined his credibility—other times his occasional exaggeration did. Even if it weren't true, I could see he believed it when he said two company-size units of hard-core VC were in the vicinity and heading east.

Such information was invaluable. Charlie sent us no notes informing us of his intentions, so J. V. relied on informants, and that left him to decide what was reliable. He'd inherited and had added to a network of local informants. They were rewarded based on information, but any time information translated into money, perhaps on a scale of so much for a company of VC, more for a battalion, and more still for a regiment, it could encourage informants to embellish in order to fatten their reward. And unconfirmed information was generally considered unreliable.

J. V. was guarded to the point of near paranoia about intelligence information. Once he caught me looking at his map and asked what the hell I thought I was doing. I said, "Nothing." He told me to go do nothing somewhere else.

It crossed my mind that I should sneak into the back room next time he tied on a good one and rearrange a few pins just to see if he'd notice. I left without protest, even though everyone in Special Forces had at least a secret clearance. I could've told him but didn't that in the Dom Rep a CIA agent had handed me a Swedish 9mm submachine gun and civilian clothes. The secret operation there could have left troopers helpless and in rebel hands had the mission failed.

Today my job was to scout it from the air, note anything unusual, or "take a look-see," as he said. It would be the first of many such flights over the mountains where I would spend a great deal of my tour humping below the jungle canopy. I folded the map and slipped it into the cargo pocket of the fatigues.

The L-19 was a small two-seat high-winger. The pilot settled it down gracefully. It carried two white phosphorus rockets on its wings. They were meant for marking ground targets. The plane was otherwise harmless except that the pilot could radio in an air strike. The pilot feathered the prop and signaled for me to hurry. I ducked under the wing strut and handed my M-16 and M-79 to him before clawing my way through to the backseat.

He was young, a first lieutenant, and seemed eager to get into the air. I maneuvered a leg over the stick and buckled in. He handed back the rifle and grenade launcher and pointed out a set of earphones. I put them on. He told me to push a button on the wire to talk. He held up his own map and asked where to. I indicated the general area.

"What're you looking for?"

"Whatever's out there."

He grinned. "Won't see what you're looking for anyhow. It's luck. Hold on."

In a minute or two we were airborne and climbing. The air blowing past my face was cool. He asked how good I was with the weapons.

"Good," I said.

"We see some Charlies, we'll go down and you can take a shot or two."

"Fine with me."

He took a direct route west up the valley, skating just above the treetops. He explained that at low altitudes, the plane is gone before Charlie can take an effective shot. I could see by the way he handled the plane that the pilot was a cowboy, as were many of the pilots who flew light aircraft in the boonies. At the end of the valley, he eased back on the stick and rose far above the canopied mountains and headed west. I unfolded the map and studied the terrain below. From above, I was struck by how high and rugged the mountains were, not the Rockies or the Andes, but nonetheless steep and treacherous. If Charlie was under the canopy, there was no possible way for us to see. The only signs of human activity were the bare mountainsides the Montagnard had burned in preparation for planting rice and the occasional village of long houses in clearings.

We crossed the first range of peaks and descended into a high plateau where the ground leveled, much of it under cultivation, mostly rice paddies. Here and there were a scattering of huts, no villages, no one working the fields. He asked if I knew how to fly an aircraft. I told him no.

"Wanna try?"

"Sure."

"Take the stick."

He turned the controls over to me and for the next ten minutes directed me how to use the stick and pedals on the floor, how to accelerate, how to slow, to turn and coordinate the flaps so that the plane didn't slide. A spell took hold of me as I eased the plane right, then circled and took it down, then up again. There was no purpose to it except doing it.

He broke the spell. "Give me the stick and get ready."

The plane veered, then headed down. Fast. I heard the whine of the prop and felt air surge through the cabin. Then I saw what prompted him to take the controls. Three VC, each with a rifle slung over his shoulder, chugged across a dry paddy heading for the nearest berm, where they promptly dived for a chestful of Mother Earth. The pilot fired the missiles, and two white clouds blossomed on the paddy some twenty yards off the mark.

The Cong scrambled to their feet and tore off toward a wood line west of the paddy. The pilot pulled back on the stick, gained altitude, and circled to cut them off.

"Give it try," he said. He took the plane down, leveled it at about three hundred feet, and held it parallel with the wood line. I tucked the butt of the M-79 into my shoulder and balanced it on the window. I had one shot and no way of judging the speed of the plane. I aimed slightly ahead of them and squeezed the trigger. The VC hit the ground again at roughly the same instant I fired. The grenade arced groundward and landed some thirty feet off target behind them.

Undismayed, the pilot said, "Let's go. Use the rifle and be careful not to hit the wing strut." He maneuvered the plane as before, until it skated just above the paddy. I fired three quick bursts, again failing to compensate for airspeed. The pilot repeated the turn, made a third run across the paddy, and came in higher. This time I got off four bursts.

I glanced back, sighted the VC running for better circumstances in the direction of the tree line to the west. One had an obvious limp and lagged behind. Another circled back to help. Before the pilot could negotiate another turn, all three reached the wood line and disappeared in the cover.

"Got one," the pilot said. "Or he twisted an ankle. No matter, bet they shit their pants."

This, I thought, was not the war I came to fight. I should be down there. That was what I'd trained for. That was my war. As we flew back over the same mountain range, I studied the land closely. I'd seen Charlie in the open. He existed. He was down there. Somewhere.

SIXTEEN

I scooped lye from a bucket and sprinkled it into the piss tube, a duty assigned to either Norwood or me, as were other dirty jobs no one else wanted. The smell of broiling meat from the striker compound again hung in the air. I was convinced they ate better than we did, and convinced also that this was the hottest day I'd yet endured, but I thought something similar to that each day. It was a windless day, bright and clear all the way to the South China Sea. I covered my mouth and nose with a bandanna, which accomplished little in the way of ameliorating the smell. Lye in contact with human urine created fumes that irritated the eyes and skin; what was hot seemed hotter, and whatever smelled stank all the more.

Every day in camp was a Monday. No Fridays, no weekends. I'd finished the late guard shift, the most recent in a series I'd done for nine or ten days in a row, often twice a night. Only those who went on patrols, which we called walks, got a full night's sleep. My effort had been limited to paperwork, sweat labor, and standing guard. As of today everyone but Cam Gamble and myself had gone on a walk, Cam because he was our only radioman. I'd not even pissed in the bushes, and the most excitement I'd experienced had come while walking guard when a rat the size of a ferret had scurried across my path and sent my heart into overdrive.

Even Norwood, now on his first operation, had taken a walk. He'd left early on patrol with the Aussie Bill Green and a platoon of strikers who were now somewhere in the vicinity of Binh Hoa, so I was anointed king of the piss tubes.

In addition to being a piss-tube day, it was a shit-burning day, so after I finished with the tubes, I poured a gallon of gasoline in the latrine and dropped a flare grenade in before gas fumes had time to build up. A black cloud funneled out of the nylon-mesh windows, and with no breeze to carry it away, the smell of burning shit hung over the compound at about nose level.

Fox tried monitoring the patrol's progress from the team house, but the radio lost contact with the patrol off and on, so bare-chested and wearing cut-off fatigue trousers, he packed the bulky PRC-25 to the top of the compound, where he sat and worked on his tan. He gazed off at the eastern valley as if he could actually see something other than paddies, trees, and the distant VC-controlled villages.

When I passed by, he asked why the latrine had to be burned today. What he meant was why at that moment.

"'Cause I was told to."

"Who told you?"

I said, "You did," which wasn't the answer he wanted to hear.

I was inventorying weapons in the armory when the firefight erupted. I hurried out. A tense gathering circled the radio, heads bowed, ears intent as they waited for a report. I joined them. Following a brief period of silence, during which it was hard to breathe, static crackled on the radio and Mr. Green said in a calm manner that the patrol suffered no casualties, but they had one Vietcong KIA and a weapon seized. We breathed easier after that. I realized at that moment that I cared more about my teammates than I'd been aware of, and years later I would explain to a counselor in a session with other vets what it feels like, how in a unit like mine the loss of one man is like losing an arm, two like losing the other arm, each life an amputation of a limb that will never grow back.

Two hours later the jubilant patrol returned. Dangling from a pole toted on the shoulders of two strikers was a dead Cong. The strikers dumped the body in the dirt and left him to the flies. Along the nine-kilometer march back to camp they had paraded their trophy through the roadside hamlets. In this land of the grotesque, a message and perhaps a provocation.

We hurried to the gate, where we listened as Green narrated details. Near a paddy east of Binh Hoa they'd encountered four VC armed with Chicom .308s. The brief skirmish ended when Mr. Green zapped a Charlie hoofing his way across the paddy toward the village. Three had escaped.

The mood among the Vietnamese, who desperately needed a victory, was celebratory. They acted as if the dead man were Ho Chi Minh himself, but he was just a kid, perhaps my age, no older, one bloodless bullet hole in his side. The flies were already making merry on his face.

Oddly, he seemed not dead, at least not dead in the sense that the bodies I'd seen in the Dom Rep had, but nature would fix that soon enough. By evening the body was too much even for the happy Vietnamese to bear, and they got around to ridding the camp of his odor. I doubted they took time to bury him. As to where and how they disposed of him, I could only guess, but Song Tra Bong did flow all the way to the South China Sea.

SEVENTEEN

Gusts whipped sporadically through the valley, the surface water on the paddies rippled, and the temperature dropped. For the first time since arriving in 'Nam, my skin wasn't filmed with sweat. The captain and Lieutenant Quang drove to the village for a dinner with the district chief. The rest of us gathered in the team house and covered the shuttered windows with blankets. I was largely excluded from the information loop, but I sensed an undercurrent at play in the room.

As the rest of us sat at the table, Mr. Whitten tossed darts, then retrieved them and tossed them again. A fizz announced another opening of Mr. Schlitz. Someone spread a felt blanket over the table. A Buck Owens single recycled on the record player, background noise I no longer heard. Norwood commented on Mr. Green's remarkable single shot that brought down the vc. We all agreed. Hell of a shot.

Cam came up from his commo bunker and reported news that a front was blowing in. News from the C-Team. Brownie said that if he were blind, he could figure as much out by stepping outside. He pulled up a chair behind J. V. and angled it so he could look simultaneously at two hands. Few things gave him more pleasure than kibitzing after the play.

Pop a beer and get 'em in the air. We needed to take the edge off, a little pinochle, nothing at stake. The deck, thick and stained from mold, clumped together, hardly what we would choose to use, but the cards were sacred to us. J. V. switched out a Buck Owens for a Johnny Cash record. Cam pulled a cold beer from the fridge and sat down. Mr. Green seated himself at the far end. Pablo, on first watch, was absent. Jake, a Montagnard crossbow on his lap, sat between

J. V. and Mr. Green. Norwood sat by me and waited for his turn at a game. Mr. Whitten continued his one-man effort at wearing out the dartboard. Reifschneider sat alone on a stool, meticulously cleaning his boots. He was headed home, a wife and children awaiting him, and he probably thought a good shine on the boots put him closer to the World.

I partnered up with Cam, the kind of bidder who would end up bankrupt at an auction. Fate pitted us against J. V. and Fox, at cards both as ruthless as mad monks in the court of Nicholas II. The humidity affected the cards. I powdered the deck again, shuffled, and offered up the cut. We arranged our cards and waited for Fox, who sat, one leg crossed over the other, and sucked on his cigarette. Finally, he said, "Pass."

As J. V. started to bid, Jake leaned over and peeked at his cards. J. V. told him to mind his own business. We were gabby, Reifschneider and Norwood being the exceptions, Norwood especially. The night before he and Brownie had been summoned to the village to aid with a breech birth. They could help neither the woman nor the baby. Brownie, who knew we weren't here to save humanity, seemed okay with that. That night didn't augur well with Norwood.

In the middle of the hand J. V., who'd already visited the back room a couple of times, looked at me and said, "It's like gettin' your dick wet the first time."

"What is?" I asked.

"Leave 'im alone," Jake said, looking at J. V.

Cam tossed down a card and said, "Take that."

Brownie said, "Bad play."

J. V. trumped the hand and scooped up the trick. The next play I dumped the queen of spades on Fox. Two tricks later the game was over; Cam and I survived his bad play. J. V. muttered to himself on his way to the intel room to enjoy a short chat with Jim Beam.

By then, Reifschneider had spent the better part of twenty

minutes cleaning his boots. From time to time Mr. Whitten had watched out of the corner of his eye. Reifschneider picked up his brush and began to buff the boots. Mr. Whitten watched until he couldn't contain himself. "Mate, your boots'll be getting dirty soon enough."

Reifschneider hit one of the boots with the brush a couple more times, then set the boots aside. "But they're clean now." He slipped them on, tied the laces, and left to join J. V.

The roof shuddered under a sudden gust, a blanket flew off the window frame, and the overhead light flickered. Brownie reached up and steadied the light. The tail of the wind rustled through the thatch. Clattering came from the galvanized roof as the thatch moved.

"Your storm, Cam," Mr. Whitten said, as if Gamble owned it.

Cam said it was my lead. I tossed down a trick.

"All you Yanks do? Play cards?" Mr. Whitten asked.

"Least we do something," Jake muttered.

A different clattering sound came from the tin roof. Then everyone looked up as a fleet shadow crossed a beam. Jacobsen swung the crossbow into action. He fired a bamboo bolt at the rat before it made its crossing. The shaft hit the tin ceiling and ricocheted before it disappeared.

Seconds later a huffing J. V. emerged from the back, his face red, in his hand the bamboo bolt. "Ain't funny," he said.

EIGHTEEN

Although we made water runs every four or five days, the Montagnard treated each of our visits there as a brand-new event. They seemed to find us entertaining, and this day Norwood and I were the stars of the show. He leaned on the fender of the trailer, rifle at the ready, and watched the forest while I stood midcalf in the Song Tra Bong, priming the hose. Near the bank, a dozen women squatted in the shade and watched. Those with babies nursed them. A few boys played. An old man smoked a pipe with a foot-long stem. Three adolescent girls hung back at the riverbank and furtively glanced at the goings-on.

We heard the rattle of the jeep approaching from the south and looked in that direction. Reifschneider braked to an abrupt stop. Dust rose from the jeep's undercarriage. Reifschneider remained seated behind the steering wheel. Brownie swung down from the passenger seat and strolled over to the water trailer, where he engaged Norwood in conversation.

The Montagnard sidestepped a pace or two from their previous locations and squatted again. I bent over and cranked the starter on the pump's engine until it fired to life. When I looked up, Reifschneider hollered something. I indicated I couldn't hear and shut off the engine.

"How much longer?" he asked.

"Just started," I said.

"Half-full's enough," Reifschneider said. "Captain's gonna need the truck."

I nodded. Brownie strolled back to the jeep.

"He wants you two in camp in clean fatigues," Reifschneider called.

Those were the most words I'd ever exchanged with him.

I didn't expect him to elaborate and didn't ask what it was about. I nodded, bent over again, and brought the pump to life.

Soon after our return to camp an Otter, an eight-passenger high-winger, passed over, heading toward the airstrip. VIP aboard. No name given. Something to relieve the tedium. Congressman, I figured, or Martha Ray, who'd been adopted as an honorary Green Beret. Wherever she visited, she sat in team houses and boozed with the men. In between the bawdy jokes she told, she asked about their lives and relayed messages to their families Stateside.

Thirty minutes later, Moses tripped into camp with his escorts, several marines and a Special Forces officer. Charlton Heston himself. I stood with the rest of the team, ready to shake hands with the actor who was surveying camps around the country to get a feel for a future role he was considering as the lead in a movie based on the book *The Green Berets*.

The captain introduced him, four or five inches taller than any of us but Reifschneider and handsome. He smiled without showing his teeth as he shook hands all around. On the screen he seemed capable of single-handedly repelling a battalion-size assault, but in person he was just a gangly guy with a well-arranged face and a pleasantly aloof manner. His handshake was tepid—not womanly, but unenthusiastic. He asked us no questions, and it became apparent he had little interest in those of us who manned the camps or what constituted our duties or what we did to stay sane. I expected more from Ben-Hur and a hell of a lot more from the Prophet, who in his fury cast down the stone tablets, thus becoming the first of mankind to break all the Commandments at once. I remembered a line he rendered in the film—"You push-pullers, over here." I'd laughed aloud at it and wondered why no else one in the theater had. As I shook his hand, I wondered who the idiot was who'd penned that line.

He seemed altogether out of place here in this land of no Bel Air swimming pools, no caterers or fountains bubbling with champagne, no makeup artists shooting spray on your face so you'd appear to be sweating, and no well-rehearsed enemy to wilt in your presence. Here sweat came naturally. What we had to offer were mosquitoes, rats, and work. Hardly the heroic stuff of Hollywood film.

The captain guided him on a tour of the camp.

In order to draw demolition pay I was required to use explosives once a month. I went from bunker to bunker searching out moldering shells to be destroyed and placing them in a gunnysack. I paused for a time and watched Captain Fewell and his guest walk the perimeter. Mr. Heston stood nearly a head taller and had a long ostrichlike stride, taking one step to Captain Fewell's two. They stopped. He stooped down, tilted his head to hear whatever the captain said. Then the actor gazed at the Song Tra Bong. Part it, I thought, Moses. If you can.

An hour later the Otter carrying Ben-Hur flew over the camp. The strikers waved. I toted two gunnysacks of bad mortar shells and ammunition near the gully we used as a trash dump. I placed a kilo of C-4 on top of the mortar rounds and a few dozen corroded .30-caliber rounds, primed the explosives with a blasting cap, and walked back to the detonator.

The blast channeled though the ground and through me. A cloud rose that gradually billowed into a feminine shape, a mini atom bomb with figure-eight curves. One that would do Hollywood proud. Too bad, I thought as I reeled in the wire, Moses didn't hang around for this.

The captain and Fox sat in the team house. The captain told me to look at the wall near the door. A chunk of concrete was chipped off a support column.

"There's more of the same in the back," the captain said. He asked if I had a comment.

"Bad construction, sir," I said.

"Less explosives," he said.

Misters Green and Whitten tossed darts. J. V. studied aerial photos spread out on the end of the table. Reifschneider thumbed cards off the deck as he played solitaire. Beside him Sheppard and Fox offered commentary. The captain sat at the head of the table with Lieutenant Bussey, Henry, our interpreter, behind him. I headed for the refrigerator and a cold soda. All morning I'd been demolishing the shed and salvaging what materials I could.

"Got a job for you, Barnes," the captain said.

I hoped it wasn't a requisition or some other construction job. Already projects were piling up. If it wasn't Fox or Captain Fewell, it was J. V. or one of the Aussies. It seemed everyone who outranked Norwood and me had a list of priorities and wanted us to "get on it." Thus far all I had accomplished was razing the shed in preparation for digging a hole for the bunker.

"Do you have something that'll cut chain?"

"Yes, sir. Bolt cutters."

"I want a gate in the fence between here and the Luc Lon Duc Biet."

Our counterparts, the Luc Lon Duc Biet, commanded the camp, but as if to suggest their inferior status, a barrier of wire had been built at the discretion of the Aussies. It prevented their having open access to our compound. Mr. Whitten, who'd never in his life while sober missed the board, sent a dart into the window screen. His face blanched, and he looked over his shoulder at the captain as if he were going to speak out. Mr. Green toed the foul line and shook his head, signaling his mate not to talk.

The captain looked at Whitten. "And it'll remain open in daylight hours."

His cheeks a bit rosier, Mr. Whitten's face returned to its usual state of gruffness.

The captain ordered Henry to have Lieutenant Quang meet him at the fence and told me to bring the bolt cutters. He and Lieutenant Bussey marched out of the team house. Captain Fewell stood midpoint at the fence. Lieutenant Quang and Trung Sí Cu, the Vietnamese top sergeant, came from their command post. The captain whispered to Lieutenant Bussey. Then the four them met at the fence, and Henry began to translate the captain's promise that there would no more fences between them and us. Captain Fewell gripped a metal post and rocked it back and forth. Quang grabbed onto the same post, and together they loosened it from its mooring. Lieutenant Bussey and Trung Sí Cu did the same with an adjacent post. When that part of the fence lay flat, the captain motioned me forward. "I want a gate up ASAP."

The laborers were preparing a stage for the coming Chinese New Year celebration, so I was saddled with the job. I cut a space in the wire wide enough to accommodate a gate. As I dug the first posthole, some curious strikers formed on the Vietnamese side. They looked at me as if asking what I was digging. I said, "I'm digging a hole to the Caribbean." They nodded as if they understood.

I was mixing cement for a footer when Mr. Whitten sauntered up. Hands on hips, he looked at the space I'd cut in the fence. "Fine thing your captain's doin', lettin' the bloody shirt-lifters in. What if one sees the wrong thing while looking for something to steal?"

"I don't know."

"That's right. You don't. Neither does he. That's the point."

"Mr. Whitten, I got stuff to do."

"So you do."

That evening the captain told me to prepare for the next operation, two or three days away. He'd be going, along with Pablo and me, and a fourth.

"Four?"

"Reifschneider. Joe knows the area."

It seemed unreasonable to endanger a man so near the end of his tour. Reifschneider should be packing to leave. I thought as much but didn't say so. Then too, if the dead VC and the weapon he'd toted were an indication of the enemy we would encounter, there seemed little to worry about.

As I drifted toward sleep, a five-hundred pounder exploded three or four kilometers to the north. A second later a slow, powerful vibration traveled up through the ground, that explosion followed in quick succession by four more. The B52s that dropped them flew so high, the whine of their engines went unheard. Ghost planes. I recalled the landscape I'd seen from the air, pockmarked by bomb craters, and speculated what it was like to be Charlie, to live where trees are ripped from their moorings and tossed aside like matchsticks.

I sat on my cot in the bunker and listened for more. Silence and anticipation, I thought, must terrify a man as much as the explosions themselves. Bullets made sense. A man in your sights. Your finger on a trigger. Well, Charlie could get a break tomorrow. A cease-fire was in effect for the coming Tet. Both sides agreed: no killing for a couple of days.

A rat scrambled between the timbers that supported the roof. Mosquitoes buzzed. I swatted one, then lay back and slept the sleep of the exhausted.

NINETEEN

That morning of Tet 1966 a wind blew in from the South China Sea, the kind of a blow that sinks a barometer needle. Reeds on the riverbank danced, and the elephant grass on the far bank of the river bent westerly. The air smelled of ocean and rice paddies, gutted pigs and chickens and of excrement and moist grass, and everything fecund and rotting. It smelled of Vietnam.

Ever since the team's third day in camp, the captain had ordered operations east. He even went on one himself. For more than two weeks I'd watched teammates come and go, operation after operation, and I clocked my days in camp doing labor while yearning to go. All but Cam Gamble and I had gone. Twice my name was on the roster but scratched because of some duty or another that needed attending. I began to have doubts about myself, wondered what I had done to make the captain doubt me. If not him, perhaps Fox. Now the captain had said I was next up. I hadn't come just to demolish a shed with a crowbar or pour lye down a piss tube. I'd volunteered to fight. I considered the upcoming operation as my real introduction to Vietnam.

The team house was abuzz, as plans for the operation were outlined. From midmorning on the captain, Johnny the interpreter in tow, shuttled between the back room of the team house and the Vietnamese command post. The camp commander visited the team house with Trung Sí Cu. In the afternoon the captain along with J. V. and Johnny drove to the district chief's headquarters in the village. More planning, more involving our allies, more of what's now called consensus building.

I signed the ledger and got a Schlitz from the refrigerator, then took a seat at the table. I seldom drank, but today we were bringing in the Year of the Horse. I watched the village girl who cleaned the team house work to dislodge a stain from the hard-packed dirt floor. She worked herself into a frenzy. In the end it defeated her. She was a shy girl, sixteen or seventeen, and as undeveloped as an adolescent boy. We called her Cô Dep, pretty girl, but one would be hard-pressed to see her as pretty. She didn't look my way as she departed.

I finished the beer. It left a foul taste in my mouth. I considered the half-dozen tasks I'd not yet started or finished. None seemed important. I decided to write Mother, mostly because I had written only once or twice in more than a year, perhaps all of three times since I'd left for basic training. I'd not even informed her or my stepfather when I enlisted. After staring at a blank piece of paper, I realized I had nothing to say. How would Mother react to hearing about a dead man strung to a pole? She had four young kids, bills, a husband, himself an incompetent parent whose life consisted of eating, sleeping, and gathering bad news for broadcast on the radio. That was their world and this was mine. I set my head on the table and napped.

Mr. Green awakened me and said that the celebration had begun. I was to come along. He backpedaled toward the door. I'd been curious for two days now, so I asked what was behind Mr. Whitten's being upset over opening a passage between ours and the Vietnamese compound.

He said, "I'm not at liberty to say."

"Captain Fewell?"

He shook his head. "Mine. Captain Fazekas."

I assured him I wouldn't repeat anything he told me. He thought about it, then took a seat opposite me. After again hesitating, he told me that Captain Fazekas, Warrant Officers Wheatley and Swanton, and Staff Sergeant Sershen went east on an operation past Nai Hon Dost and encountered a contingent of VC. As the strikers with Swanton and Wheatley rounded up civilians in the village, the platoon came under heavy fire, and a striker was wounded, though not seriously. The Vietnamese officer in charge balked and quit in the midst of battle. "That Quang, the officer over there," he pointed to where the celebration was under way, "he was with Fazekas."

He explained that the firefight intensified. More strikers were hit, and Swanton took a bad chest wound. Wheatley called for an air evacuation and support from mortars.

"My captain tried to get to them, but . . ." He paused, then said, "They buggered on 'em, the whole lot of them. That's it."

I started to rise. He held a hand up. I sat back down. He said that Wheatley dropped his weapon and dragged Swanton away from the firefight and across a rice paddy to a stand of trees for cover. The Vietnamese remaining with them tried to urge Wheatley to leave Swanton behind, because he was obviously dying.

"Instead of leaving his mate, Wheatley took two grenades in hand and pulled the pins. Waited for the bloody slopes, he did. Captain couldn't get to 'em, 'cause *your* captain's good friend Lieutenant Quang wouldn't . . . Cowards, Barnes."

I told him I was sorry.

"Got no reason to be. They were my chums. Come along, now." He walked to the exit and held the screen door ajar. Before stepping out, he said, "You're a good mate."

"So are you, Mr. Green. Tell them I'm writing a letter. I'll be there."

The clouds had closed in the valley, and a light mist fell. He capped his head with a slouch hat and stepped out into the rain.

I sat in the dim light and wrote nothing other than a request that Mother send a bottle of some new treatment for athlete's foot that I'd read about. The rash on my crotch was getting worse, and foot powder hadn't helped. I told her I hoped the family was all doing well. Safe stuff to write. I signed my name to the letter and sealed the envelope.

The team was staggered around the table with the Vietnamese. The captain, seated between the district chief and Lieutenant Quang, glanced up me and immediately turned his attention back to the camp commander. Trung Sí Cu nodded as I stepped under the tarp. He pointed to the seat next to him, then offered his hand to shake as I sat. I looked across the table at Pablo. "Real food," he said.

I'd not had full sleep since arriving and had labored ten or twelve hours each day, living off Spam or bacon and C rations. I filled my plate with some rice, seasoned meat, and greens. Trung Sí Cu passed me a bowl of *nuc maum*. Though it stank, I sprinkled my food and tasted it. It was better than it smelled. I ate that first serving and filled my plate with whatever was in reach. I remembered how much I loved food and vowed that when I got Stateside I would eat prime cuts only, fresh vegetables, and piles and piles of pasta, wonders I had taken for granted.

A young woman in a red *au dai* and white-silk pajamas mounted a makeshift stage that faced the canopy. She stood demurely behind a microphone as a soldier adjusted it. When the soldier stepped aside, she began a lilting ballad, sung in a thin soprano. It seemed to please the soldiers, and when she finished they applauded. Then Lieutenant Quang, frail and no more than twenty-five, mounted the stage. His thin wrists showed at the sleeve as he gripped the microphone. He leaned forward and spoke. The speakers screeched. He talked louder, which only amplified the feedback. The soldier who'd assisted the girl hurried to the stage. He smiled sheepishly and adjusted the angle of the microphone.

The lieutenant began a speech presidential in length if not in tone and obviously improvised. Whenever he paused to think of what next to say, the audience clapped, which he must have interpreted as their urging him to go on. Johnny's interpretation was only slightly more comprehensible to us than the speech itself. Then, after twenty minutes of stops and starts, Lieutenant Quang finished, but for an embarrassing moment no one realized it, until someone had sense enough to clap and spare him embarrassment. The gathering stood and applauded, I suspected, mostly because he'd finally finished.

He invited Captain Fewell onto the stage, but before the captain could join him, the sky to the east thundered. A few sprinkles fell outside the tent, but the Vietnamese were committed to celebrating, and the coming storm didn't hinder their spirits in the least. One stood and began belting out a tune. It was apparent no one had ever been kind enough to tell him he couldn't sing. Nonetheless, when he finished, the audience clapped enthusiastically. Another, little better than the first, sang and was also applauded. I wondered if the rice wine had rendered them tone deaf.

Lieutenant Quang urged Captain Fewell to stand and sing. The captain's face reddened as he tried to decline. Lieutenant Quang insisted. Things were otherwise going well, so our captain pushed back his chair, cleared his throat, took a sip of wine, and commenced singing "The Star-Spangled Banner" in four or five keys, none of them the right one. The tone-deaf audience shouted and clapped, so, encouraged by the reception he'd gotten, Captain Fewell tackled "The Eyes of Texas." Two Vietnamese stood and joined in, improvising lyrics and melody. I acquired a sudden and unexpected appreciation for the Buck Owens record that had annoyed me before.

Someone, perhaps the captain, decided all of us should

take a hand at singing. Jacobsen surprised us all. Although he couldn't whistle on key, he sang "The Tennessee Waltz" in perfect pitch, sang it so well that it temporarily silenced the Vietnamese. The Aussies appeared left out, so when my turn came, I sang "Waltzing Matilda," the rare tune whose lyrics I knew. Misters Green and Whitten joined in, as did J. V., who'd visited with Mr. Jim Beam before the party and was a stumble away from a fall. Cam Gamble joined after the first chorus, as did some Vietnamese. We sang the remaining verses and choruses in two languages and a half-dozen keys.

It had rained for a time, but that had softened to a mist as the day crept toward evening. Everyone had pretty well exhausted his musical deficiencies, and the supply of rice wine had dwindled to what was left in a man's glass. We sat in numbed silence, Norwood, Captain Fewell, and I the only sober ones. I looked at Fox, who sat squinting at his hands, an unlit cigarette in his mouth, his expression morose, lips moving as if he were muttering a prayer. In general, the others were in similar condition, though Jake and Pablo, both in good spirits, handled booze the best among the team. I admired that.

Someone offered a toast. Like the singing, that too passed around the table. Mr. Whitten toasted the queen. Everyone drank. Fox sat up straight and pulled out a lighter. Captain Fewell raised a glass to the Vietnamese. Everyone drank. The Vietnamese toasted us. Norwood sat grinning as if waiting for a punch line. I probably had a similar expression.

J. V. stood and lifted his glass. He searched the tent with his bleary eyes. As words started to form in his mouth, he lurched to the right, grabbed the table, and straightened himself, then grinned and tried again to speak, but before the words came, he collapsed facedown on the table. Except for the captain and Lieutenant Bussey, everyone found it amusing.

Jacobsen lifted J. V. onto his feet, then onto a shoulder, and sacked him out of the tent. They were halfway to our compound when the first real cannonade of rain came. When the rain hit him, J. V. came to and demanded to be let go, but Jake held on firmly and proceeded up the incline. He slipped now and then, but recovered before he fell, and never dropped his package.

I stood at the edge of the canopy and watched rain spill down. The canvas top flapped in the wind. The rain pelted it in a deafening monotone. The roof of the team house barely fifty feet away was a blur. The pretty cô who'd sung earlier opened an umbrella and fled in the direction of the village with a young soldier beside her. They vanished in a curtain of rain as if swallowed by the storm. I'd heard tales of the monsoon, but none of them had prepared me for this.

Brownie came up beside me and said, "Guess we're stuck until the rain lets up." He lit a cigarette and exhaled. The wind shifted, the canopy shivered and pulled a support stake loose, and the apron of the canvas above him dumped a stream of water on his head. The wet cigarette dangling from his lips, he looked over and said, "Didn't plan for that."

I needed sleep for the morning's operation but couldn't hit the rack just yet. The rain left a pleasant chill in the air. The night invited reflection. I paused on the way to the bunker. By day the land was the stuff of a Gauguin painting, but at night it was all Conrad—dark, seeped in ambiguity, and mesmerizing. Even in pitch-black I could see steamlike tendrils rising from the surface of the paddies adjacent to camp.

The sight might have been mystical, if not for the soldiers from the Popular Force's outpost celebrating Tet by firing tracer and illumination rounds into the sky. I watched for a time. All night we'd heard bursts of gunfire now and then from the hillside. Isolated as they were on a mountainside, the defenders probably got nervous. Nothing about the place had changed since I last looked in daylight, but through a veil of mist in the dark with the weapons going off, it took on a different character. Even at night a South Vietnamese flag, three red horizontal stripes on a yellow field, flew above it.

In daylight, those manning it had a clear view of every village and path from Tra Bong to Vin Thuy. The soldiers occupying it conducted no patrols or operations. The defenders, drawn from the local populace, numbered between twenty and thirty. I could only guess from there that they were mostly Buddhist. There may have been a Catholic or two. Chances were good that one might have been a communist. Tracers from the outpost etched a path across the sky, faded, and petered out. On any other night, the defenders might have been sleeping, but tonight was Tet, and if you were Asian, it was a time to go wild, to scratch an ear and bay at the moon or, in the case of the defenders, to shoot up the sky with rockets and bullets.

Jake sidled up beside me. "Can't spend the night here," he said. "Morning comes early."

I nodded, told him I was on my way. He headed off to hunker down for the night. But I lingered a while longer and watched the outpost.

In the bunker I slipped on the web gear. I attached grenades to the straps, two white phosphorus and two fragmentation, jostled the pack to ensure its balance, and slipped off the harness straps. Outside a striker fired a burst. How long did they celebrate? Were there twelve days of Tet, as there are twelve of Christmas? Did tomorrow officially end the cease-fire? I wondered what kind of meat I ate at the party, hoping that it wasn't dog. I took off my boots and fatigues and lay on the bunk, thinking about the coming day. My first operation. Would it be like Norwood's, a quick firefight, a kill and home for dinner? Overhead, rats scurried about in their network of tunnels. For a time I listened to them and the scattered shots fired by our strikers.

The sound of mortars exploding boomed up the valley, accompanied by machine gun and small-arms fire. In the dull middle ground between sleep and consciousness, I heard the sounds. Then Whitten shouted into the bunker for me to man my post. Since arriving I had rehearsed the drill in my mind over and over. I swung my feet onto the floor and slipped on my boots and buttoned my fatigue shirt, then grabbed my M-16, and entered the trench. It was raining, and I'd forgotten my poncho and steel pot. I went back for them.

Jacobsen, in T-shirt and trousers, was setting the bipod on the mortar. An outgoing mortar round exploded near the river. Strikers throughout the camp fired their weapons, scoring the sky with tracers. Unperturbed by the weather and other events, Jake said he was going to instill some fire discipline in them. Then he said, "Let's put a little light on the subject."

Unhurried, the captain, occupied in thought, walked past the pit without speaking. I grabbed an illumination round out of the magazine. Jake cut increments by guess and set the delay. I pulled out another round and waited. He said one was hanging and dropped it in the tube. Seconds later a blazing light burned a hole in the black sky. I handed him the next round and climbed atop the parapet to see the flare hanging over the swollen river, too far out. I told him and he adjusted the angle. I glanced to the east at the PF outpost at the very instant a mortar round exploded inside the post. Fox slogged by and shouted for us not to waste any flares. J. V. followed him. I hopped back into the pit.

With nothing for us to do but wait, Jake started shivering. He said he'd be right back. A few minutes passed before he returned wearing a poncho and stood above on the parapet. I climbed up beside him. Though a deadly ordeal at the other end, viewed through the misty sky the battle was indistinct and dreamlike. Tracers from small-arms and automatic fire crisscrossed the sky. Trip flares lit up the perimeter as sappers probed the defenses to see how much fight the defenders had in them. Mortar rounds exploded inside the defenses, first the flash, then a delayed bang, like the sound and image out of sync on movie screen. By then sappers had penetrated the outer wire. A flare flashed, then another. A recoilless rifle barked its unmistakable sound.

On his hurried way to the team house Cam slowed long enough to say we would get no air support. The whole of I Corps was boxed in. Something too obvious to be said.

Then the far hillside went black and silent. Norwood shook his head and walked away. Jake and I returned to the pit and hunkered down, while inside the team house the captain, Lieutenant Quang, Lieutenant Bussey, Fox, and J. V. were deciding how our team and the Vietnamese would react.

Over the next hour the gruesome aftermath was telegraphed up the valley, executions announced a single shot at a time, followed by a pause, then a shot, and so on, leaders first, then others who didn't accept the chance to convert. Join or die, the politics of a gun to the head.

Mr. Whitten called out that he was coming into the pit. "Bloody wet," he said. "The cheek of these Vietcong." He lit a cigarette, concealed it under his poncho, and blew smoke skyward. "Shame this happened the day of the captain's party." He took another drag off his cigarette. "I'm relievin' you, Barnes. Your good captain wants you to be ready for the morning."

Past midnight, now the day after Tet, I scrabbled about in the dark. Down the valley they'd killed unarmed men, their reason — *because they could*. It was a piece of Vietnam to take to bed and think about. I shed my poncho, hung my .45

in its holster on the frame supporting the mosquito net, then dried my rifle, slipped out of my boots, and flopped down for a brief, restless rest.

TWENTY

Mr. Green shook my cot. I opened my eyes. It was still dark. His vague shadow hovered outside the mosquito netting. I pulled my poncho liner over my head. He shook the bunk again, this time harder. "Time, mate," he said in his unflappable manner.

It took a moment to remember what had happened the night before and realize I was to get up, prepared to go to war. My first operation. Great timing.

"Coffee's ready, bloody bad as it is." He rattled the frame to the mosquito net and said the captain and others were preparing. He'd stood last watch and probably went without sleep, but his voice was cheery.

I sat up sharply. "I'm awake now. Thanks."

I booted myself, slipped on my tiger-striped shirt, hoisted up my backpack, and was harnessed up in a few seconds. Jacobsen shouted he was coming in. He brought two grenades, which he stuck on my shoulder straps, saying I couldn't have enough. I jogged the load—a final check for balance. Including grenades, I'd be packing fifty pounds. He told me to turn around and held up the backpack as I adjusted the straps, then he asked how it felt.

"Heavier."

"Good," he said.

I stepped out into a mist-filled air and hurried in the direction of the team house. I nearly bumped into the captain coming from the other direction. He carried his m-16 but wasn't yet harnessed up. He looked at me, his expression grave, and said, "I was on my way to find you. There's a change in plans. I'm taking Brownie."

Not realizing what he meant, I nodded, as if agreeing with a good idea.

He diverted his eyes to my backpack. "You can take off your gear."

Then it dawned on me that I wouldn't be going. My cheeks flushed. "But sir . . ."

He shook his head. "They may need a medic," he said, meaning those in the outpost, which struck me as odd. They were all dead.

He saw that I was balking. "Take off your gear. It's an order."

"Pablo can stay," I said. "It's my turn."

"Pablo *is* staying." His tone indicated that the matter was incontrovertible.

I stood planted in an inch of mud, confounded and angry. A medic? What for? We'd heard the executions. If he was going down looking for survivors, he wouldn't find any. For that matter, if he went down the valley, it was at best unwise. The Vietcong assault on the outpost might be a diversion, using a small unit to draw a reaction force from camp into an ambush. Good military sense said that lacking air support and without knowing the size of the enemy unit, it was best to cancel the operation. A bad decision would be to march into the unknown. That was how a French battalion had been lured into an ambush and destroyed on Highway 1.

Still, I wanted to go. It was my operation. "Why me? I . . ."

He left his reasons unsaid and brushed past me.

I heaved my gear in the bunker and kicked the footlocker. I stepped out into the trench as Brownie rounded the corner. The why-me expression on his face told the other side of the story. Two or three days before he'd been on an operation, his second. Jogging by, he muttered something but was gone before I realized he'd said, "Great day for a hangover."

A moment later Jake came along, backpack slung over his shoulder. The captain had picked him to take Pablo's spot. I reached inside the bunker, grabbed my rifle, and walked up the incline. The clay was like butter. It dissolved under my boots. I looked to the east. The valley was as I'd last seen it in daylight—fairyland green and unmarred.

Below on the Vietnamese side of the compound, the soldiers milled about, their faces hidden under the steel pots or other headgear, a force of some sixty or seventy, most of them diminutive, more like a gathering of Boy Scouts than men-at-arms. Their backs to me, their lean bodies hidden under wet ponchos, only their legs and boots showing, they looked like plastic bushes. If not for the urgency of the moment, the sight might appear a parody of war. Pushing roughly through the ranks, squad leaders shouted and lined them up in two columns, staggering intervals between each soldier. At one end Reifschneider, a foot taller than the Vietnamese, wove in and out of the ranks, lifting ponchos, tugging at a grenade on one soldier's straps, checking ammo pouches on another's. In similar fashion Brownie worked his way forward from the opposite end.

The three-quarter ton idled at the entrance, waiting as the guards unlocked the chain and spread open the gate. The gate finally swung open, and Sheppard and Norwood drove out to meet a C-3 flying in with supplies—despite the weather and news of the night's battle. Reifschneider, Brownie, the platoon leaders, the lieutenant, J. V., and the captain circled around Lieutenant Quang, who marked something in the mud with a bayonet. They talked, Johnny translating, until everyone nodded.

Jake, holding a squawk box, stepped out of the team house and jogged to the formation. The radio, a handheld remnant of the Korean War, was effective in the best weather conditions at some six kilometers over flat ground. In this weather it should limit the patrol to going no farther than the cluster of huts west of the village of Lang Ngang, both out of range of our mortars.

Lieutenant Quang stood, erased the mud with the toe of his boot, and spoke to the captain through Johnny. They walked back to the formation as Brownie and Jake integrated themselves into the columns. Reifschneider positioned himself inside the columns beside Captain Fewell. Lieutenant Quang nodded to the platoon leaders, who shouted to the strikers. Their weapons clattered as the soldiers chambered rounds. The leaders shouted again, and the columns faced left.

J. V. and the lieutenant plodded up the slick roadway to our compound. Behind them, the front gate sat open. Soon the patrol filed out. Weapons rattling, the columns marched on either side of the road. I watched until the column reached the turn and vanished in the mist. I didn't believe in premonitions, but I had one nonetheless, an ugly one that soured my stomach.

A wasp-shaped Caribou appeared under the cloud cover, passed over the camp, made a soft turn, and leveled off for its landing. Though we needed what was on board, bringing supplies in under these conditions might go bad. We didn't know where Charlie was. Could be down the valley licking wounds or sighting a mortar on the airstrip or waiting for Norwood and Sheppard to truck supplies past the village. Bad decision followed by bad decision. So far only the bad coffee seemed like a good idea.

Lugging the PRC-25, a hungover Fox, his face starched and drawn, slogged his way up to the top of the camp. We passed, going in opposite directions. He said he'd be monitoring the radio and told me to have Cam come see him to string an antenna. Before descending the steps to the commo bunker, I glanced back. A hand shading his eyes, he stared numbly where there was nothing to see but sky and ground fused into a slurred mass.

I relayed to Cam what Fox had told me and headed to the team house. Mr. Green stood on the sandbag wall surrounding the team house. He poured out the black liquid contents in a canteen cup and said, "Coffee's inside, Barnes, if you don't mind a mouthful of grounds." He gazed down the pipe of the valley and muttered, "Bunch of bloody fools."

J. V. stirred sugar in his coffee. He told me to sit. "You see Fox?"

"Up monitoring the radio." I aimed my thumb in the general direction.

He held his cup in both hands and talked into it. "Well, Joe and Jake, they . . ."

The door opened, and he didn't finish the thought. Mr. Green entered and raised his empty cup. "Think I'll heat some water for tea." He asked if anyone wanted some. I declined and ladled myself a cup of coffee. As Mr. Green said, it was worse than bad, but I drank it nonetheless.

Sheppard and Norwood returned safely with the supplies. They reported that the road from the east was flooded with Vietnamese carrying sleeping mats and baskets filled with their belongings. The refugees pointed east to their home villages. "Beaucoup VC," they said. In returning from the airstrip, Sheppard and Norwood crossed paths with the captain. They'd warned of the claims of the refugees, but despite this the captain turned the force east.

Trung Sí Cu raised his brow and showed his gold caps in a half-hearted smile. "*Chào Ong, Trung Sí,*" he said, greeting me. Johnny was with the captain, and Henry was elsewhere translating. I returned the greeting, hoping I wouldn't be pressed to say more than that.

Cu lit a cigarette and held it between the first and second knuckle of his middle and ring fingers. Whatever troubled him, it had him agitated. I would have to deal with it. He gestured for me to follow along and headed down the track to the main gate. The laborers squatted outside the wire, staring off at the mountains. Ong Dao stood. His eyes trained on me as Cu spoke slowly, addressing the old man. He finished by saying, "*Mua,*" which meant "Go away."

Ong Dao didn't understand or didn't care about the gravity of our situation. He flailed his arms and harangued Cu, who responded with his own animated diatribe. This went on for a minute, and when one paused, the other took over, their voices getting louder with each exchange. Finally, Ong Dao turned his back to Cu, who kicked the ground and spattered mud on the back of Ong Dao's black pajama bottoms.

Cu looked at me, then up at the sky, before he renewed the argument. I waited until he cooled down. I somehow figured out that Dao wanted pay for the day and wouldn't go away without it. I had no control over money but came up with a quick fix and indicated I would return. I did, with a pilfered carton of Camels out of a drawer in J. V.'s sacred room. I gave Cu a pack and handed the carton to Ong Dao, who gave each laborer a pack and kept the remainder for himself. He wasn't fully satisfied, but he and Cu had both saved face. He led his laborers off.

It was sprinkling again. At the top of the camp Norwood and Pablo waited nearby as Fox tried to raise the patrol on the radio. I was about to tell Fox about the laborers, but before I got a word out, automatic fire erupted down the valley, at first a few indecisive bursts, followed by several heavy exchanges, punctuated by the unmistakable double report of a recoilless rifle.

Fox pressed the microphone button and called Jake's code name. He got static. He adjusted the squelch and called again. This time Jake's near-inaudible voice came over the radio.

"Say again," Fox said.

Jake said, "We're goin' to attack."

The radio crackled and went silent. The distant valley erupted in machine-gun and small-arms fire. The occasional explosion punctuated the violent clash. It was obvious the force the patrol had encountered was hard-core and large, company size at least, perhaps a battalion, and for the second time in ten hours we stood in camp and listened to a battle, this time with a great sense of anxiety and a greater sense of helplessness. Fox pressed the mic button and called again, asked for coordinates, paused, and repeated the request a half-dozen or more times. When it was obvious Jake wouldn't or couldn't respond, Fox dropped the microphone and stood, shoulders slumped, eyes on the curtained horizon.

A gray mask hung over the tops of palm trees. Though there was nothing but a deep, gray emptiness, we stared down the valley. The volume of the firefight grew. I clutched the stock of my rifle and swallowed down the acid in my throat.

Within minutes the sounds of the battle trailed off until the valley went silent. Fox knelt down and gathered the microphone in both hands, repeating Jake's call sign over and over. When it became obvious that the patrol had lost communication, he dropped the microphone and stared at the PRC-25 as if it were its fault. All of us stood in silence for a moment in a state of near trance.

Fox was the first to snap out of it. He looked at me. "Barnes?"

"Yeah, Top."

He looked toward the far end of the camp and searched

absentmindedly in his pockets for a cigarette. He found one, but his Zippo didn't work. He dug his fingers deeper this time and came up with a pack of matches. The pack was damp, and he tried several before one sparked on the sandpaper. He cupped his hands over the flame and puffed the cigarette to life. All the while I stood waiting for him to finish whatever he'd started to say.

Lieutenant Bussey tramped up the incline. Binoculars dangled from his neck. "C-Team said jets and helicopters can't fly in this," he said, offering up news that wasn't news. Fox told him we couldn't raise the patrol.

His gig being psy-ops and winning hearts and minds, the lieutenant was a decent guy who was ill-prepped to take command under these conditions. The muscles in his neck knotted. He moved his lips as if speaking but made no sound. He held the glasses to his eyes and scanned the valley, then let them drop to his chest. "Nothing from them?"

Fox shook his head and said, "I'm sending Barnes," he pointed to the hillock to the east, "to bring in that mortar out there. If the VC overrun it, I don't want our own mortar used on us."

The lieutenant again looked through the binoculars at the defenses, three bunkers on a stub of dirt protected by eight or ten Montagnard, three strands of concertina, a double apron, and a 60mm mortar. "You figure the Yards can't hold it?"

I saw what Fox was seeing. A squad of marines probably couldn't hold it for long.

Fox looked at me. "Take C rations along. Give 'em some."

I turned and headed down the incline to do as told.

"Wait." Fox squinted out of his sagging eyes. "What do you figure the distance is?"

I looked. "Sixty meters."

"Pace it out. When you return, sight it in on your mortar."

I nodded.

Under other circumstance I would have thought Fox insane. As if possessed, he kneeled beside the radio, holding the mic to his lips and mouthing curses under his breath like a widow offering novenas at the altar of a saint to save a soul. He thumbed the mic button and called blindly to the patrol, then cursed the weather or the radio or Captain Fewell for his impulsiveness. "Shit. Fuckin' hell. Flannel-mouth mother-fucker." The radio, no matter how often he spit out call signs and demanded an answer, remained stubbornly silent. Still he called to them fitfully.

The silence down the valley extended into an hour, then two. It and uncertainty worked on us worse than the sound of battle had. Manning our posts, we prepared for Charlie to hit us as he had the outpost. Each passing hour shaved away some of our hope that our teammates had survived. Still, men had survived worse. I'd heard a litany of examples, including that of Hector Camacho, who'd escaped imprisonment in Cambodia and found his way back through hundreds of miles of dense jungle to Vietnam.

So as Fox called them in fitful desperation, I dwelled on the day's events and the decision leading to them, in the end condemning the captain for not being circumspect. Certainly, he'd studied the history of war here, the deadly mistakes the French made. He should have considered weather and timing. As an officer, he was obligated to weigh the variables. Looking skyward, I would think how the darkness would work to their advantage. If the four of them stayed together, surely they would have a chance. Look at what Camacho did. Nothing was settled. Reifschneider knew the territory, Brownie didn't rattle, the captain was as determined a man as I'd ever met. And who was more capable than Jake? Hell, they could hide in the foothills or go farther east and reach Camp Starlite, or breach the river, hole up in brush on the far bank through the night, then cross to camp in the morning. Then I took a closer look at the river, a torrent of displaced tree limbs and foaming currents. The strongest of swimmers couldn't cross it.

We'd spent one largely sleepless night. Another lay ahead. We were about to settle in for the wait when the calm broke. Gunfire resounded down the valley for minutes, followed by three quick explosions. I inhaled, exhaled, swallowed, and held my breath. I keened my ears, but all I heard was my pulse and the thrum of rain on my poncho. I breathed again, then again, listening alertly for what I didn't know, but the only sounds beyond the pit were those of the rain pelting the ground and Fox's strained voice calling into the microphone in a tone that sounded like something less than panic but short of resignation.

A fierce wind rose from the South China Sea and pushed black-bottomed clouds inland. Across the nearest paddy the fronds of palm trees slapped back and forth, and the water churned violently. Rain, cold and hard, angled in from the east. It forced Fox to retreat to the team house.

In the pit I hunkered under my poncho and turned my back to the slanting rain. Water gushed over the sandbag walls and swirled around my ankles, and disconnected thoughts swirled in my head. Right now, Charlie's probably licking wounds, burying dead. There must be dead. From the sounds of the firefight, a lot of them. Remember what you know, I thought. What you know and your weapons are all you have now. Instructors at Bragg harped on the fact that Charlie is patient. Remember that, too, boy. He'll come when he's ready. Or maybe he won't. And nothing you can do will alter that.

I hopped back into the pit and sloshed around, wondering

what to do with myself, though there was nothing really to do but be patient and to wait, even though waiting wasn't what we were best at. The temperature had dropped noticeably. My fatigues from the ankle to the thigh were soaked, as were my boots. The poncho repelled most of the rain but did little to break the chill. Wet and shivering, I went to the bunker to change socks and boots and put on dry fatigues. I realized what I was doing was as absurd as Reifschneider's polishing his boots as Mr. Whitten carped on him about their just getting dirty again. Those polished boots carried Reifschneider east through mud and water to whatever fate he'd met, but for a moment they *were* clean, and maybe that meant something.

I changed fatigues and socks, then slipped into the boots. At least for an instant my feet were dry, a small but welcome comfort. I laced my boots, tied them, and grabbed some more ammunition for the M-16 and .45, three grenades. I left with a fresh canteen of water.

We stood our stations. For us there was nothing but the grim master Duty and the matters that occupied our thoughts. One was defending the camp, the other concern for our teammates. We clung to hope despite all the signs that told us it was a fool's hope. Maybe the patrol got lucky and our teammates were hiding in the brush, waiting for the cover of nightfall before they attempted a return. I wanted to believe in luck. For them. For me. I'd heard of a player holding the dice for a half hour in Vegas. There was the story of Hector Camacho and his unbelievable escape. He had to have been lucky. Sometimes luck dictates a good outcome. Aristotle said as much, claimed that a man has to have luck, that it is an ingredient to a full life. Sometimes it favors soldiers, too. Then sometimes it doesn't. The French on Highway 1.

TWENTY-ONE

I spent the hours from midday to near dark alone. Rain came in torrents, then as dusk neared, it settled into a monotonous drizzle. To the west the last of the light leaked into the mountain peaks as the sun set. The sky turned into an inky shroud, and soon our own hands were all but invisible to us in the oily darkness that followed.

We now numbered ten round-eyes and some sixty Vietnamese and Yards, to a man all of us anxious and exhausted. Other than rain and the occasional nervous trigger finger popping off a round, silence and a state of gloom settled over the camp. Pablo stood a post in the strikers' compound and manned an 81mm mortar. Misters Green and Whitten watched over the sights of a machine gun aimed at the rice paddies, as did Sheppard. Norwood trained the barrel of the A-4 in our bunker on the riverbank. The lieutenant assumed his new role in his bunker, which was now the command post. On occasion Fox or J. V. tromped by on his way to give Cam a message to send. Sometimes Cam hurried along to relay a dispatch from the C-Team, none of which offered us hope of relief.

Although uncertainty itself isn't an emotion but a state of mind, it sparks emotions, especially those primitive ones connected to survival. That night and in the days that followed I would come to understand that fear, discomfort, and uncertainty were endemic to soldiering and had been since the first day tribal man warred with tribal man. The soldier's a high-wire artist without a net who lives for the next step because all that's left for him is the next small step measured by heartbeats.

Sometime later I ran out of the adrenaline that had

kept me going. When I'd depleted all of it, I was sapped of strength, and my body began to betray me. Shivers came first, then a feeling that I'd been hollowed out. I wrapped my arms around my chest and leaned into the sandbagged wall. I fought to keep my eyelids open, laboring against an almost overwhelming exhaustion.

J. V. entered the pit and stood a yard away by the entrance, peering up at me from under the brim of his steel pot. "Wet enough?" he asked, his jaw protruding.

Loaded down with weapons and ammunition — .45, M-16, two bandoliers of grenades — and unshaven, he appeared surprisingly alert. I didn't answer. "You ready?" he asked.

I blinked and this time answered. "Yeah. Ready enough, I guess."

He pulled aside the cover to the magazine and checked the store of rounds. In preparation, I'd broken seals on the casings of a dozen HE and white phosphorus.

"How long you been here?"

"Can't say. Long time. Any word?"

He shook his head and hollered, "I tol' 'im, right out! He wouldn't listen!" He rubbed the stubble on his jaw.

He stood and looked at me as if trying to recall a piece of trivia that would come to him. This little war of his was no longer about colored pins on a map. Four members of our team were out there. Finally he said, "If they come, I'll be in here with you."

I nodded.

"I'm here just to relieve you. There's food inside. Go eat. But don't be long."

A pot of rice sat on the table, cooked but cold. Strips of Spam fried like bacon floated on a bed of grease in a skillet. I rubbed my hands together. It took a minute before I could coordinate my fingers well enough to hold the utensils.

I spooned some rice onto a plate, forked a piece of the fried Spam, and sat at the table.

The rice went down. So did the first bite of Spam. I gagged on the second. The smell of Spam seemed everywhere — on my hands, my hair, my wet fatigues, like the stench of dead, a nauseating smell I would never forget. Thinking that maybe someone else's stomach might handle it, I scraped the Spam back in the pan, and I spooned the last of the rice onto a mess plate and chased every bite down with a swallow of water. Finished, I returned to the pit.

Alone again with only a mortar for company, I hunkered down and listened to the rain on my hood. This was the rain God sent to destroy skeptics and sinners, the rain my step-grandfather, the Reverend Ames, preached about from the pulpit. I wished I believed in prayer. I wished I could muster enough faith to ask that my teammates' lives be spared, perhaps pray for the rain to stop and for Charlie to go home. But this *was* Charlie's home. And I was one of those skeptics God was intent on punishing.

The rain came quick and needle sharp. The temperature sank. I'd never imagined 'Nam's being cold, but it was. It seemed about sixty degrees. My fingers went numb, and I worried that they might be useless if they got any more numb. I remembered the sudden storm that came when a mass of clouds flowed over Pikes Peak and descended on Colorado Springs. I was hanging wet clothes out to dry, and when the wind blew in, it numbed my fingers and hands. I fumbled with each sheet and towel and shirt and diaper, securing them with clothes pins, even as the wind whipped through the yard and ripped the clothes off the line. I was thirteen and too afraid of being punished to dare stop. I ran around, picking up the wind-strewn clothes and rehanging them, only to see the futility of my efforts because I couldn't press the clothespins open. I finally gathered up the laundry basket and went inside, where I sat on the staircase to the basement, rubbing the purple out of my fingertips. The items that stayed on the line froze, and two days later I went to the hospital with strep throat. And now another storm and my fingers were numb again. Water channeled in from the trench. I took off my boots and the soggy socks, then put my boots back on. Socks or no socks, it was the same.

Our Vietnamese fired intermittently, even in the direction of the village. Each machine-gun burst set off a chain reaction. For the next hour or more there were gunfire and uncertainty and the unyielding thip-thip of rain on my poncho hood. Occasionally, I stood atop the parapet and stomped my feet. There was nothing I could do for my fingers.

Norwood came into the pit and said something I couldn't hear. He held out his hand and motioned for me to take whatever was in his palm. My hand closed over a small plastic packet.

He leaned close and shouted, "Keep them dry! Take one or two to stay awake, no more!"

"Anyone radio in?" I asked with little expectation.

He pointed to his ear and shook his head. "Don't forget to take them!" He left.

I stepped into the trench to piss. No need to find a piss tube. Rain would wash away any urine. Hell, it might wash the camp away. What's a little piss? Finished, I stepped back. The impressions my boots left instantly filled with water. I buttoned up my fly, climbed onto the parapet, and stomped my feet to get blood circulating.

It was the blackest night I'd ever witnessed. I wanted Charlie to come if for no other reason than to end the wait. I dropped into the pit and went about my job, pulling the pin on an illumination round and firing it. The flare popped open north of the camp and lit up the riverbank. I couldn't take my eyes off it, watched until it died on the ground. For a time afterward white and red spots danced in front of me, and I could see nothing else. When my sight recovered, I looked at my fingers, the tips pale and shriveled as raisins. I imagined the fingernails emulsifying. Water was the universal solvent, and this rain was trying to dissolve away nails and flesh and the entire camp, sandbags and equipment. I leaned into the sandbag wall and sank down in the pool of mud and water. Somewhere on the other side of the great spinning ball others were walking in sunshine, their feet dry. My chin sank to my chest.

"Hey!"

I looked up.

"Get up," J. V. said.

He extended a steaming canteen cup to me. I couldn't see or hear him very well, but I was thankful for his company, something I would have bet against the day before. It was midnight or later. Eighteen hours before our teammates had marched out. I pulled myself to my feet. He said something inaudible. I reached out and cupped my hands around the metal. His brew, campfire coffee, full of grounds. Feeling returned to my fingers. I held it below my chin and felt the steam drift up. I took a sip of it, strong and remarkably terrible, but wonderful all the same.

"Take the pills Norwood gave you!" he said and left me.

I sipped on the cup and let the drink warm me. I swallowed it down, grounds and all. In no time I was deaf again to all but the thip-thip-thip on my hood and the intermittent gunfire of the strikers. I decided to put another flare above the perimeter to calm their jitters.

I pulled the pin and reached over to lift the cover off the mortar. As I did, the round slipped from my hand. I grabbed it, held my breath, and lifted it out of the slime. I let the rain rinse off the mud. Stay alert, I thought. Don't die from stupidity before Charlie gets you. Then something clicked off. Rain dripped off the rim of my helmet. I awoke cross-legged in the slurry, a mortar round resting between my legs like some freakish dildo. How long I'd been out, I had no idea. Any sense of time had been washed away in the monotony of rain and darkness. I remembered dropping the round and realized the pin was out. It's armed, I thought. Fucking idiot, you are unfit.

I looked up into the drizzle, then at my knees. I wondered, have I truly been asleep? Did I faint, swoon? Syncope, break off, pass out? I knew the words. Crossword words. Was it just exhaustion? I recalled a kid named Beck in basic training who went to sleep while on marches. He passed out in the bleachers at the firing range, his rifle clattering, his body hitting the ground with a dull thud. The cadre went on instructing the platoon as if nothing unusual had happened.

I held the round gingerly, rolled onto my feet, and lifted the cap off the mortar. I slid the round into the tube and plugged my ears. The flare lit the perimeter as I uncapped my canteen. I opened the plastic packet and swallowed a pill, then a second for good measure. Unsure if two were sufficient and if four were too many, I opted for three.

In short time, I felt not just renewed but energized. The pills, aided by some profanity, kept me alert. I cursed at the blackness and the rain, cussed out the captain for leaving me behind and leading my teammates into a certain ambush. I cussed out Charlie. I wanted to kill, and I wondered about the morality of that. Thou shalt not kill. What number was it in on the tablet? Number 1 was the Lord's name. I hadn't honored him or my parents. Not for years. I had little regard for my stepfather and didn't even know the son of a bitch who'd given me my last name. I'd stolen and I'd lied. And I'd coveted. When you're a kid deprived of most everything, you covet because there's so much to want and so little to have. If I killed, it'd just be another black mark on my sin board.

The river was an unlikely approach, but I decided to light

it up again all the same, maybe discourage Charlie from setting up a mortar on the opposite bank. The flare popped deep over the river. The halo of light left an afterglow in the sky. Shadows lengthened eerily, and the mortar pit seemed deeper and darker. Then the flame fizzled on the ground. Something crawled from under fronds on the roof of the team house. A two-foot man? His shadow wavered. When I blinked, he disappeared. It took a moment to clear my thoughts and realize it had been the shadow of a rat, standing on its hind legs and tail.

After that my thoughts meandered in an amphetamine-induced psychosis, and the images that came were odd and disconnected, some half hallucination. I thought of Jake, who in part had come here for combat pay, rations-nonavailable pay, overseas pay, money he needed to buy a red Caddy convertible. I imagined the smooth-running, candy apple–red beauty, top down, him behind the wheel, his smile big to match his joy. The car would be pristine, engine tuned like a symphony orchestra. I was in the antechamber listening to Lela belt out an aria, rain surrounding her, not a drop of it hitting her. Does she still sing? Does she think of me? After me, she took up with Jay, her school choir mate. Broke my heart, the bitch. I saw them holding arms, smiling at each other. Then I saw a rotting corpse blocking the sidewalk on a narrow street. It stood up and walked toward me, and I ran away but couldn't outrun it.

I snapped out of it, rubbed my wet hands on my face, and wiped away the image of the dead body, only to have a dozen new images fly at me out of the blackness—a woman charged with a .45 in hand. She fired a bullet at my forehead. It moved so slowly I could track it. And I couldn't prevent the inevitable. An airplane engine howled. I looked at the sky, still black, and realized the sound was in my ears. My hands had quit working. I'd lost control of them, too.

I walked in a circle in the pit and shook off the feeling, but an odd fear lingered. It was unlike the fear a driver experiences in a near collision, not the heart-thumping slamming of a foot on a pedal and sound of screeching tires on pavement. Nor was it like the moment when one shakes hands with his own mortality. I didn't believe I would die, not then, not there. Shivering under my poncho, what I feared mostly was that my hands would betray me and I wouldn't be able to defend myself.

What, I thought, if the rain wasn't trying to dissolve my hands, but rather wash away their sins, an act of purification? Did God send Noah's rain to purify the earth? Or was he just pissed? Even Noah must have gotten pretty tired of rain—and scraping up animal shit. Divine wrath may be an illusion; the rain was not. If it worsened, I thought, I could build my own ark, leave the camp to Charlie, float on down the Song Tra Bong, hit the South China Sea, get a little beach sun.

You're a heretic and one jaded SOB, I thought and laughed. Although my fingers were numb and my hands trembled, an unexpected calm came over me. I adjusted the angle of the tube, got another round, and pulled another pin. The HE landed on the other side of the river. If Charlie was there, I wanted him to know it was in his interest to lurk elsewhere.

The rain fell, a constant thip-thip on the nylon poncho. I ran out of ironies to consider.

My heart began to race. I had to move to get sensation in my feet and hands again. This seemed more important than anything. I climbed out of the pit and walked in a circle, flicking the fingers of one hand, shifting the rifle, and flicking the fingers of my other. Numb fingers and feet and the thumping of my heart were one matter; wild and insane thoughts were another.

I jumped back into the pit. A hand caught me by the

shoulder. I pushed it away. Then two held me in their grip. I wheeled around, ready to fight. But no one was there. The mortar was tipping to the side, and the rifle strap and my poncho were hung up on the tube. Too many pills. Stupid you, one probably would have done you better. I had to do something to clear my head.

A flare round went up from Pablo's pit. It hung over the paddies to the south. The rain had slowed to driblets that shone like tinsel as they fell. Think straight, idiot. I pulled back my hood, removed my helmet, looked up, and closed my eyes. Rain washed over my face. My wits gradually returned. I had an odd thought. I hadn't been bitten by a mosquito. The smallest, dumbest creatures had the good sense to find shelter and wait out a storm.

I thought, I'm okay. I can taste coffee, swallow down grounds, and I can see in the dark. I have X-ray vision. I'm invulnerable.

TWENTY-TWO

Night dissolved into a sunless dawn. Fox continued trying to raise Jake on the radio. Cam still relayed storm updates from the C-Team. The rest of us stood our posts. We needed no weather report. Ours was: sky grim, humidity smothering, prospects dubious.

Then two at a time we went to the team house. Cam emerged from his hole in the ground to update us with news about air support and the arrival of a reaction force slated to fly in—neither likely anytime soon. He carried the long night on his face.

We were a silent bunch gathered to share cold C rations and hot coffee. I wondered if Charlie was celebrating. I'd pictured the VC as dour little fanatics decked out in black garb as a symbol of their dark nature. They demonstrated barbarous cruelty against captives or those who didn't support them. They charged barriers surrounding camps and flung their own bodies on the razorlike wire so that others behind them could breach the walls. How did fanatics celebrate? Do they drink and cheer victory?

Fox told me to sack out for a couple of hours. The floor of the bunker was surprisingly dry. I removed my boots, wiped and powdered my feet. I was too exhausted to do anything but stretch out and give myself over to sleep. An hour later someone shook my cot and disappeared before I could see who. I pulled on a pair of dirty but dry socks, slipped on the wet boots, and shuffled out into the day.

Fox called me over. "Find Norwood. Take the truck," he said, "and go there." He pointed east. "Don't go beyond the wash. Maybe you'll find one of them." The look in his eyes didn't indicate he had much faith in that happening. "Take a few Vietnamese with you, and be careful."

I warmed the truck's engine and waited until Norwood climbed in. As soon as he was seated, our reluctant escorts crawled over the tailgate. "*Sau lam,*" one said, meaning "bad." They too had friends out there and had spent their own hard night looking out into the rain. Norwood didn't speak, his silence, like mine, saying all that was needed. Fox had made a bad decision telling him to go, not a blunder like the captain's, but bad. In a sense, I was expendable, someone to man a mortar, but if Norwood was killed or badly wounded, the camp would lack a medic. Medics and radiomen were treasured assets. We carried that fact with us as we passed through the gate.

The tires dug channels in the slurry of clay and splattered mud against the fender wells. Mud built up in the tread until it was nearly impossible to control the steering, even in four-wheel drive, but I wasn't about to crawl up the road and get ambushed. I held the steering wheel as steady as possible and stayed on the throttle. We encountered an exodus of women and children from the Binh Hoa village complex. They struggled alongside the road, their backs and shoulders loaded with sleeping mats and baskets of goods, and gazed at us with muted disdain as we passed.

About a half mile outside the village proper, one of our strikers scrambled out of the brush and stepped into the open, then another, both weary, dazed, and weaponless. The second waved as he crossed a hedgerow. They climbed aboard the bed and sat trembling in the back, their eyes doing a jitterbug as if wired on speed. "VC," they uttered, "beaucoup VC." Uninjured, still in uniform, they'd likely dropped their weapons in battle and fled. That they may be cowards was of no consequence. It was not my place to judge, but I did all the same. I would have left them there, except they might have information about our comrades. A few hundred yards later a third striker emerged and climbed over the tailgate. He jumped off after seeing that we weren't turning back toward camp.

We reached the wash, normally a trickling runoff. Water sluiced down from the foothill in a stream four feet deep and twenty across. It seemed impassable and left me wondering how the refugees had breached it. On the far side at the edge of the road three women, two young *côs* and a wrinkled *bà*, kneeled around a body. The soldier, stripped of clothes and boots and naked save for his boxers, lay dead, killed three ways, bullet holes in his side, chest, and head.

The *bà* wailed and wept. Her wails rose above the sound of the rushing water. The others joined in, a lament offered by sisters and mothers and wives, one we would hear more and more as the days progressed. We'd seen all we could and dared go no farther. I turned the truck about. The wheels spat mud. The right front tire lost traction and brought the truck precariously close to a drainage ditch. The strikers clung desperately to the truck walls until the tires found a bite.

On the way back we came upon the striker who'd jumped from the truck. He stood on the roadside, signaling us to stop. Our escort from the camp hooted at him. I sped by, splattering him with mud.

Nightfall, same as the night before—cold, wet, lonely, different only in that we held no hope for our teammates and the camp was quiet since Cu had ordered his soldiers to conserve ammo and threatened to confiscate theirs if they didn't. I decided not to swallow any pills.

During the day a handful of survivors from the battle had straggled in, but there were no signs of our teammates' surviving or any reliable accounts of them or their condition. Between sketchy accounts of the battle from the strikers and Henry's lame translations, an accurate account was impossible. What didn't come clearly out of their mouths registered unmistakably in their eyes and trembling lips as they spoke. They felt no shame. "Beaucoup VC," they said with awe and terror in their expressions. I looked down at them with my own list of questions.

How could people of the same blood be so different—Charlie a brave fanatic, our allies unblushing cowards? Nguyen, you were scared shitless, weren't you? Pucker factor of nine or ten. Dropped your rifle, sucked your balls into your belly, and jetted yourself to the nearest pathway out. Boogied on your buddies. And Diep, where'd you leave your grenade launcher? Brownie probably needed you. So, Tien, when the shit hit the fan, did you take a breeze? Your name's Hùng, Vietnamese for "hero," huh? Change it. What's the word in your tongue for *coward*?

In Mexico when a dog quits in a fight, the owner kills it. It has no worth. If it quits once, it'll quit again. It was sung in corridas, in lyrics with a message for those dogs who'd run. The words weren't meant for dogs, but of course for men. Batterham had told me. The cadre at Bragg knew it. Here it was.

Some of us perhaps found hope in mumbling for divine intervention. I muttered a few prayers myself but invested scant hope in them. In our history together, God and I had agreed on little. I decided it best to put my faith in bullets and grenades. What I wanted most was for Charlie to come. I wanted to do what the stragglers who'd returned to camp had not, kill Charlie—him, them, a bunch of them, not a bunch but every single motherfucker in the district, hell, the province. I wanted to do what it was apparent the strikers didn't. Fight.

My grumbling stomach went unheeded. I fed it anger. Gone, four Americans and fifty, maybe sixty, strikers. I thought of the wailing mother who could do nothing with her rage but cry. Sorrow is a wound. Madre Dolorosa. I couldn't wail or cry, so I transferred it to words, wishing they were bullets and grenades instead.

Words I was taught not to say, I chucked them. Even the most forbidden were inadequate. No *motherfucker* strong enough. So I cursed in Spanish. I used phrases that once made little sense but now rang true as nothing else could. I repeated them. *Cabrones. Pinche tú madre. Toma mí verdiga.* And one that I never fully understood before this night: I shit in the milk of your mother. I muttered those sweet profanities like prayers accompanying a rosary. Prayers better serving me if Charlie were in my sight blade, my finger on a trigger.

I shit, again and again, in the milk of your mother.

Forget the purifying rain. I wanted to wash the world clean with vulgarity. I wished I knew a dozen other tongues or could invent a new and better language for this rage. But for now—*Me cago en la leche de tú madre, otra vez y otra vez.*

I was certain if the rain extended into another night that my fingernails would dissolve and so would most of me. What would be left was rage enough for me to do what must be done. But Charlie wasn't coming. That murderous little fucker sat warming his belly with rice wine.

The words kept my mind alert. I keened my eyes to the dark. Come on, Charlie. You fucking piece of *caca de pero*. I will kill your ass. Do you understand? *Me cago en la leche de tú madre*. Anger that big. Rage enough to kill with words.

"*Me cago . . .*" I ground out the hours of the second-longest night of my life.

TWENTY-THREE

Scattered clouds remained in the east, but in the mountains and the valleys north beyond the mountains, the sky was nearly blue as far as we could see. Even in our valley the lid was lifting. The truck idled, its wheels sunk in mud nearly to the rim. My only dry clothes were a T-shirt and pair of tiger-striped trousers I'd cut into shorts. I sat in a swath of sunlight that warmed the airstrip. I'd taken off my boots to dry my feet, a rare pleasure.

Fox sat in the jeep, talking to the pilot through the PRC-25. I rested my back against the fender of the three-quarter ton and measured the coming day. The MIKE Force, on standby for two days, was a minute or two away. What we wanted to gain from their arrival was a warm meal, a good sleep, and the opportunity to go down the valley and find our friends or at least kill a few of those who'd killed them.

We heard the plane's engines, even and powerful. It was a comforting sound. A minute later it slipped through a crack in the clouds some ten kilometers away. I tossed the smoke grenade. A soft violet mass flowed out of the canister, separated, and rose listlessly. The Caribou lined up on a glide path and came in full-flaps. It approached like a crab with wings, edging forward, drifting sideways. Momentarily, it seemed suspended, and then its landing gear touched down and it rattled over the metal plates. Spitting up mud, it pitched toward the end of the runway. An instant later the props reversed.

We drove out to meet the plane. The tailgate dropped. The crew chief told us beer and steaks were onboard, as if that would heal what was behind us and ahead of us. He stepped aside to accommodate the departure of the passengers. The Nung, Chinese exiles and full-time mercenaries, streamed out and formed two files. They had an aloofness about them that gave them the look of invaders instead of rescuers. Their predecessors had fought for Koumintang, and war was their craft, passed from father to son. They knew nothing else. They'd seen this before, or at least something so similar that distinctions were inessential. Ours was just another camp manned by exhausted men. The mercenaries spread out at disciplined intervals. They wore clean, dry uniforms and were well fed and equipped with the best American armament — M-16s, M-60s, M-79s.

After an exchange with Fox, the Aussies pointed the formation east and went to the head of the columns. Backs straight and eyes to the front, they marched off. Already I resented them.

I swung myself into the driver's seat and backed up to the tailgate — steaks and beer for those who drank it. It took the loadmaster and us mere minutes to empty the plane of cargo.

As the sergeant handed over the final crate, he said, "Eggs? Pretty sweet."

I laid the crate on top of the others. "Yeah, that's us."

We were on the road before the plane rattled down the runway and thrust itself over the edge. It dipped momentarily over the village before gaining enough lift to climb.

The Aussie commander, Captain Fazekas, flew in by helicopter. Rifle and pack strung over his shoulder, he jumped down before the chopper settled. It was obvious he'd come not to our aid but to take charge. His face full of I-told-you-so, he looked about the camp, then marched in long strides uphill to our compound. He consulted in private with the lieutenant and Fox in the back room of the team house as the rest of us got our first full hours of shut-eye in days.

While we slept, the leaders huddled in the back room and after two or three hours found themselves at loggerheads. Fazekas stubbornly insisted that he was sent to clean up what he viewed as the mess we'd made of *his* camp and that he would make all decisions on strategy and that only his people would participate in any operations. Fox and the lieutenant were equally insistent that our team participate in any rescue or recovery operation. In the end they could make no headway with Fazekas, so they went over his head and reported the dispute to the C-Team by radio.

Near evening a plane arrived carrying Major Truesdale, C-Team executive officer, and Sergeant Major Hodge. I drove the jeep to the airstrip to ferry them to camp. The Caribou's engines feathered, and the plane came to a stop, then turned back. I pulled the jeep alongside the ramp and helped unload their gear. The major, a former college lineman, at six-three and 240 pounds, still looked the part twenty years later. He filled the passenger seat as he settled into it. He looked at my mud-caked boots and my tiger-striped fatigues cut off at the thighs but said nothing.

Sergeant Major Hodge tossed his pack in the back and climbed in after it. His dark-brown hair cropped into a flattop and boyish face belied his stern, no-nonsense manner. In a unit like ours, filled with wild men and free spirits, he was a Bible-thumping moralist and by-the-book NCO. He too took note of my clothing and said, "You're out of uniform, Barnes."

I knew his reputation. He frowned on things most us thrived on, including but not limited to fornication, foul language, and drinking alcohol. I rarely drank, and there was no getting laid out here, but I was well versed in foul language, especially ways to use *fuck* in a sentence—as a noun, an adjective, and a verb in the subjunctive and both active and passive voices. I thought of it in the passive—as in "I'm about to be fucked."

"Sergeant Major, it was this or naked." I pressed the accelerator, kept my eyes aimed to the front, and drove slowly. I didn't have to look back to see that he was glaring at me. I avoided senior noncoms and officers whenever possible. Hodge now topped my list of those to avoid.

Outside, the Vietnamese camp cook squatted before the grill. The air smelled of steak and potatoes. Inside, we gathered at the table and sat in silence. Those with food on their plates sliced off bites of steak or potatoes and forked them in their mouths. They chased the food down with beer. The idea of rewards for surviving seemed obscene. We should have been in harness and scouring Binh Hoa for our teammates. Between bites we glanced at the back room where Major Truesdale and the sergeant major had set up shop and one at time called team members back and debriefed them.

Vietnamese were interrogated in an adjacent room by an interpreter who spoke nearly impeccable English. The accounts, inconsistent in details, were consistent in terms of bleakness. Nothing they offered indicated our teammates had survived. J. V. told me one had said, "Trung Si *Hep,*" meaning Jake, was killed at the onset. Though prepared to hear that, I still took it hard.

After the food was gone, we kept our seats and waited, passing the time by playing solitaire or tossing darts. A bag of mail had come on the plane. Some read or answered letters.

Envelopes addressed to our missing teammates lay unopened on the table.

Within the hour the members of our team were called to the back and debriefed until only Norwood and I waited. When the sergeant major summoned Norwood, I went to the bunker to see if my fatigues had dried. I changed clothes and returned. A few minutes later Norwood, subdued and seemingly irritated, stepped out, shut the door, and walked up the hall. I wondered what was asked and what was said, but he didn't volunteer anything and I didn't ask.

Dusk neared. I waited for my call to the back. Sergeant Major Hodge appeared at the end of the hall but didn't summon me. Instead, he walked to the door outside, held it open, and motioned for me to join him. I knew him mostly as the one who'd wanted to ship me to A Shau, and before picking him up at the airstrip, I'd spoken to him only once in passing. He held the door ajar and waited. He told me to get some sleep, that there was no need to ask me questions. I nodded and thanked him. For what, I didn't know.

I moved to leave. Before I could, he raised a finger. "Are you all right with Jesus?"

"What?"

He repeated the question. I shrugged and said that I hadn't put much thought into it.

"Well, now's a good time." He motioned for me to step outside.

He shut the door and laid a hand on my shoulder. He smiled. I smiled. He said he'd brought some Bibles along and hoped I might want one.

I looked in his sincere eyes and said, "Got one, Sergeant Major. Use it as a doorstop." Whether I intended it as humor or an expression of frustration, it was in my worst interest to say it, but I didn't care. I'd moved beyond that kind of caring.

"I don't know . . . ," his hand slid off my shoulder, "how long we'll be here, but you'd best avoid me."

"Yes, Sergeant Major," I said.

I'd been fed, and I was free to sleep as long as I wished. I was exhausted but wired on caffeine. The clouds had lifted in the late afternoon. The valley was still cool. I buttoned my fatigue shirt and scaled the incline to the top of the camp, where I sat on the parapet surrounding the motor pit. Stars, startling in their clarity, reached from horizon to horizon. It was the type of night that under other circumstances would inspire contemplation, but tonight stars were just stars.

The Nung had set up camp in the storage tent beside the team house. I watched the fluttering shadows on the canvas walls. They laughed loudly as they slapped down cards on a makeshift table. One threw back the tent flap to allow in air. The candles flickered in the slow breeze, and a continuous stream of cigarette smoke circulated above the men's bowed heads.

They seemed impudent and disrespectful. Then, too, why should they care? They'd done this work of theirs for two decades and would be doing it after I left. To them my team-mates were just four men who'd come to serve out a year and leave. One stepped out of the tent and urinated, his water splashing noisily on the still-damp ground. Someone inside the tent scolded him. He hollered back, shook the dribble off, and buttoned his fly. After stretching, he went back inside the tent.

J. V. approached from behind and offered me a cup wrapped in cloth, said that he had made it from a chocolate bar and some powdered milk. He seemed uncharacteristically subdued. I took the cup and thanked him. It was hot, so I set it aside.

"You gonna try it?"

That was more like the J. V. I knew. I picked it up and transferred it from hand to hand before I took a sip. It wasn't bad.

He took a seat. "They're lookin' to lay blame. They ask you 'bout drinkin'?"

"Not me. No one talked to me."

"You must'a said somethin' to Hodge. He was askin' Fox and the lieutenant about you."

"What?"

"Wants to know if you're . . . Well, doesn't matter. Stay away from him." He lit a cigarette, cupped it in his palm, and looked at the Nung tent. "Havin' themselves a time."

I glanced in that direction. An arm stretched outside to pull the tent flap closed. Soon after the candles went out, and a hush fell over the camp. It suddenly became so still I could hear J. V. inhale smoke. For the first time in days I heard mosquitoes and crickets. He and I sat, him smoking, me sipping his not too bad hot chocolate and looking up at the immense sky. When finished, I handed over the cup, thanked him, and promised to avoid the sergeant major.

TWENTY-FOUR

We were greeted with a morning of emerald fields and sharp-cut peaks defined against the sky. Steaming tendrils rose from the surface of the paddies outside the wire. Inside the wire the camp filled with the sounds of steel clattering as men lined up. Behind the sounds was a sense of urgency and expectation. Sheppard was going out with the Nungs and Aussies to Binh Hoa. Once again I was trapped in camp and facing a morning of tasks. The unfinished and those not yet started.

Work offered some semblance of order to us. Norwood began checking rat traps. Fox trudged to the top of the camp with the PRC-25. Mr. Whitten boiled himself an egg. The lieutenant drafted the first of the reports. I cleaned the mortar pit of used canisters, then stood at the perimeter of the compound and watched the MIKE Force march off, following the same route our teammates had taken three days before.

Ong Dao and the laborers waited outside the gate. As the last Nungs exited the camp, he led his wards inside. We walked to the excavation that would become the bunker. His wrinkled eyes sank when he saw the hole filled waist high with rust-colored muck. He pointed to the nearest trench, then the hole, and held his closed fists several inches apart. He moved his arms in an arc to indicate shoveling a channel to drain the water. He awaited my go-ahead.

"You're a crafty old sonofabitch, aren't you?" I said softly.

When I nodded to indicate approval, he turned to the workers and barked out instructions as if they had somehow provoked his ire. The men gathered up picks and shovels and began digging. Ong Dao placed two fingers to his lips to indicate that some cigarettes would be appreciated and then, rendering something akin to a smile, assured me all was in good hands.

Two FACs, the eyes in the air, hummed in from the east. With no idea where to start my own day, I headed to the supply tent. Piss tubes needed lye, latrines needed burning out, weapons needed cleaning and oiling, trash needed dumping, the radio needed manning. Lunch was ahead. I returned to my bunker, took my rifle from where it hung, sat on the parapet, and began stripping it. At present it was something I could fix, and I'd be needing it if called upon for the next patrol.

Fox sat atop the hillock like a shaman on a healing vigil and kept his eyes peeled to the east where Bird Dogs circled and guided the MIKE Force. The pilots had spotted bodies lying in the open. Between tasks I went and asked if he wanted a break. Twice he left, hurried to the latrine, and promptly returned. The other times I asked, he shook his head and asked if I didn't have something to do.

By midmorning the MIKE Force had reached the site. He was on the horn when the MIKE Force announced they'd located the bodies of two Americans and a dozen or so strikers. Fox asked if anyone could identify them. Sheppard said, "Reifschneider and Brown," and asked for a medevac.

Fox left me to monitor the radio and disappeared down the steps to the com bunker. He returned in short time and stood with his hands on his hips, eyeing the distant landscape. After several seconds, he looked at me with one slitted eye and said, "Find Norwood and gather a squad of strikers." He aimed a bony finger in the direction of the truck. "Take the truck east."

"That's all? Just drive east?"

"Yeah." He held up a palm to stop me. "Joe should be on a plane to Saigon by now."

"He didn't talk much," I said. It was the way I most remembered him.

"I respected for him for that."

"Top, what're we supposed to do there?"

"I want you to . . . I don't want these people thinking we're hiding."

"Got it." What he meant was that after the strike force left, we'd still be here.

People crowded the road, kids holding hands, infants in the arms of mothers, old men and women, boys driving water buffalo and even a milking goat. Toting their possessions rolled up in bamboo mats, they hurried as they looked backward like frantic animals fleeing a forest fire.

We spotted two military-age young men in the crowd. I

stopped the truck and signaled to the strikers accompanying us. Norwood sprang down. I did the same. The young men saw what was developing and backpedaled. One turned to flee, but I collared him in a few strides. The other broke free of the strikers, but they stayed on his heels. Mine seeing he couldn't escape fell limp on the ground. I lifted him to his feet by his shirt. Some refugees squealed protests. A few tried blocking my path. I held him by the collar and bulled my way through to the truck. I motioned for him to climb in. He refused. I picked him up and tossed him in.

The strikers, Norwood beside them, prodded the other toward the truck. He too refused to get in and shook his head defiantly. A striker thrust the butt of a rifle into the man's ribs and was about to strike again when I stopped him with a wave of my hand. He spit out a string of curses in Vietnamese. Like us, he'd lost friends, and these two might have had a hand in it. The prisoners wisely squatted in the middle of the truck bed and stared off so as not to provoke the strikers.

In camp Cu took charge and shouted questions into one prisoner's face. Unmoved by the theatrics, the prisoner stared off. The sergeant backhanded him and ordered the strikers to take the prisoners to the Luc Lon Duc Biet command post.

Two Huey medevacs and a gunship churned up the valley from Quang Ngai. The dead on the battlefield numbered more than the helicopters could handle. Fox told Norwood and Pablo to take the three-quarter ton out to help the Nung bring in bodies. I watched these events evolve and waited for Fox's attention. Finally he took notice of my standing nearby. He asked what we saw in the village. I mentioned the two Vietnamese we handed over to Cu.

"You did what?"

Even though his question was rhetorical, I repeated what I'd said. It sounded no better to him the second time. He shook his head and thought a moment. "Don't mention that to anyone. What'd you see?"

"Refugees."

Around two o'clock the task of ferrying the dead began. The sun was intense. Water steamed in the potholes. Though the road remained slick in spots, the clay was drying up. The absence of dust was the only blessing. A chopper arrived with bodies and hovered over the strip as a white-masked crew chief and gunner lowered bodies to the waiting Vietnamese. Among the dead were Lieutenant Quang and the district chief, shredded by shrapnel. Some men from the village and Popular Force soldiers toted the bodies from the airstrip to the wall surrounding the district chief's headquarters and laid them down. Villagers assembled nearby in search of loved ones. The dead came mostly from the Popular Force unit, full-time farmers or tradesmen and part-time warriors.

I monitored the radio and kept an eye to the east where the L-19 circled the hostile village. The pilots directed the MIKE Force to other sites where bodies lay. Relatives sat among the remains, crying over the remains of a brother or a husband or a son. They'd awaited what all the circumstances told them would be bad news. For some it had come. For others the wait went on.

Among the grieving was the *cô* who sang at the celebration. She squatted beside an older woman who wailed inconsolably over the remains of a young soldier. I wondered if he was the one who'd held the umbrella and escorted the young woman out of camp. Two men lifted the fallen man onto a makeshift stretcher to bear him off. The young woman wiped her eyes with the back of her hand, then stood and helped the older one to her feet. They fell in behind the men with the stretcher, the older woman leaning into the young one, who stared groundward.

Major Truesdale and Lieutenant Bussey ran relays from the team house to the com bunker, sometimes one coming and one going at once. The major, six-foot-three-inches of him, charged down the steps and banged his head on the cap of the door, not once but each and every time. And each time he looked up at the beam as if to ask how the hell it got there. He did the same when passing to the strikers' compound, where he tangled with barbed wire and required first aid. Some among us figured he would be the next American casualty to depart.

Fox monitored developments over the PRC-25. He grumbled about the MIKE Force, how they didn't stay in contact. He looked like a suffering ascetic as he leaned over the radio. He shouldered responsibility, real or imagined, for what had happened. Those were his men. Among his implicit duties as top sergeant was the responsibility to keep officers from making hasty decisions. The squelch crackled on the radio, and an Aussie asked if any black soldiers were on the team.

"Could it be a Montagnard, over?" Fox asked, referring to the dark skin.

"No. This man's too big, over," the Aussie answered.

J. V. parked himself in his room of colored pins. He had interpreters now to help debrief the surviving strikers, more having straggled in overnight. Their stories remained vague. Beaucoup VC. A battalion? Could have been a regiment. Could have been a company of hard-core North Vietnamese. Could have been Gabriel with a band of angels. J. V. had a pin representing one or more of each on his map.

Cam Gamble relayed messages to the team house. Among the rest of us there was a feeling of haplessness and resentment. I wondered, would I be out there on patrol had I been amenable to accepting the sergeant major's offer of a Bible?

The Nung under direction of Captain Fazekas evacuated Binh Hoa and villages to the east. That furthered the flow of refugees from nearby hamlets. The patrol drove laggards out and searched huts, but Charlie had slipped out of the valley, probably fleeing to safe havens before the MIKE Force landed. It appeared now that either the VC never had designs on our camp, or if they did, they changed their minds when Captain Fewell marched the reaction force into their snare.

The Aussie captain, now freed to do what perhaps he'd wished to do but couldn't when he lost two of his own, called in an air strike. Three silver F-100s in formation screamed up the valley in response to his call. They tilted their wings and climbed toward the mountains to the west. The flight leader announced that they'd arrived with a package and needed instructions on where to put it. Hearing that, I waved my slouch hat at them. Bring it, flyboys, bring it.

The formation circled. The jets swooped down and, one at a time, leveled. South of the airstrip they cranked off bursts of 20mm rounds. The sound of their afterburners as they rose up shook the ground. It was the Fourth of July, half-time at the Rose Bowl, New Year's in Times Square, and better. The Vietnamese watched, fingers pressed to their lips. When the planes passed over Tra Bong again, the grievers returned to the business of the dead.

On the third pass the pilots unloaded the cigar-shaped canisters from their bellies. The first plane's fell end over end, flipping groundward like a diver who'd lost equilibrium. A wall of orange flame engulfed the edge of Binh Hoa. Black smoke roiled up from the flame. The Vietnamese at the airstrip covered their noses and mouths with bandannas. It took some time, but the fallout drifted west, and the air smelled of burned gasoline. It stung the eyes and skin.

Families carted away bodies on anything that could be improvised as a stretcher—bedding, mats woven over bamboo poles, the springs and iron frame from a bunk. Some were solemn and dignified, others distraught and effusive.

Fox called us back to camp. Along the route we slowed for a procession of villagers. I steered patiently through them, stopping when necessary. In the village center two women were repairing the roof of a lean-to. The blast from one of the jet's afterburners had blown fronds off it. One stopped, looked at us, and spat betel nut on the ground. Smoke wafted in from Binh Hoa.

It was nearly five o'clock when the MIKE Force filed in like laborers who'd put in a good day and earned a beer or two. In passing, they looked disdainfully at the Vietnamese, then went straight to their tent, where they shed gear and lit cooking fires. The round-eyes retired to the team house and recapped the day.

What Sheppard and Mr. Cameron, one of the Aussies, found near Binh Hoa matched stories gleaned from battlefield survivors. Between them, they pieced together the evidence and concluded that Reifschneider and Brownie, separated from the captain and Jacobsen, had survived into the evening and gathered in a defensive position in a flat field near Binh Hoa. To the north was an outcropping of rocks where a farmer had planted a garden. Near their bodies were the district chief, Lieutenant Quang, and a dozen or more Yards, stripped of weapons and uniforms and discalced. Sheppard counted at least fifteen striations on the rocks where outgoing rounds had struck, indicating that they'd put up a fight and settled into a defensive posture for the night. Somehow, around dusk, sappers crawled to the edge of the rocks and heaved grenades.

"The bodies weren't stiff," he said. Brownie was found sitting, one leg propped over the other at the knee, a wet Salem dangling from his lips. Reifschneider lay nearby. A few yards away were the district chief and Lieutenant Quang, both dead from self-inflicted grenade shrapnel. Brownie's and Reifschneider's bodies were riddled with wounds, and the VC had stuffed cigarettes in them. The image wouldn't leave me. Stuffing cigarettes in wounds. It was hard to imagine desecrating the dead for a laugh. Besides, that would imply Charlie had a sense of humor. Too unimaginable. No, Charlie was a bleak little man. He was sending a message to the living: this is what he does to Americans. I thought of the VC body carried as a trophy by the strikers. Perhaps cruelty was customary here, and this beautiful and alien land just produced cold-blooded people. Or perhaps twenty years of war did. No matter the cause, the blood that flowed through Charlie's veins was cold, and the temperature in mine was dropping. The fact was absolute and irreversible: Brownie took my place and died. I was alive. I should have been thankful for my good luck, but it didn't seem at all like luck.

The days lay hard on us. No one spoke. We had to eat, so we did. The sergeant major sat at the table. I gathered up my plate and utensils and slipped outside to the wash pan. A moment passed before the door swung open. He stepped out and looked my way. I pretended not to see him and scrubbed harder with my brush.

He reentered the team house. I changed my mind about avoiding him. Inside, I made myself obvious by walking around the table to get to the refrigerator. I grabbed a Schlitz out of the refrigerator, marked the roster, and took a seat across from him. I wondered how he might reconcile the events of the past four days: Brownie and Reifschneider dead; the captain and Jake question marks. It seemed to me one had to at least ask why God and man had learned so little since that fiasco in Eden. I took a slow drink from the can. The beer was even more bitter than I recalled. I swallowed it down all the same.

TWENTY-FIVE

The heat had returned, and the simple act of breathing was labor. Helicopters churned down the valley en route to ferry in more dead. At midmorning Norwood handed me two cotton balls swabbed with Vicks and told me to twist them and stuff them up my nose. Before we drove to the airstrip and the business of handling bodies, we had ten days of trash accumulated that needed disposing. We filled the three-quarter ton with the plastic bags, drove to the ravine that served as our dump, and heaved the garbage down.

We'd been monitoring the radio. Nothing new had developed for an hour when the search party had found a couple of Vietnamese dead. No contact. No sign as yet of Captain Fewell or Jake. Pablo, Sheppard, and Mr. Cameron were combing fresh areas down the valley as a spotter plane circled. The longer they went without sighting our missing teammates, the more I convinced myself that the captain and Jake had survived and were hiding.

We were tossing bags away when Sheppard announced that they'd located more bodies, among them an American. Jake, they assumed. They would send him to camp temporarily for bagging before flying his remains to Da Nang. That would free up the helicopters to deliver the other dead to Tra Bong first before leaving. As the helicopters throbbed in the distance, Norwood and I kicked the last garbage bags into the ditch.

We reached the LZ as the chopper neared. Norwood stepped down from the truck, under his arm a folded body bag. He grabbed his medical bag. I told the pilot to come in on purple smoke, pulled the pin, and tossed the smoke canister. Norwood handed me a pair of surgical gloves, then slipped on a pair.

Stirring a wall of dust, the chopper touched down and settled on the LZ. The pilot kept the blades rotating for lift-off. Norwood and I ducked under the rotors and rushed to the crew door. A masked crew chief guided the handles of the stretcher carrying Jake into my hands. I pulled on my end as Norwood waited for the other handles. Jake had taken on a few pounds in death. We toted him some feet away and turned our backs as the pilot wound the engine and laid the stretcher gently on the ground.

The din from the turbo and the whipping blades was deafening, and dust roiled up. Two seconds later the ship was up and gone. Despite the menthol prophylaxis in my nose, the stench nearly brought up my breakfast. Flies swarmed us by the dozens. Though we swatted at them, they weren't discouraged.

Norwood pursed his lips and nodded. I didn't want to look. I looked anyhow. Flies had done a good deal of mischief, but not enough that we couldn't recognize Jake. Days before he'd helped me assemble a carbine the way a watchmaker might. He'd aimed a crossbow at a rat and missed. He'd written a letter home. Maggots wriggled out of a gaping wound in the back of his head. Except for Jake's tiger-striped trousers, Charlie had stripped him of all else, including dog tags. Above a bullet hole a wisp of sandy blond hair showed at the peak of the forehead.

He'd lain for five days facedown in water. Lividity had set in. His flesh was discolored and swollen. A portion of his skull on the back side was missing. His eye sockets were hollowed out, and his eyelids sank into the cavities. Parasites had eaten away at the soft tissue, brain, lips, ears, eyes. They'd stripped him of flesh and organs.

We had to lift him off the stretcher and ready him for the trip home. Norwood unfolded the nylon coffin, spread it beside Jake, and unzipped it. I grabbed the ankles. Norwood said, "On three," and took Jake's wrists. He counted. On three we lifted but got Jake no more than a foot off the ground before Norwood lost his grip. Jake's head and shoulders hit the ground.

Norwood's face screwed into a grimace as he looked at what was in his hand — several inches of skin from Jake's wrist had sloughed off. I cleared my throat to speak, but nothing came out. Norwood tossed the rotted skin aside. We looked down at Jake's remains as a pair of black feelers probed the air and then vanished back into an empty eye socket. An instant passed, then two long black mandibles issued from the bullet wound in the forehead, and a black beetle nearly two inches in length slowly crawled out. It moved like a fat man waddling down the line at a buffet. I bent down and flicked it onto the ground, where it reared up and snapped its mandibles at me. Its head shell popped as I ground it under my toe.

When the helicopter returned, we handed the stretcher to the crew chief. He gave us a new stretcher in return. Then we watched solemnly as the chopper climbed and turned east. Then I mounted the driver's seat and started the engine. I needed something to keep me busy. The color drawn from his face, Norwood settled in his seat. The days showed like years in his eyes and, I figured, in mine as well. We'd seen up close what we had to fear.

The image of the beetle reeled about in my head. Already, it had become bigger — three inches, soon to approach four. Huge and defiant. We had work left and needed food and sleep, but the insect wouldn't let me sleep peacefully that night. *There must be something you can do, boy — if not something urgent, then something small but necessary to rid yourself of the beetle.* Rid yourself? No, not then and not for some time long after.

That evening we heard how Pablo and Sheppard had found Jake lying facedown in wet reeds on an incline. Sheppard had tethered straps to an ankle and wrist and stepped back. Then he and Pablo lay belly down a safe distance and pulled the straps until the body rolled faceup. When certain the Cong hadn't booby-trapped him, they called in choppers from Quang Ngai. I was glad it was they who'd recovered our teammate. For the most part, the Aussies were good men, but they didn't know Jake—better that his teammates be the ones to send him home.

Later, Captain Fazekas stood atop a bunker and gazed at the valley. With the swagger of an actor delivering lines, he said, "When I was here, my men could go anywhere in the valley, unimpeded." No one mentioned the firefight that took the lives of Swanton and Wheatley, but we all knew what had happened. Whether the Aussie leader meant it as an affront to us or not, it was. Sheppard, in particular, found it a bitter epitaph to the day.

That same evening the gate I'd built between our compound and the Vietnamese command compound was chained and locked. It would remain so from then on.

TWENTY-SIX

Lt. Neil Davidson arrived February 2, as temporary team leader. Following a sketchy briefing of the camp's circumstances, he'd flown in by helicopter. He shook hands with each of us, then spent a lengthy interlude in the back office with Fox and J. V. After his briefing, he took a look around as we poured lye in piss tubes, gathered corroded ammunition, or in my case supervised the digging of a hole. He was young and smart, an ROTC type wise enough to recognize the uneasiness that pervaded a camp that had become the ugly stepchild of I Corps.

We'd lost four, 25 percent of our men. The Vietnamese had suffered some fifty dead, and we in camp were back to the business of being busy. Refugees had trickled back east, and reconstruction in Binh Hoa was under way. The dead were buried or on their way to be, but Captain Fewell remained an MIA, reportedly captured. No one expected to see him alive. The captain's legacy came in the form of a directive from the SFOB to all A-Camps that said no more than three members from a team could take part in a single operation.

The real lesson of January 22 was that little purpose existed in our being there other than racking up body count. Grenades and bullets, the rest seemed high-minded ornamentation and rhetoric meant to justify our presence. I questioned whether our other efforts weren't merely absurdities, beginning with the notion of winning the hearts and minds of a people who mostly wanted a bowl of rice a day and to be left alone. Politics and decisions dictating the conduct of the war worked to Charlie's advantage. In the meantime, soldiers dangled from strings while the puppet masters making policy wiggled their fingers.

We couldn't sit in camp and wait for Charlie to hit us. We had to go after him. He was down the valley. He was in the mountains. But for now the camp couldn't mount adequate operations. We needed replacements. Until then, the days must consist of work, the nights of cards. The new lieutenant joined us at the table that evening as we slapped down cards and scooped up tricks.

Some things were the same as before. We grunted and moaned over bad plays and close losses. Cam bid hands haplessly, win or lose. J. V.'s thoughtful strategies often turned against him. Norwood's slow play irritated opponents. Still, we played cards, and the more we did, the more the mood in the room darkened. We needed noise and complaining, needed distraction. We spoke in terms of luck or bad breaks, referring to the last hand, but much more. Cards, like war, reduced to luck no matter a man's skills. No one wanted to be alone with his thoughts to think about that.

TWENTY-SEVEN

When the MIKE Force departed Tra Bong, Don Cameron remained to temporarily reinforce the team until the slots left by our dead were filled. Stocky and congenial, he had dark hair and the sunbaked Outback look one would imagine on an Aussie. He was all soldier and fitted well with us. I was glad he would be in charge on my first operation. After a leisurely breakfast, we left — Misters Green and Cameron, three squads of strikers led by Trung Sí Cu, and young Barnes, as the Aussies called me. A heavy dampness hung in the air, and the sun was in our eyes.

Intelligence sources claimed the force that perpetrated the ambush — a battalion-size hard-core regional force — had since left the Binh Hoa area. Nonetheless, we had prepared ourselves for an encounter with something more than the farmer-by-day, guerrilla-by-night men who'd killed Swanton and Wheatley. Marine air support was on standby, and a Bird Dog would be aloft once the patrol crossed the village's eastern edge. Our objective was to determine if any sizable enemy units remained in the Binh Hoa area, and then, if we made no contact with Charlie, we were to proceed five kilometers to a spot between the Cham Temple and Vin Thuy, where, according to J. V.'s sources, Captain Fewell was last seen.

On this first mission since the ambush the strikers squeezed the stocks of their weapons tightly and carefully studied shadows in the passing landscape. A stocky Yard who barely stood up to my chest toted the 57mm recoilless across his shoulders. Upright, the weapon was taller than he. Cu had ordered him to stay near me at all times, and he did. Whenever I turned my head, he smiled up, a smile almost as broad as his face.

Sometime before 0600 we cleared the outer fringes of Tra Bong, where the valley spread wide to the north and crossed the trickle of water that marked the boundary. The lead squad broke off into fire teams and covered each flank. The next two formed staggered columns on either side of the road. Trung Sí Cu sent a Yard to the front some twenty paces, then shouted the order to proceed. We advanced cautiously up the valley in the open, three to four paces between men.

The paddies and farm villages to the north were havens for VC. To the south the dense undergrowth and rocky shelves were well suited to hiding snipers. Anything from a lone rifleman to a regiment of guerrillas could be concealed up there. I scanned from side to side, everything, the hedgerows that ringed the villages, the bushes in the hillside. An inexplicable sense took hold of me as if I'd done this all before, walked the road and seen the foothills, though I never had.

We advanced within a kilometer of where Brownie's and Reifschneider's bodies were recovered. The FAC arrived on schedule and circled overhead. Other than a few women in the paddies just south of the village of Binh Hoa, there was no sign of human activity anywhere. No children. No men. The women, feigning disinterest, bent over and watched us pass.

We marched another five hundred meters or so, and then another, and reached a crook in the roadway as we neared Lang Ngang. Everything seemed peaceful, but nothing seemed natural. We came out of the turn. A bullet snapped overhead. The shooter had waited until the column was halfway around the curve. He fired another. Cu shouted, and the strikers hit the ground in the brush at the road's edge. I went to a knee and studied the hillside. Judging from the sound, the shooter was using a BAR. He fired two more shots that kicked up dirt to my right, ten or twelve feet away. I spotted his muzzle flashes in the shadows on an outcropping below the tree line. I aimed and waited. When I saw the next flash, I squeezed off three rounds in succession. Then I hustled to a spot behind some scrub and waited.

He was still up there. I'd missed and I knew it. Charlie was a phantom who vaporized at will, and I'd just witnessed it. We took incoming from a different angle. At least two were above. Up the road the Aussies and strikers with them returned fire. About fifteen yards to the front at the toe of the hillside, I spotted a rock formation from where I could fire the 57. I looked over my shoulder for the Yard carrying the reckless. He was behind me and ready. The 57's rounds were distributed among four others squatting in the cover of nearby brush. I crouched and went to the nearest one, got his attention, and motioned with my head for him to follow. As if we'd rehearsed for this very moment, he and the others shot to their feet and trailed me up the incline.

We crouched in the brush. I opened the breach and loaded the gun with a high explosive and then balanced it on my shoulder and waited. The sniper hadn't fired for at least a minute. I figured he was gone. I couldn't be sure exactly where the Aussies were, other than somewhere behind and to the left of me. They had the radio and were in communication with the Bird Dog, who most likely had spotted the snipers' exact position, but that wasn't helping me.

No one fired for some time. We waited and watched. I steadied the barrel and eyed a crevice about 150 meters away below the tree line, a spot I figured ideal for a sniper. A solo shot chipped away leaves in a nearby bush. I set the crosshair on the crevice and aimed slightly low to compensate for the short distance. He fired. I fired. The round exploded — on line, but too high. I'd overestimated the range and hadn't compensated enough, but I'd put it close enough to make him consider his own mortality.

All around strikers were firing up at the brush on the hillside, and they didn't bother with aiming. I reloaded the reckless. From behind me Mr. Green asked, "Are you all right, mate?"

"Fine." I pointed to the notch between the rock formations. "He's up there."

"Probably not now, Barnes."

We waited until certain there would be no more incoming.

I felt no great satisfaction as I unloaded the weapon. At best, I'd been close enough to take an hour or two off his lifetime, hardly the revenge I'd imagined. A metallic taste settled on my tongue, the aftertaste of adrenaline gone amok. I felt my heartbeat slowing. Mr. Cameron joined us, and Mr. Green radioed in coordinates for an air strike. The L-19 circled. We crouched behind whatever cover was available and waited for the marine F-100s out of Da Nang. Soon they scrambled up from the coast, and the FAC marked the target with a rocket.

Nearby some strikers chewed on rice balls. Others indiscriminately fired weapons. That drew the wrath of Trung Sí Cu, who strutted up and down the road, berating them. He kicked one's ankle and shouted. When the strikers lowered their weapons, Cu, obviously embarrassed, looked at Mr. Green and shrugged.

The jets ripped up the hills with their full arsenal and departed. The patrol spread out on an assault line and ascended. We reached the area where the sniper had nested, and Mr. Cameron and the strikers secured the base of the outcropping, while Mr. Green, the Yards, and I swept the area. We found what we'd anticipated. Save for rocks, what remained was burned bush and brass from a 30.06, the only sign of Charlie. We knew he was nearby — somewhere beneath the earth. We just didn't know where.

We trekked another few uneventful kilometers and assessed the damage done by the jets in previous days. Then we marched back, fifteen to sixteen equally uneventful kilometers. All in all, my first walk had been a bit of a laugher. I'd expected more. And yet I felt unburdened.

As we entered the compound, someone snapped a picture of the Aussies and me. The reckless rested on my shoulder. Cameras and war. Photos from the front line. I'd written a paper on the work of Mathew Brady for a college history class at Texas Western. The Civil War was the first recorded by camera. I wondered if Vietnam would become the first to be captured on camera by soldiers themselves. Soon enough it would be the first captured for viewing on home television.

A night before going on an operation and a night after, those who went weren't required to pull a guard shift, but we were shorthanded. At dinner Fox informed me I had midnight watch.

Gathered about the table, we listened to Mr. Green sketch out the day. As a subject it quickly died, and the team settled into small talk. The real conversation was left unspoken. Three were accounted for. One was not. Filling an empty seat wasn't so easy as it might seem. You can't just occupy space vacated by the dead and missing, so we filled the blank spaces with thoughts and a tense politeness. One empty chair in particular was troubling. We knew the others' fate but not the captain's. Where was he? I wondered. Then the answer came. He was in my head, just as the others were, precisely where they would remain as long as I lived.

When the night closed in, I went to my moldy lair, lifted the mosquito net, and lay thinking of revenge. Even though vc bodies laid wall to wall and stacked floor to ceiling wouldn't fill the four empty spaces in the team house, I wanted to kill at least that many.

TWENTY-EIGHT

Three days after the fiasco with the sniper J. V. rattled my bunk and shined his flashlight in my eyes. He said he had coffee waiting. I set my feet down on the dirt floor and fumbled about for my boots, then gathered up web gear and weapon. I was hot to go. On the way out of the bunker I banged my shoulder and nearly fell.

Mr. Whitten, waiting in the team house, poured boiling water into a mug for tea. I poured a cup of coffee and drank it with a slice of stale bread. The operation promised to be what I'd come here for when I volunteered for 'Nam. The team had yet to receive replacements, so the least-critical position to the camp, meaning me, was doing double duty. Mr. Whitten would not have been my choice to lead the operation, but his name was top on the roster.

The mission was simple enough and seemed workable. Lieutenant Davidson and Fox had laid it out in detail, including points for commo check. The theory was to catch the vc in Binh Hoa by surprise by approaching from the river side, a one-day affair, up and back in time for dinner and cards—easy unless Charlie had been alerted and was waiting for us.

Mr. Whitten finished his tea and said, "Let's go, young Barnes."

Besides us, the patrol consisted of twenty Vietnamese and Henry. We formed inside the gate and left two hours before sunrise. It was moonless and dark enough to cross undetected as we approached the river. We stationed a striker with a BAR and two others to cover the crossing, then sent three across to secure the other side. Saying he would cross when the main body was on the far side, Mr. Whitten remained behind with Henry and the radio. I lined up the strikers and positioned myself in the middle of the column.

The strikers waded in, keeping a one-yard or better space between themselves. Normally, the river was shallow and easily breached, but here the channel narrowed and the bottom dropped sharply. A few yards from the bank, the lead man sank waist deep. At midcourse water rose to the chins of most of the strikers and well above my waist. We held our weapons overhead and plowed forward. In some five or six minutes we reached the reeds on the far bank, where it was steep and slippery. One of those we'd sent ahead took the weapon of each man as one by one they used vine tangles to hoist themselves up.

In another five minutes we were all atop the bank. I spread the strikers out and waited as Mr. Whitten and the others crossed. Instead of turning it over to a striker, he packed the radio on his shoulders. I judged from the sound of his heavy breathing that he had difficulty sloshing his load through the high water. When he reached the bank, I relieved him of the radio and gave him a hand up. "Bloody buggers. Drippin' wet," he said as he settled onshore.

We couldn't risk moving on in the dark, so I told Henry to spread the strikers in a half circle along the river's edge and take up defensive positions. Mr. Whitten radioed camp and said we were safely across the river. We waited until daybreak, and then Mr. Whitten radioed that we were advancing to the next check-in point.

The strikers slipped into harness. I sent a Yard as point man to the front and two on each flank, and then Mr. Whitten and I fell in at midcolumn. Two strikers between us, we headed out. We entered the tree line where the underbrush proved surprisingly thin. The ground, softened by rain, muffled our steps. We progressed slowly to the next checkpoint, mostly because every dozen steps or so, Mr. Whitten stopped and scanned the brush. Although I appreciated his caution, I saw no need to stop. The Yards accompanying us were plenty alert, and all the frequent stops accomplished was to spook the Vietnamese. Soon Mr. Whitten's actions began making me nervous. I worried, not that something was wrong but that something wasn't right.

By 0830 the temperature was climbing toward ninety. The canopy thinned, and sunlight angled through the gaps. The patrol hit the wood line and encountered a clearing about a hundred meters wide. Mr. Whitten stopped the column at its edge, where the scant vegetation, a few stunted brambles, provided little concealment. With a kilometer remaining to travel to the next objective, we couldn't stay put, and in any case it was unwise to do so. I suggested sending a couple of men ahead to the far tree line.

Mr. Whitten shook his head. "Best keep the buggers together. We'll all go."

He passed his decision through Henry to the platoon leader, who signaled the soldiers forward. We advanced no more than fifty meters before Mr. Whitten again stopped, studied his map, and then after a brief time folded it and motioned to the radioman. He kneeled beside the man with the radio and unfolded the map again. Whatever he had in mind was a bad idea. I hurried over to him and asked, "Mr. Whitten, why are we stopped?"

He held up a palm and pressed the mic button with his other hand and sent the camp a set of coordinates, saying he wanted advancing fire. I was dumbfounded. We weren't a conventional unit assaulting a fixed position, and we'd made no contact with Charlie. The best that could result was his compromising our position. Besides, my best estimate placed us at the fringes of the 81's outer range. I told him it was a bad idea.

"We're not moving without it," he said.

I'd heard that tone in his voice before—Warrant Officer Whitten in charge, veteran soldier, at your service. Though he outranked me, he was dead wrong. I suggested we turn north, stay in the woods, and circle downhill. It would add no more than a half hour to the operation.

He fixed his gaze on the far tree line and said, "We're not advancing there."

The strikers were jittery enough. It wouldn't help matters if they saw us arguing. I kept my own counsel and nodded. He pressed his thumb to the mic and asked for a round.

The tree line lay a hundred yards ahead. The patrol proceeded toward it slowly. Halfway across a faint pop came to us, announcing a round was on the way. Then we heard the round burst and felt the ground shiver behind us. I grabbed a bellyful of earth and waited. The air smelled of nitrate. I stood up slowly and looked back, where smoke was already dissipating, some twenty meters away. Ten meters closer and the rear of the column would have been hit.

Before I could speak up, Whitten had called in an adjustment and said, "Fire three for effect."

He ordered Henry to get the strikers moving. Those nearby squatted and shook their heads. I urged them up, and the column advanced some five or six paces before we heard a familiar pop, a delay, and this time the whistle of a descending round. I dove to the ground and covered my head with my arms. The blast was ear-shattering. Two strikers in line immediately in front of me tumbled backward. Dirt rained down. I lay motionless, looking ahead. I could barely hear for the ringing in my ears. I didn't move, just breathed, one breath, then another.

The ground smoldered, marking where the round had hit. Maybe three feet in front of me a striker clutched his leg at the thigh and moaned. His helmet lay beside him, a half-dollar-size hole torn in it. Another striker lay in front of and perpendicular to the first, a chunk of shrapnel lodged in his shoulder. A ragged piece of shrapnel steamed on the ground by my boots.

Farther still Mr. Whitten lay belly down, his hand clutching the mic as he shouted, "Cease-fire! Cease-fire!"

By then another round was on the way. It hit in the middle of a half-dozen strikers. Mr. Whitten hollered again for a cease-fire. Thinking that was the last of the firing, I rose up to my knee and surveyed the damage. Just under half the patrol lay wounded. Four were in serious shape, others less so. Mr. Whitten stood and shouted, "Bloody hell!" His red cheeks redder than I'd ever seen, he cursed Pablo, called him a bloody idiot, and threatened to shoot him.

Cussing wasn't going to change our circumstances. Whether it was his purpose or not, the mission was ruined and needed help. I hurried to the radio, called for a medevac, and requested two choppers. At least we were in a clearing that would serve well as an LZ. Unfortunately, it also served to make us vulnerable to an attack.

Whitten calmed enough to have Henry form the strikers in a circle and secure the landing zone. I started bandaging the man with the wounded thigh and told Henry to let the others know a helicopter was on the way. As he translated, he turned his back to Whitten, tapped an index finger to his temple, and mouthed, "*Diên cà dàu,*" meaning Whitten was crazy or dumb.

After dressing his wound, I administered morphine to the striker with the hole in his shoulder. Despite his nasty wound, he seemed unconcerned if not pleased, which puzzled me for a time. As we waited, I considered my own luck. Two strikers had taken metal that might have otherwise hit me. As the wait dragged on, Mr. Whitten sat to the side, ranting and vowing retribution.

When the chopper neared, I smiled at the wounded. Some smiled back. Others smiled at one another, which gave me pause to think. As the whoop-whoop of the blades got louder, I understood what had inspired their smiles. A few days safe in some hospital was preferable to being out on a fucked-up patrol with a raging, red-faced round-eye.

I rested my rifle barrel against my thigh and tossed a smoke grenade. When the helicopter came in sight, I pulled the pin and tossed the canister. As soon as the craft sat down, the healthy strikers, grinning and chatting as if on holiday, helped their comrades aboard. Once the injured were evacuated, we formed a column and retraced our path to the river, another bad idea from Mr. Whitten.

Fox sent Pablo out of camp to Da Nang until Mr. Whitten cooled off. Sometime that evening the Aussie wrote an after-action report. My version was that Charlie hadn't paid a penny's worth of blood, and the patrol suffered eight wounded without firing a shot. I never saw Whitten's version of the events, but I heard what transpired at the other end of the radio. Norwood, assisting Pablo in the pit, had rechecked all the calculations. The truth was Mr. Whitten had called in bad coordinates.

In less than a month I'd seen enough to realize poor judgment calls and ineptitude were predictors of a woeful outcome. I slept restlessly that night, thinking of how the months ahead might bring more bullshit my way and perhaps leave me bleeding on the ground and waiting for a medevac. If killed, it would be because it was my turn.

TWENTY-NINE

The only thing permanent at a camp was impermanence. Men flew off, replacements flew in, no sentimental scenes, no hugs, no Hollywood-film good-byes, maybe a handshake and a "So long" or a "Good luck." On moving day a man simply packed his fatigues, boots, and weapon and took them with him. Those were his furniture. When one arrived, it was no different: "Hello and here's your bunker. By the way, you stand guard from 0100 hours to 0300 hours."

One February morning the first replacement flew in by helicopter. Following habit, the strikers waved as it passed over the river and turned upwind. A few minutes later Fox pulled the jeep to a stop by the water trailer. His passenger wore staff-sergeant stripes and an open smile and had loves-this-war stamped all over him. The little bit about him that didn't say all soldier said wild man. It was obvious Fox was pleased to have him aboard as he introduced him around as Hank. Henry Luthy's arrival was actually a return to Tra Bong. He was a medic and had been chosen to replace Brownie because he knew the area. He was muscular and had the easy stride of an athlete. He reminded me of Joe Hague, who in practice scrimmages smashed someone with a tooth-rattling tackle, then smiled as he offered a hand up, which he'd done to me more than once. I figured Luthy might make things just a little more interesting.

Fox, who praised no one that I could recall, said, "Hank's the real deal. Good man."

Right away, Luthy made himself at home. He knew his way around, went right to his bunker, then sized up the compound. That evening he sat in on the pinochle game. He was good-natured and kept his conversation loose, ribbing J. V.

and Fox and mocking bad plays. After one hand he bowed out of the game and kibitzed. He wasn't Brown, but he was welcome all the same. It was the first time spirits had been up in days. By the time the team was ready to rack out, he'd established himself. Already he was scheduled for an operation.

1st Lt., soon to be Captain, Richard Gregory — slim, around thirty, with thin reddish blond hair, already balding — arrived soon after Luthy. He shook hands with each team member, then turned his attention to Lieutenant Davidson and got down to business. As he walked perimeter with Lieutenant Davidson and the new Vietnamese camp commander, Lieutenant Gregory seemed more like a junior-high civics teacher on a field trip than the leader of an A-Team. But he was a leader, one with an astute eye. Everything he saw told him this wasn't where an officer could best build a career, but that didn't faze him as he went about sizing up the camp and the team. He'd likely arrived with an earful of bad reports, and looking around probably confirmed much of what he'd heard. This was Oz minus a good witch, a wizard, or ruby slippers, and this was where he had to command.

He consulted at length with Fox and J. V. Then he invited comments from everyone but Norwood, Cam, and me. Mostly, we were excluded from the important parleys, those that dealt with operations and planning and which of us might be chosen to be the next potential KIA.

That evening we played cards in the smoke-filled team house. Lieutenant Gregory asked to be dealt in. He was calm and deliberate when he talked. He played cards thoughtfully. He wasn't the kind to tell jokes or anecdotes. He contented himself with playing one game, then bowed out. That evening he'd scheduled himself for the next operation. He wasn't here merely to give orders, which sat well with us.

Other than the quick introduction, I'd not spoken to him, but he stepped outside with me when I left. It was sunset but not yet dark. He asked how long before I finished the big bunker. I said it was progressing but couldn't pin down a date. He said in his quiet way to waste no time completing it. Then he asked what else I thought the camp needed to shore up the defenses.

"We need a minefield in the wire."

We had to resort to the use of toe poppers, harmless-looking two-inch plastic discs that could take off the ball of a foot or a heel or shatter the lower leg, depending on what part of the foot stepped on the detonator—heel, ball, or toe. Perhaps because toe poppers didn't kill, they were thought humane. Instead of sending a man directly to eternity, one might cause him to bleed to death or sentence him to a life on crutches or an artificial limb. What minimal damage they inflicted might be enough to impede an assault. He asked where I'd place them. I pointed north where the approach was most level. "Higher up, they might wash away in a good rain."

He didn't speak for a time, just eyed the perimeter, then said, "Get on it."

Even before we lost four in the ambush, Paul Sheppard had decided life on A-Team, or at least in Tra Bong, wasn't for him. He'd requested a transfer to Project Delta to perform cloak-and-dagger mischief anywhere the generals who ran Military Assistance Command Vietnam wanted. His request was approved. With no adieu, he packed his gear and choppered to Da Nang in February.

Staff Sgt. Douglas Malone, his replacement, flew in soon after Shep's departure. Shorter than average, medium build, Malone proved to be a know-it-all, and that put him at odds with J. V., who had the corner on knowing everything.

Malone was congenial. He liked cards and beer, two standard requirements. Like Shep, he was a light-weapons specialist, which meant the team remained short a heavy-weapons specialist, so Pablo and I kept our assigned mortar positions if the camp was struck.

A few days later Jake's replacement flew in. Sgt. 1st Class Willy Hunter was black — one among few in all of Special Forces then. He had broad shoulders and a sledgehammer stare in his eyes. His backpack on his shoulder, he ducked under the blades of the helicopter that brought him, toting an m-16 in one hand and a duffel bag in his other. I introduced myself and offered to help with the duffel bag. He held it aside as if I were trying to steal it and gave me a sideways glance, then tossed his gear in the back of the jeep, and climbed aboard.

My first impression of Willy was that no one, even a Martian, could be more different from Jacobsen. Giving him the benefit of the doubt, I credited his rudeness to having been assigned to Tra Bong.

I slid behind the wheel, started the jeep, and looked at his name tag. "Sergeant Hunter, what should I call you?"

"How often do they send out patrols?"

I put the jeep in gear but didn't let out the clutch. "Lately, regularly."

"Good. Willy. Call me Willy."

"For William?"

"For Willy."

"Okay." I pressed the accelerator and turned the jeep about.

Willy Hunter proved to be as reticent as Luthy was gregarious, and he did little to ingratiate himself to anyone. It took several weeks before he became an accepted part of the team but much less for him to earn my respect. Right away he looked to see what work needed doing. He was the first one to step up, grab a shovel, and work beside me and the laborers. Though not a combat engineer, he understood the intricacies of construction — slump factors, steel reinforcement, cure time. He dug holes and mixed concrete, and he knew machinery. The more I was around him, the more I saw that he *was* like Jake, except nothing about him said he would ever crack a joke or laugh at one.

Over the months he would sweat, climb mountains, and lie in ambush alongside me without ever revealing that he'd volunteered to come to Tra Bong. In fact, he'd requested a transfer the day he got news four Americans were killed in an operation in Binh Hoa. I'd lost teammates and friends; Willy had lost a close friend, perhaps his closest, and had come to Tra Bong solely to avenge Jake's death, information he would offer more than three decades later.

THIRTY

The second week in February, our team was near full strength. It lacked a second radio operator, so Cam's daily duty was doing double duty, either buried in ditty-dots, running messages to and from the team house, or pulling guard at night. He lived on coffee, short naps, whatever sugar he could get, and pinochle. Card games were about his only communion with the team.

The big bunker, a new bench for the latrine, water runs, garbage runs, rat traps, guard, disposing bad ordnance, teaching Vietnamese how to fire a rifle from the shoulder without flinching, stringing wire, raising a new fence, defoliating elephant grass, and clearing fields of fire filled my days to the point that my own fuel gauge was straddling the empty line. I'd mapped out a minefield and gotten approval to go ahead with it. Gregory wasn't MacArthur or Patton, but he was less concerned with winning hearts and minds and more devoted to fighting Charlie. He knew how to get the most work out of us. In my case he'd said I wouldn't be scheduled for a patrol until the minefield was in. That served as my motivation.

The day the toe poppers arrived on a supply plane, I went to work. Charlie wasn't above sneaking in and stealing a few mines to use later against us. Because the laborers couldn't be trusted, it was left to me to dig holes and lay each mine. We couldn't risk the minefield's being compromised. I put the laborers to work on the bunker and carried the box containing the mines and what tools I needed out to the wire. The mines had to be laid in clusters of three and four, two rows deep, between two barriers of concertina wire, their locations carefully mapped.

I measured and dug, pacing off and charting each placement. I wiped sweat away, opened the next container, and dug. Squat labor. Dirty. As I planted the mines, the irony of my mission wasn't lost on me. The good guys were restricted to using these, whereas Charlie could plant an A-bomb, provided he could get his hands on one, and place it wherever he wished. He could take us captive and put a bullet in our heads, castrate us, even impale us on a wooden stake, all of which he'd done. None of which we could do. One war. Two sets of rules.

By afternoon of the second day the minefield protected a hundred-meter strip of land facing the river, a small feat in the big scheme. I duplicated the minefield map so that a copy could be forwarded to the SFOB. The other I handed over to J. V., who secured it somewhere in the back room. The following day my name came up on a patrol roster. I would be going out within the week. That afternoon I poured the first of the walls of the big bunker. Two weeks after the patrol I was scheduled for a flight out into Da Nang. A day and a night, a big reward for doing labor. Lists, schedules, plans laid out in the future. First the patrol. Cam would be going. I wondered if he considered it a break.

We readied ourselves to leave about an hour before dawn. I carried the 57 recoilless and four rounds for it down to where a platoon of Yards and Vietnamese waited in the outer compound. I turned the gun over to the Montagnard who'd carried it on the previous operation and distributed the rounds to two others. In my bunker I harnessed up, my web gear weighted down with four grenades and eight full magazines, then joined the patrol as it formed to leave, taking a spot in front of the Yard with the recoilless. He smiled at me. I smiled back.

Trung Sí Cu paced up and down, giving his charges a final look before shouting the order to march. The guard opened the gate.

As we left, Lieutenant Gregory asked, "Where's your headgear?"

I shrugged. "I forgot it, sir," a lie because I hadn't forgotten but chose not to wear it.

He looked at me as if to say it was a topic open to later discussion.

Going were thirty strikers, Cam Gamble, Lieutenant Gregory, and myself, our objective the ridge about seven clicks to the east. There, according to J. V., a squad of locals had set up a machine-gun nest to fire at planes. Informants claimed it was constantly manned. The eastern horizon began to lighten as we moved through the sleeping village to the outskirts of Tra Bong. Lieutenant Gregory was behind the Yard with the 57 and one pace ahead of Henry and the striker carrying the radio. Cam marched near the rear of the lead squad. This was his first walk, and we were headed farther into Charlie's backyard than any operation had to date and into an area that would remain a scourge for months to come. Occasionally, he would look back.

Eager if uptight, Cam was ready to see action. Since Hausenfauk had been sent to Ba To after our arrival, Cam had been the team's sole radioman, and up to now his single duty had been manning the commo bunker. I couldn't recall his leaving camp, even a short trip to Da Nang for a rest. The rest of us had tans that ranged in darkness from khaki golden to earthen sunbaked, but he seemed paler now than when we'd boarded the plane to fly from Pope Air Force Base. If nothing else happened on the mission, at least he could get some well-needed color in his cheeks.

Shortly after we left the village, Cu, tough as hardpan, ordered out flank security and shouted to the strikers to spread their intervals to four paces. He strutted up and back like a game cock, here and there prodding soldiers to keep the spaces even. He'd been a soldier since his teens when he'd battled the Japanese and later had fought alongside the French and now fought the Vietcong. He'd been tested in more than twenty years of near-continuous war and knew his troops were scared and had reason to be. Three weeks before four Americans and some fifty Vietnamese died on this same route. Like us, he hoped the strikers felt enough anger and had guts enough to fight. Just in case, he bolstered their courage by displaying his own and demanding discipline.

The skies were clear. If hit by a superior force, we could call in jets and have them strafe the area within ten to fifteen minutes. It was always a discrete call. If we brought in a strike before the vc were committed to attacking, the enemy would evaporate into the trees and mountains. At least we had the option, something Captain Fewell and the others never had.

My ever-smiling guy with the 57 stayed at my heels.

Whenever I glanced back, his face expressed what he couldn't say in my language—I'm your man. Don't worry, you.

Halfway to Binh Hoa the sun's corona cracked over the flats. A kilometer later, the sun's glare off the mirrored surface of the paddies nearly blinded us. Women waded in the shallow paddies, one with a nursing baby slung across her breasts. In their seeming unconcern they noted every detail—our numbers, the armament we packed. Trust no one, the sergeant at Bragg had said. The enemy is everyone—male, female, child.

Soon the thermometer would eclipse a hundred degrees and rise even higher as the sun climbed. We passed the crook in the road and roughly the same spot where I last took fire. The outpost sat abandoned on the ridge, a bleak sight in the early dawn, its bannerless flagpole a reminder of what had happened. Then Lieutenant Gregory called in for a FAC.

We cleared the bend in the road without incident and neared our objective. The point man stopped. Lieutenant Gregory had Henry call Cu over. They consulted the map. The lieutenant radioed in our coordinates and informed Fox that we were near the final objective and preparing to advance. Between us and the objective lay a hundred-foot barrier of brush and elephant grass. Cu split the unit in two and pointed to a rocky abutment below a stand of trees. He ordered the first unit up, and when a soldier balked, Cu grabbed the man's harness straps, slapped the back of his head, and shouted, "*Di di mau!*"

We progressed without incident through the elephant grass until positioned to the west of and just below the ridge where the machine-gun nest was reportedly located. The lead squad split in half and ascended a narrow course up the rock wall. Once the front unit secured the high ground, we followed. The target lay across a depression thick with brush. We dared not cross it for fear of being trapped and cut to shreds by automatic fire. That limited our choice to going uphill, where we'd gain the advantage of shooting down.

A footpath spiraled up a narrow crevice to a rocky shelf some thirty feet above us. Lieutenant Gregory pointed to it and consulted with Cu, then sent Cam up the narrow trail with a fire team. He called for a spotter plane, and the lieutenant reported our progress. He was still on the horn to camp when the machine gun cut loose and the firefight erupted.

I signaled that I was going up to see what was happening. Lieutenant Gregory shouted to me, but the intense shooting drowned out whatever he said. I nodded as if I understood, then signaled to the Yard carrying the reckless to follow. Grinning, he crouched and scurried up behind me. Then, as if reading my mind, those packing the 57 rounds in their harnesses followed.

The shelf was nearly flat and about forty feet long, and narrow, at its widest point no more than ten feet. A convex bank of granite rose up about twenty feet from the floor of the shelf. Cam and two strikers huddled at its base as incoming fire chipped stone above their heads. The other strikers were spread along the flat stone, lying flat or clinging to what little perch was available. Their situation was precarious. Crouching, I hustled to a point farthest east on the shelf. The squat boulders there offered some cover and view of the far bank where the automatic fire came from. I kneeled and, using a boulder for cover, peered over.

The strikers nearest the edge pointed across the gap and shouted at me. The machine-gun position was well concealed, most likely near a tunnel or a network of tunnels, and its crew had wisely removed tracer rounds from the feed belt, so I couldn't pinpoint the exact spot of the source. I did, however, hear its bullets crack overhead before they caromed off the stone face behind me. There seemed as much danger of us taking a ricochet as from a direct hit. Wherever I looked the cover was too little for me to fire the weapon without exposing myself. I figured to become a target once I fired the reckless. I needed the first round to count.

Bullets pinged off the rocks or cracked overhead. I needed a better look. I waited as the machine gunner fired several successive bursts. Then when the shooting ceased, I crawled around the boulder to the edge of the shelf. The gunner fired a burst. I didn't spot a muzzle blast. Rounds dinged off the boulders behind me, but I saw all I needed to see. Nearly level with us the palest wisp of smoke drifted from a thicket roughly a hundred and fifty meters away.

The FAC had arrived and was circling. Jets would soon arrive, but no doubt before they did, the machine gun would be gone and Charlie would vanish into his underworld. I decided to use the grapeshot first, which would scatter a pattern of lead over the area. If the machine gunner didn't return fire, I would follow with another grapeshot, then follow that with an HE. Cam remained crouched behind a boulder. I backed away from the edge, crossed over to where Cam waited, and signaled for the Yards to bring the 57 and ammunition. To get an accurate shot I would have to kneel or sit at the edge of the shelf. The Yards set the rounds beside me, and I handed a grapeshot to Cam, picked up an HE, and shouldered the 57. I figured he would know what to do better than any of the Yards.

I kneeled at the edge, hoping to get off two shots in succession. I told Cam to load me up. That's when he informed me he didn't know how to operate the breach.

"Gimme the round," I said. I had no choice but to lay the reckless across my knee.

I rested the barrel on the rock, opened the breach, and chambered the round. A Yard was squatted down directly behind me. I waved him and the others away so as not to injure anyone with the backblast. I didn't even bother with using the scope, and there was no time for precision. I propped the weapon on my shoulder, aimed the barrel, and waited. I figured the crew had seen me by then. My pulse raced, but I kept the barrel steady. Bring it, Charlie. But the gunner didn't fire right away. I had to be a tempting target, a blond man, an American among a dozen Yards.

Out of the corner of my eye I saw Cu standing in the open a step away, exposed, a target Charlie couldn't resist. When I saw the brush rustle, I squeezed the trigger and quickly loaded another grapeshot. Charlie fired. I fired.

He didn't fire again after my second shot. I waited for the breach to cool, then loaded the high explosive. I took my time and using the scope spotted what looked like an arm. I took a breath and let it out as the wobble settled in the barrel. I fired and backed away from the ledge.

It would have been a pointless risk to cross the divide and needlessly expose the strikers, just to confirm the kill. Cu ordered his wards to fire in the general direction of the machine-gun nest, just to make certain. Or perhaps it was the crafty old sergeant's way to instill them with some well-needed confidence.

Though I'd been unaware of it, the FAC had been circling overhead. Cam and I climbed down to join Lieutenant Gregory. While the lieutenant chewed me out for going up top, the marine pilots arrived in F-100s, and one said they were ready to cook if the spotter plane would mark the target. The FAC fired a Willy Pete on the far bank. The jets promptly delivered a load of 40mm and rockets on the spot, then some bombs, and finally a little napalm to punctuate their departure.

The heat and the smell from the napalm carried across the ravine. I took my olive-drab handkerchief from around my neck and wiped the sweat off my brow. Cam smiled. Cu smiled. I smiled. I could never know with certainty that I'd hit the machine-gun crew. I simply reported what had happened, everything except that Cam didn't know how to load a round in the breach of a recoilless, something I would teach him before we ever went down the valley together again.

It was noon before we descended the ridge to the road. Women no longer worked in the rice paddies. Vietnam took a siesta this time of day, all but our small force. The return to camp went faster than the departure. The soldiers seemed different. We'd taken no casualties. They needed this. It wasn't a victory exactly, but it certainly wasn't a defeat. That was reason enough to stand taller and walk faster.

When we reached camp Luthy, who'd been manning the radio, reported that the pilots could see my blond hair from a thousand feet up. That didn't sit well with Lieutenant Gregory, who gave me my second reprimand of the day, saying that from then on I was to wear headgear anywhere I went and added, "And that's an order."

I said, "Yes, sir," and turned toward my bunker with the reckless to clean it.

"And when I tell you to stay with me, you stay."

"Is that what you said, sir?"

My name was on the roster for a late guard shift — punishment, I figured, for not hearing well or wearing headgear. I liked this lieutenant, so I shrugged it off and headed for a shower to wash the day off. Norwood was occupied with a trapped rat. I paused to watch. The rat, average by the standards of the camp, was perhaps twelve inches nose to tail and a pound in weight. It was a furious devil, hissing as it tried biting its way through the wire with its square teeth. Norwood sprinkled his catch with gasoline, set the gas aside, took out a match, struck it, and lobbed it at the cage. The animal screeched as it burst into flames.

He used a rag to spring the door on the trap and free the rat. The rodent scampered a few feet, rolled on its side, and balled up. Its squeals were like those of an infant. Its paws drew up into little fists and disintegrated. Its determination to live was nothing short of amazing. A moment later all that was left of it was its charred remains. Norwood smiled.

<hr />

THIRTY-ONE

From the mountains to the coast the sky was overcast on the morning of March 9 when I flew on a C-123 into Da Nang. Ahead was my first break, two and a half days to clear my head. Because my birthday was six days away, I pretended the break was a present, a vacation of sorts. But there were no vacations without work in Vietnam, not for a member of an A-Team. No sun. No beach. At best, a hamburger or steak and a night or two of uninterrupted sleep.

Actually my time away was mostly a scrounging mission — buy beer and whiskey and trade for whatever food a few Montagnard crossbows and spears and two bottles of scotch would net on the underground marketplaces. That morning I went about the business of collecting food and supplies. I'd signed for sixty dollars in scrip from the team fund that was meant for purchasing beer and whiskey. I had written instructions from Fox that included the name of a contact at the C-Team who'd help. The sergeant looked the crossbows over, took the best among them for himself, and told me the rest would do me well as trading material. In exchange he provided me a truck and a petty officer's name. I drove to the PX, where I purchased a pallet of beer and four bottles of whiskey, two scotch and one each of bourbon for Fox and J. V., then rambled over to the naval base, where I contacted the petty officer who ran the navy mess hall.

The chief petty officer was in his forties and balding. To break the ice I gave him a bottle of scotch as an act of goodwill, and then we began negotiating the trade. His forehead was splotched with dead skin, and he scratched at it almost constantly as we negotiated. He was pleased with the prospect of having more souvenirs to sell, said they were bragging material for sailors on shore leave who couldn't get enough of them. He looked my wares over, liked the spears, and said he'd take the crossbows, though they seemed inferior in craftsmanship. I gave him the list that Fox had written up. He studied it a moment and in exchange for the weapons offered a dozen steaks, three tins of powdered eggs, a case of Vienna sausage, a box of smoked oysters, a few loaves of bread, and a carton of Spam.

His offer came up short. I asked about getting a box of pork chops. He said that wasn't possible. When I mentioned having another bottle of scotch that I was going to trade elsewhere but could make available to him, he raised his eyebrows and upped the number of steaks to three dozen and offered to secure it all on a pallet and have a couple of seamen load the supplies in the truck. Then he asked if I was hungry and what I'd like to eat.

I scarfed down the first good breakfast I'd had in ten days—ham, three eggs over easy, and wheat toast with marmalade—and decided the navy had the army beat to hell when it came to food. Then on a full belly I drove the goods to the airstrip and stored our food beside another pallet that contained a resupply of ammunition. My errands done, I took a shower. The water was cold, but there was an endless supply. I lathered and shivered and scrubbed, then dressed and headed to the club. By then the skies had blackened and the ceiling had dropped. Earlier I'd seen others who were in from A-Teams for a break. The bleak weather raised doubts whether they or I would be able to fly out.

I was concerned, as I entered the clubhouse, that the steaks might go bad. They were packed in dry ice, but that gave me little confidence about their staying frozen if the flights were delayed a few days. I had no desire to explain rotten steaks to Fox or J. V. The club, a converted mess tent with a plywood floor, had a crude pine bar that was supported by columns of ammo crates nailed together. Five A-Teamers were inside. They glanced when I came in but didn't speak, just turned their attention to the speaker on the wall.

Something was abuzz. What it was I had no idea. I ordered a Coke and took a seat. The others loitered at the bar, looking down, then up, then off, their eyes pausing for an instant to take in the loudspeaker. I asked what was up. One said a camp was under siege. Another added that the MIKE Force was on standby to go in. No one seemed clear on any details, except that the camp was A Shau and communication from camps to the C-Team was on hold.

Then the squelch crackled as Sergeant Hoover, the radio operator from A-102, called in to the C-Team. We listened as if transfixed as he gave a briefing of the situation at A Shau. Boxed in, surrounded by North Vietnamese regulars, the camp was taking barrages from mortars and rockets, and the weather was worsening, the ceiling near zero, too low for jets or any accurate bombing from above the cloud layers. Charlie had antiaircraft weapons in place on mountain slopes above the camp. Small-arms fire was intense on the perimeters. The defenders were down to dwindling supplies of ammo and their own resourcefulness. I'd not given A Shau much thought before then, but I did now because I was reminded that was where the sergeant major had intended to send me until Jacobsen convinced Captain Fewell to intercede.

The radio went silent. The bunch of us stared at the speaker, thinking, speculating. We remained silent and defensive, intent on the speaker, when three young marines entered and sidled up to the bar. They propped their weapons against the bar, slapped money atop the counter, and ordered beer. One commented on the silence and said it was time to party. His beer in hand, he headed for the jukebox, which had gone unused the entire day. He dropped some change in the coin slot and pushed buttons. When the music started, he ambled back to his buddies doing a half-dance, half-walk as he did.

Among us was Sergeant First Class Pau Pau, an imposing six-foot, four-inch Samoan. He held his beer in hand, leaned against the bar, and stared at the interloper. Our club was open to anyone in uniform, but this day wasn't one for celebrating or hospitality, not to a group of boisterous marines, not given what was transpiring a hundred miles away, not even if they meant no disrespect.

"Hey, what's what?" the marine said to Pau Pau.

"Nothin'," the Samoan said.

"Man, 'at's what we intend, nothin'. So what the fuck's goin'?"

The Samoan squared up with him and said, "Drink up and leave."

"What? Hey, brother, you . . ."

"I'm no brudder of yours, and don't talk no more. Drink."

Pau Pau stepped over and took the beer can out of the marine's hand, laid a wad of scrip on the counter, and said drinks were on him. But just one round. The marines looked around. We were on our feet, ready to back up our own. One among us told them one of our camps was under attack. The big mouth's buddies said they understood and drank up, but the talker took his time. He stared at Pau Pau as he sipped. The others picked up their M-14s and advised their buddy to do the same. He hesitated, but they had better sense than he and grabbed his arms and pulled him away.

By late afternoon word came that at least two Americans died at A Shau. The team's fortunes went from bad to dire. Colonel Facey, our C-Team commander, entered the club.

I was nearest the door. I stood and hollered, "Attention!" Those who were seated stood, and those already standing faced him and squared their shoulders.

The colonel said, "At ease. Continue. I'm just looking for someone." He turned to leave.

"Sir," I said.

"Yes."

"If you need someone to go in . . . Well, I'm ready."

Pau Pau said he too wanted to go. Without hesitation those remaining volunteered. The colonel said he appreciated our offer, then said that arrangements were under way, that we were needed in our own camps, and that all A-Team members would be sent back as soon as possible. A Shau might not be the only target.

Late that afternoon, as soon as there was a break in the cloud cover, I flew out.

Action was at a standstill, everyone on alert, and like all teams in I Corps, we were restricted from running patrols and confined to camp. The entire Tra Bong Valley was boxed in with clouds. It had rained and then sprinkled intermittently, and now a mist hung over the camp, weather less fierce than in January, but reminiscent of it. News was the beleaguered A-102 team had survived the night. The other news was that casualties had been high the previous day.

This, the C-Team worried, might be the big offensive that had been rumored for weeks, the final drive that the Americans and Vietnamese anticipated from the vc and their northern allies. Half of us at a time congregated in the team house, monitoring dispatches from A Shau. Anger and frustration festered beneath our subdued conversations. The developments two hundred miles away were as close as the man sitting next to you, as close as the memory of January 22. Special Forces was a brotherhood. Some among us knew men in A Shau. Knowing a man or not made no difference. We took any loss among our unit personally.

Norwood sat across from me. I played solitaire with one ear to the speaker, turned over cards, sipped bad coffee, and listened as events play out. No one played darts. J. V. and Fox were as sober as I'd yet seen them, as was Luthy. Occasionally, one or another among us left to take a turn in a mortar pit or check on the status in the Vietnamese compound.

The day progressed grimly. At noon the team gathered to eat. No one had an appetite. We stirred rice and canned stew around on our plates. Mumbled. Afterward, I went outside for an hour. Returned. Someone else left. As evening neared the loudspeaker broadcast a last dispatch from the radio operator. Charlie had breached A Shau's final defenses. Hoover reported that North Vietnamese were outside the bunker, that he was destroying the radio equipment and the onetime code pads. Then all communication was cut off. The survivors abandoned the fight and sought escape in the jungle.

It was around five thirty, dinnertime elsewhere in Vietnam.

Over the next days the tale of A Shau's collapse unfolded in skimpy, often unreliable, details. We heard of the bravery of Bennie Adkins, who, although wounded, pulled his comrades out of the line of fire, then manned a mortar pit, and alternately fired mortar rounds and automatic fire on the assaulting North Vietnamese. The worst information of the team's plight enraged us. In their panic to escape, some Vietnamese defenders trampled one of the Americans. Others tossed a wounded American off a helicopter in an effort to climb aboard and save themselves. I made special note of this.

Of the seventeen Special Forces soldiers in the camp, five were missing in action and believed killed. The remaining twelve all received wounds, most of them severe. Adkins and the others who escaped on March 10 found cover in the rain forest and headed in the direction of Hue. They evaded capture until rescued two days later.

Then came disturbing information. Days before the assault two North Vietnamese defectors had reported a heavy troop buildup, information confirmed by pilots taking overflights into the valley. Colonel Facey had repeatedly requested reinforcements for A Shau. Headquarters at I Corps, the corps commanded by General Wall, denied several requests. Fogged in, outmanned, short on ammunition, with many strikers having deserted or even defected, the Americans were left hanging. The only ground help they received was the MIKE Force, following a week's delay.

We brooded and we speculated on what prompted the decision not to commit marines. Interservice rivalry? Failure in the chain of command? Incompetence? Dismissal of intelligence? All of these? What generals decided was often based on diametrically opposite choices—to act out of caution or to act with expediency. Choosing expediency over caution might lead to a tragic result, but choosing caution over expediency might well lead to the same result. All we knew for certain was that based on some general's decision marines might not come to our aid, not because they didn't want to but because of failure in the circuitry at the top. The other truth we knew already—the life of a trooper out here meant little, except to those who were out here.

THIRTY-TWO

Fox lifted his weedy leg over the bench and sat. The corners of his mouth were creased into a smile. He said, in his inimical and bemused way, that someone was waiting to see me at the main gate. I asked if it could wait until I finished eating.

"Don't think so."

I turned my spoon upside down and studied the pasty oatmeal clinging to it. "You may be doing me a favor, Top." I planted the spoon in the mound of oatmeal in the bowl and headed for the gate.

Mr. Whitten was about to enter as I passed through the door. He said I should hurry. It was early yet, but already too hot for exertion. I didn't recall his hurrying anywhere, ever. I walked all the slower and looked back to see if he was watching. But the screen was shut.

Inside the gate a dozen or so strikers had surrounded a benign-appearing living antique and a boy about ten, both clad in the standard black pajamas. The youngster stood behind the old farmer. Trung Sí Cu, standing inside the circle, spoke to the old man, who responded in a rapid, high-pitched voice. He held something in his hands, offering it to anyone, it seemed, who would take it. But whenever he stepped forward, the soldiers backpedaled.

When I stepped up to the ring of men, the farmer showed me a corroded Bouncing Betty, its three-pronged pressure detonator rusted, its arming pin missing — death in a can if he fumbled it in any way. Cussing under my breath, I slipped between two wary strikers and neared the old man. Behind him the boy peered out. Both were fortunate. Luck was all that could account for the mine's not having exploded thus far.

Seymore, our new interpreter, strolled up and said, "Fox, he say come see what say." He noticed the mine in the old man's hand, came to an immediate halt, and backed up two steps, then another step slowly, for good measure. He said, "Numba' ten, *sau lam*."

I smiled at the old man, whose wrinkles were about his only feature. He smiled back and revived his earlier chatter. "What's he saying, Seymore?"

Seymore, now standing on the other side of the soldiers, said, "Want money. Crazy old man, Bahn."

Neither Seymore nor Henry could pronounce "Barnes," and I'd given up on telling them how to say it. "How much?"

"No know."

"Ask."

The old man spoke to the kid, who in turn addressed Trung Sí Cu, who then carried on a conversation with the boy.

I thought of the day instructors at Fort Belvoir introduced us to the basics of disarming mines. I'd been too hungover from a weekend in DC to handle the simplest operation and bungled the exercises so badly the instructor threatened to flunk me. I didn't have to worry about disarming this one. I would have to walk it outside of camp or blow it up in place. It wasn't even safe to look at. First I had to get it out of the old man's hands without wrestling it away.

"Seymore, tell him to set it down carefully and step away."

Instead of delivering my words in a reasonable way, Seymore shouted. The old man stumbled back, but the boy caught him in time. The others started chattering wildly among themselves. I hollered for silence. It startled everyone. The old man looked at me.

"Tell him *now*, Seymore. And be nice."

The old man listened, nodded, and smiled politely, but made no effort to dispose himself of the mine. "Repeat it," I said to Seymore.

The old man shook his head and said, "*Cum*," meaning "no."

He raised the mine overhead and circled about. The strikers raised the barrels of their rifles and backed away. Cu shouted and stepped toward us. I waved him off, turned to the old man, and smiled. He seemed as anxious to rid himself of the mine as I was displeased to take it. I wanted my tone to convey that neither he nor the boy should feel threatened. I kept my eyes on him and spoke softly. "Seymore, tell the others to go now, okay?" I extended my open palms. "Tell him to give me the mine."

The delighted strikers scattered. The old man looked at me as he talked through Seymore. He spoke for a half minute and shook his head.

"He say . . ." Seymore stopped in midsentence as the man took a step forward.

I held my ground. Seymore retreated a couple of steps.

"Seymore, what does he want?" I asked, but Seymore merely backed up farther. "Stay and tell me what he wants."

"He want sell to American."

"Tell him okay, but not to move. Tell him to let me take it."

Seymore translated. The farmer shook his head as he responded.

"What now?"

"He want money first. Want know how much."

If there was a standard price for rusted mines, I had no idea what it was. I tossed out the figure of three thousand dong.

Seymore translated. The old man shook his head and counteroffered five thousand.

I lacked any authority to negotiate, but said all the same, "Three thousand five hundred."

The farmer shook his head and turned as if to leave.

I said the first thing that came to mind. "Tell him he's done a brave thing."

Seymore spoke. The farmer stopped and listened, then turned around. His goatee and mustache twitched as his mouth turned up in a smile.

"Tell him four," I said. "Because he's brave."

Seymore said, "Four too much."

The difference of a thousand Vietnamese piasters, some eight or nine dollars, wasn't worth getting my ass blown up. If necessary, I'd pay it myself. "Seymore, I don't give a shit how much. Tell him four."

Seymore made the offer, and the old man nodded.

"Now, tell him not to move. I'll do everything."

The young boy watched the exchange with a kind of detached curiosity as I cupped my hands around the base. The exchange completed, I held it gently as the old guy stroked the backs of my hands with his callused palms. When he let go, he offered me a polite bow.

I told Seymore to lead them to the team house and have someone, anyone, pay them. The boy following close on his heels, the farmer trudged behind Seymore, his arthritic gait telling of how feeble he was—and lucky. I wondered how far he'd come.

Cu gave me a gold-toothed grin, then departed. I held the mine at arm's length and looked at it. I wavered between blowing it in place and taking it to the disposal pit. I opted to destroy it right there at the gate.

I brought down the tools of my trade and turned the mine into a cloud of black smoke. I was reeling in wire when they passed by on their way to the gate. The old guy proudly showed off a fistful of piasters. The colorful bills seemed to give his step a touch of youthful spring.

J. V. cornered me as I entered the team house. "How much you think an old mine's worth, any damn how?"

"Guess that would depend."

"On what?"

"Whether or not it blows up in your face."

Mr. Whitten stopped tossing darts. Fox nearly choked on his beer. J. V.'s face turned red. I got myself a soft drink and left. Outside Norwood asked if I would help burn shit. I said I would, but it seemed pointless. The flies would come back. We'd still have the runs. The camp would stink. The business of war would go on. I told him sure. Burning shit, what the hell?

There was too much shit in this country to burn all of it. All we did was burn a little of our own at a time. Or blow up the crap left to rot from other wars. I hated Vietnam. It had taken the lives of my teammates, but oddly enough I was developing a grudging admiration for the people, especially the elderly, who never seemed to give up, despite all the shit. Old men, I thought, the brunt of jokes where I was from. Not here, *and life here, boy, well, it just ain't fucking sweet.*

THIRTY-THREE

As late as April the team remained short a second commo man. Finally the C-Team sent one out. That was some good news. The events of January 22 still affected those of us who'd endured those days, but none of us more than Cam. Now he could get out of camp, go on an operation, maybe even take a well-earned two days off in Da Nang.

The new guy arrived, M-16 in one hand, duffel bag in the other, a hot-dog smile, and an attitude that said green in every way. He stepped down from the chopper as if playing out a scene in a war movie. I sized him up pretty quickly, a city boy, twenty at the outside, black, thin as a runway model, and too cocky. That was what he *was*. What he wasn't was qualified to be on an A-Team. The tab below our unit insignia on his beret indicated as much—support staff. He'd completed basic training, radio school, and the jump course at Fort Benning, just enough training to buy him a ticket to 'Nam, where skill with code was desperately needed, and nowhere more than in Special Forces. Like Batterham, he'd slipped through the back door into a slot on an A-Team and was pleased as hell with his beret.

He introduced himself. Jimmerson, Jimson, Jim-Something. In welcoming him, Cam seemed content to have help, and Willy, who was probably tired of being the only ebony key on an ivory keyboard, was overtly pleased with the newcomer. I didn't have much use for anyone who didn't train for our mission. Out here the work never ended, and everyone pulled his weight and more. I didn't feel up to the task of babysitting him on a patrol or operation. I shook his hand, but the expression on my face said, Get the smirk off your mouth, Cherry. Men have died in this valley, and more may.

Willy took young Jimmer-What's-His-Name under his wing and led him to a bunker, where they stashed the new guy's gear. Before the new guy even got a peek at Cam's com bunker, Willy guided him through a tour of the camp, our compound first, then the Vietnamese. Willy pointed out one feature or another, chatting away more than any of us, based on three months of his stoic reticence, would have thought him capable of.

They came into the team house for lunch. I sat at the far end of the table and watched as Willy briefed the kid on where to initial the beer roster and what was expected as far as guard duty and other details went. I relaxed. I figured if anyone could shape the kid up, it was Willy, who was as no-nonsense as a head nurse in a psych ward. If Willy approved of him, I felt obligated to give him a chance. After all, if he held up his end, it would benefit us all around. Cam would get needed rest, and Willy would have a student. Still, I held some reservations.

After lunch Willy took it upon himself to show his protégé how to strip and clean the machine guns, which were due maintenance. Jimmer/Jimson followed along, watching earnestly as Willy spread a poncho atop his bunker, then went below, disarmed the machine gun, and brought it up. Willy told his understudy to fetch the rest, starting with one from the captain's bunker. If nothing else, the kid had enthusiasm. He couldn't get to it fast enough and ran off to get the weapon. I thought someone should bring it to his attention just how hot and humid it was and that the machine guns weren't going anywhere anytime soon.

I was restocking a mortar pit when I heard a burst of three. Willy and I stopped what we were doing and headed in the direction of the sound. We converged as the newbie came running from the opposite direction. He stopped and made an effort to speak, but couldn't do more than offer a throaty groan. He held his arm and circled about maniacally. Finally he screamed, "Jesus, oh, Jesus!" Willy and I gripped him by the shoulders to restrain him and get him to sit down. We were struggling with him when Norwood arrived.

He'd taken at least two of the rounds. Bone and muscle exposed, his arm was shredded by through-and-through wounds to the elbow and midforearm. There was some blood, but much less than would be expected. He stopped struggling and whimpered through clenched teeth, saying, "My arm. My arm."

Norwood said he'd gone into shock. We lifted him to his feet, and Norwood guided him to the first-aid bunker. Willy looked at me as if he wanted to speak but didn't, just shook his head. He seemed in shock himself. Drawn to the commotion, the rest of the team gathered. Fox demanded to know what had happened.

Willy found his voice and, for the first time since arriving at Tra Bong, lost some of his composure. "I swear I told him be careful, told him what to do step by step."

Fox asked me. I shrugged. En masse we walked to the captain's bunker. The barrel of the A-4 was still hot. The air smelled of nitrate, flesh, and the pungent stink of iron so common to human blood. Fragments of bone and skin tissue lay scattered on the ground. What had happened was obvious to all of us. The newbie, in trying to remove the machine gun, had grabbed the gun's barrel. He didn't have the training or the good sense to figure out that any weapon in camp was locked and loaded and ready to fire. Nor did he know that the A-4s didn't have trigger guards. Cam left us looking at the evidence and called for a dust-off.

The barrel was still hot. A couple of feet away lay more shredded flesh and a chip of white bone. The recently promoted Captain Gregory assured Willy that accidents happened, but Willy seemed unconsoled. Though he wasn't responsible, he readily took the blame for it on his shoulders.

Norwood juiced the newbie up with some morphine and stopped the bleeding. An hour later I helped him lift the new guy aboard a chopper and exchange him with the crew chief for a new stretcher. Norwood had managed to close the artery before Jimmer-What's-His-Name came out of shock and bled to death and probably saved his life. No one would likely save his arm. The newbie never even saw the commo bunker. Already his days as a radio operator were over, as were his days as a soldier and any future he had as a tennis player or golfer, unless he could learn to play with one good arm.

Norwood shook his head as the dust-off lifted. We watched it climb. The strikers waved. One helicopter in, one out, a six-hour turn-around, and a million-dollar wound that would give diminishing returns the rest of the newbie's life. Already, I'd forgotten his name.

Back in camp, Norwood set out rat traps. He was determined to do some damage to the rat population. Someone commented that the new guy was lucky he wasn't standing in front of the barrel. Lucky, in the sense of good luck? I said, "We were just lucky we weren't walking by at the time." I wanted to see no more like him jumping down from the side door of a helicopter as if come to save the day.

Willy never mentioned the incident again. Had he brought it up and asked, I would have said none of it was his fault, that out here, where we lived, a poorly threaded decision away from death, eagerness had no place. Nor did incompetence. The kid simply didn't belong, in the sense the rest of us did. If asked about it years later, I would have told Willy it was just proof of the absurdity of the conduct of our war.

THIRTY-FOUR

The legend at the bottom of the maps of the area around the Tra Bong Sheer cautioned that the color green was challenging, "dense forest or jungle [and] indicates more than 25 percent of the ground is concealed by canopy with undergrowth generally impassible on foot." What the maps didn't say was that the high forests surrounding us were part of a supply and infiltration corridor linked with the Ho Chi Minh Trail. Nor did the maps tell us where Charlie was. We had to go look for him. At least that was the case with some of us.

Among us were those who humped mountains and those who didn't. J. V., the captains, the Aussies, and even Fox took occasional walks in the flats to the east, where they popped a few 5.56 rounds at Charlie and ordered in an air strike, but the long-range stuff into the high peaks that surrounded us on three sides was delegated to Luthy, Norwood, Willy, or Malone, occasionally a lieutenant, and me — but mostly to *me*. As months accumulated, the long patrols, with few exceptions, began to blur together. I remember a few distinctly and the very last vividly, but I can't conjure up a memory of the first, where we went or what happened. Nor can I put a precise number on the times I woke up three hours before dawn and ascended the steep, often slippery, foothills in the dark, but it's safe to say it was more than a dozen and closer to twenty. What I can say is that the areas I humped were largely impassable for most round-eyes.

The ritual was the same. As soon as we left camp we sent a Yard on point and followed him as he led us in the manner their people had for centuries, straight up one side and straight down the other, peak after peak. Yards were tenacious climbers who made the loads they carried on their shoulders seem weightless. I came to admire them.

I remember nothing of my first mission into the mountains, what we accomplished or didn't, but I know it had to have been a test, the Montagnard stoically eyeing my every step, just as I would later see how they judged others, just as I would come to judge newcomers. I imagine at first they looked for fear or hesitance, then for fatigue. I must have met muster, because from then on humping mountains with old Cu and the Yards under the forest's dense canopy constituted much of my experience in Tra Bong.

The stump-legged Yards endured heat as if cold-blooded and assaulted slopes as if they had four legs. By my third or fourth patrol going through the largely impassable, they'd stopped watching me. We often operated out of radio range, twenty, thirty kilometers from camp or farther, two- and three-day sorties mostly to the north and west, seeking signs of troop movement. In the outer reaches we stumbled upon uncharted Montagnard villages inhabited by people who'd never seen a round-eye.

We waded through sparkling streams fouled with

parasites, fought knifelike undergrowth, picked leeches from our bodies, and cursed the nasty and frequent insect bites. We humped sixty or more pounds of ammunition and gear. We scarfed down rice balls the Yards shared with us. We alternately hoped for rain to cool the jungle and for none to fall because it transformed the ground into slurry. At night, our weapons strapped to our arms, we lay in coffinlike darkness on the sides of mountains, shivered, and slept in increments — ten, twenty minutes, never a full hour. Come morning, when the land seemed its most mystical, as sunlight trickled through the canopy, we harnessed up and humped some more.

Without his spotting us first, we hoped to sight signs of Charlie, but the VC played on our patience with his secretive ways. A phantom of the jungle, he rarely left much of a footprint, but we saw considerable evidence of what he contended with — craters the size of swimming pools and trees uprooted from five hundred–pound exploding postcards sent by Uncle Sam. On occasion at night we would hear a five-hundred pounder land, then another, one ridge away. Then we'd feel the force of its blast come up through the ground, a low, rumbling vibration that entered the spine and crawled up through the amygdala to the conscious mind. You couldn't hear the blasts or see the damage without wondering if you yourself might not fall victim if the air force missed a calibration by one or two degrees, the only solace being that you would never feel a thing, just go from this life as vaporized sinew.

I can't say when or how it happened, but I learned to trust the jungle — its animals sounds, its stillness, the way an odor hung in the air, the touch of a boot on damp earth. I trusted it in a way I no longer trusted the camp. I came to think as Charlie did. *If he can live in the rain forest, boy, so can you. If he can move silently, so can you. If he can see in darkness, so can you.* Out there invisibility was possible. Charlie managed it and so did we. A sergeant in Training Group at Bragg had said you knew the training worked when you could hear a spider spinning a web and single out one blade of grass in a lawn at night. I finally understood what he'd meant. It was a special way of being alive, and I was alive in that way, in a way I'd never before been or would be again. And the constant discomfort reminded me of that fact. In the boonies discomfort was a friend that kept a man alert, a fact we accepted.

I acquired that thing people call the third eye or sixth sense. Though it was never a point of discussion, Luthy and Norwood and Willy were much the same. Out there we shed personal history as well as thoughts of the future. Our concerns were the next creeper, the looming overhang, the treacherous thicket, the obvious trail to avoid. We heard the tiny snap of a branch, felt the ground without looking where to step, smelled two-day-old cigarette smoke. As the Montagnard on point stepped into drifting shadows cast by the canopy, we could see — in a microinstant — into brush on both sides of us and at the same time see ahead. We became not supermen but what men were before they surrendered themselves to civilization.

I gradually came to feel invulnerable. But then something invariably reminded me of how vulnerable we all were, how the rules of war applied to us but not to our enemy.

As months piled up, those of us who'd come to Tra Bong in January wanted a change of scenery. It was nearly June, and Norwood, Cam, and I would be eligible for transfers the first week of July. Though weeks away from my eligible date for rotation, I already planned on leaving. My options included safer assignments in C- and B-Teams, but pushing paper in a support role in the rear had little appeal. I hoped for an assignment that would keep me in the boonies, perhaps transfer to Project Delta as Sheppard had and operate clandestinely.

Others didn't wait a full tour before leaving. At less than four months Lieutenant Davidson ended his stay, leaving us again without an executive officer. The day he departed, I was somewhere west beyond 108 degrees longitude plucking leeches off my legs. With the lieutenant gone, the camp was again short. Luthy and I trudged in with a platoon of Yards, caught news of the lieutenant's leaving, grabbed a meal and a pillow. In the morning Captain Gregory called me into the operations room and told me to sit. What now, I wondered?

He usually got straight to the point, but this time he came at the subject obliquely. "You know you're entitled to a transfer elsewhere, right?"

"Yes, sir."

"But you don't have to. You can opt to stay."

"Yes, sir." He was right. It was normal to take another assignment but not required.

"You've done good work. The bunker's almost finished. I appreciate that minefield."

I nodded. He was sprinkling flattery for a purpose. I saw where he was headed.

"You handle yourself well on patrols."

"I'm thinking about Project Delta or the Nung Force, sir."

"If you stay here, you'll be a big asset to the camp. You know the situation and the terrain."

I wondered if similar words had been used to get Reifschneider to stay. I was waiting for him to pull the pin on the sales pitch, and he finally got to it.

"I was thinking," he said, "along the lines of you advising the Combat Recon Platoon."

"The Recon Platoon?"

"In essence, you'd be in charge."

"I don't know, sir." The pitch included a little bribery.

"I've made arrangements for you to take the platoon to Dong Ba Tinh for a two-week school. You can say no. But I'd like to keep you here. Keep someone who knows the place."

The two-weeks advanced training was for their benefit. For me, it would be a break from the camp. I'd spent much of the last two months in the mountains on patrol. I had confidence in the Yards and was pretty certain they felt the same about me. What he said about others leaving was true. I didn't know what J. V. or Fox had in mind, but Norwood's and Gamble's six months in country would come at the same time as mine. Norwood planned to transfer, and Luthy would soon be off to other duty as well. I'd been thinking for some time about some special-ops assignment, and I didn't especially want to stay in Tra Bong, but there was the matter of loyalty. Captain Gregory had been a good team leader, loyal to his men. I felt obligated to him. That made me hesitate, and he took my hesitation as a tacit yes.

"So, it's settled. You'll stay."

"I'm not sure, skipper." That bit of equivocation set me up.

"Sergeant Cu," he said, "asked specifically for you. He'll go to Dong Ba Tinh with you."

Cu? I'd gained a lot of respect for him. He'd been fighting since before the French Indochina War and was a bale of barbed wire with a lot of heart. I was barely twenty-two and would be in charge of a platoon of Yards, working with him. The idea was tempting. Cu had requested me?

"I'll think about it, sir."

The captain and Cu had confidence in me. I considered the captain's proposal all that day and slept with it overnight. I'd proven that I could follow orders, could perform in battle, and was competent and hardworking in camp. I awoke realizing that I'd been selected because I merited selection. As a troubled and abused child I'd never felt I had any value in my family, and doubts of my self-worth had haunted me throughout my childhood and into adulthood. But now I was asked to make decisions, to be the one the Yards looked to for leadership in the field. I saw it as a chance to allay any doubts that remained from my childhood and a chance to avenge my teammates' deaths.

In the morning I told Captain Gregory I would stay, and that afternoon Trung Sí Cu and I, along with Seymore, walked to the bunkers that housed the Recon Platoon. Cu lined them up. All were a full head shorter than I, and five out of six in each squad were Montagnard. The sixth in each squad was a Vietnamese who acted as squad leader. I stood before them, eighteen in all. They waited, curious. I looked at Seymore. "Tell them we're going for training to Dong Ba Tinh," I said. "Say it's because they're the best soldiers in camp."

He repeated my words. The Yards smiled. Then I looked at the squad leaders. "Tell them I'm their adviser. No one else."

They smiled politely, mostly because it was their custom.

"Tell them that if we get hit by the vc, I'll stay with them no matter what happens."

Seymore repeated what I'd said. The squad leaders again smiled.

"Tell them that if anyone runs during a firefight, I will personally shoot him."

I looked each squad leader in the eye. No matter how much they feared the vc, I wanted them to fear me more. Seymore looked at Cu and spoke softly in Vietnamese. Cu shrugged and pointed to me.

Seymore said, "No can say."

"Say exactly what I said, and you remember it as well."

He hesitated.

"Tell them."

He translated. The smiles disappeared. For a moment the platoon stood silent, and then a squad leader voiced his objection to Cu, who shouted him down. Then Cu addressed them. Finished, he shook my hand. I asked Seymore what Cu had said to them.

"He say you *diên cả dàu*. Say he like you, and if run, he shoot who you don't."

THIRTY-FIVE

The war seemed to go on uneventfully in our area of operation. Though shorthanded, we had sufficient strikers to run operations out of the camp. A firefight here, a firefight there, a couple of vc captured, our war in the valley settled into a curious thing. Weekly, a platoon- or company-size unit tromped down the valley in the direction of Binh Hoa. My Yards (for they were now my Yards) and I went on a few. Charlie sniped from positions on the side of the foothills and vanished before jets arrived. I took a walk somewhere in the mountains about every other week. In the mountains we saw signs of infiltration but made no contact with the enemy.

Someone from the team was always out on patrol. It was a good thing, in the sense that it's best for an athlete to stay in the game in order to be his sharpest. Captain Gregory seemed to understand that. He saw our purpose here as warfare and was less keen on winning hearts and minds, just as the locals to the east weren't keen on us in any way.

By early April the captain's patience was exhausted. While on patrol, we took fire from Binh Hoa and from the hillside both. The firefight lasted for some twenty minutes, then for the first time since January when the Nungs had gone in, we entered the hamlet, rounded up the villagers, and marched them to the road. Then the captain called for birds. The jets put on a beautiful display—40mm's, a few bombs, and the final brushstroke, the napalm run. Flames and black smoke engulfed the hamlet as we crouched near its edge and listened for secondary explosions. When the flames swallowed most of the village, we celebrated its end with a drink of water from a canteen, but any satisfaction gained from burning Binh Hoa dissolved within the week when its inhabitants returned and raised new hooches up. Soon after the home-grown snipers returned to the hillsides, and it was war again as usual.

When not on an operation, I performed the duties of the day, working mostly on the bunker. Uncomplaining and unsmiling, Willy helped. I'd come to understand him or at least his reticent ways. Whatever came his way he took stoically and moved on to the next matter. He was equally adept with a mortar or a mattock. Some days we worked side by side. Some days, only one of us was there, and on that rare juncture when we went on an operation together, nothing on the project back at camp was accomplished. Still, by early May the bunker was a hulking structure of reinforced concrete with four-foot-thick walls behind a barrier of sandbags and four gun ports with clear fields of fire. We began construction of the tower.

None among us who'd been in Tra Bong on that Tet morning in January had forgotten our dead or that the captain remained unaccounted for. The ill-fated operation was now referred to in after-action reports as the Lost Patrol. We'd invented no name for it, but we had memories and a residual anger that festered in us, mostly because we couldn't act on it. Troubling our minds was the unanswered question of what had happened to Captain Fewell. In May information from one of J. V.'s double agents shed light on the captain's fate.

According to the informant, our captain had been wounded early in the battle. Surrounded and unable to defend himself, he'd been taken captive. The informant didn't know the extent of the captain's wound, but he knew details of his grisly end. He'd been bound and held captive as the battle progressed. Then that evening his captors dragged him to the Cham Temple, where they questioned and tortured him. Then one beheaded him.

The VC, through arrangements negotiated by the double agent, agreed to allow a small unit to enter the temple grounds unmolested. The next day a patrol, led by Luthy and Norwood, hiked to the pagoda and recovered the remains—the captain's head and an orange landing panel used to guide helicopters in. The rest of his remains would go forever unaccounted for.

John Fewell had had a particular fondness for Norwood, and so, apparently, did the captain's wife. Norwood, at her insistence, was assigned to accompany the remains home for burial, an all but unprecedented action, as custom called for officers to escort the remains of officers.

Norwood left for America on a helicopter that brought 1st Lt. James E. Jockims, Lieutenant Davidson's replacement. The new lieutenant had some rough edges. He had tattooed arms, liked his early-afternoon beer, and spiked his conversation with four-letter words. His arrival marked another leadership change. Shortly after Jockims arrived, a second officer flew in, one wearing captain bars on his collar. He was an inch taller than me and forty or fifty pounds heavier. Even as Captain Gregory introduced him around, we knew, without its being said, why he was there.

Gregory had wrangled a commitment from me to stay at Tra Bong. I'd consented in large part out of loyalty. I felt betrayed. Fucking luck, I thought. Mine was nothing if not consistent. If I stepped outside during a downpour of beauty queens, a linebacker would land on my head.

Just as in the past, the change of command was swift.

Captain Horan seemed underjoyed about his assignment and had reason to be. He was an Academy graduate and had landed in a camp that said "career dead end." He just didn't seem to be one of us. It wasn't so much that he was any more aloof or authoritative than other officers. He had an aura about him. We noticed in short time that he wasn't comfortable among us. That translated to our being uncomfortable when he was around. Whenever Gregory had entered the team house, behavior and talk went on as usual, but Horan's presence silenced us.

On the other hand, he proved a talker, his favorite subject being himself. Early on, he mentioned that he'd finished near the bottom in his class at West Point, adding that had he tried harder for last place, he would have earned a dollar from each cadet in the graduating class. Norwood and I wondered if Horan's revealing that was to remind us he was an Academy man, or was it some off-the-cuff effort at self-deprecation or humility? Was he simply trying to be one of the guys? Nothing else about him suggested that was the case.

Fewell, Gregory, Davidson, all the team leaders I'd had before, enjoyed commanding men like those who made up our team. You could tell by the way they'd talk and listen and laugh when laughter was called for that they respected each of us. And while we respected rank, we offered our trust only to those who merited it. By the end of two weeks under his command, some of us would fabricate a reason and excuse ourselves to leave whenever Captain Horan entered the team house.

The underground inhabitants of Tra Bong had even less regard for the new team leader. Although we remained wary of them, we'd learned to live with the rats. They played tag at night on the roof of Horan's bunker. In the team house over dinner that first week the new captain brought up the subject to Norwood. Wasn't it his responsibility to eradicate them? Norwood explained how ineffectual poison and traps had become in the battle, but Captain Horan couldn't grasp that short of wiping out the camp with an air strike, rats were there to stay.

"We could solve it by feeding them," I said.

The captain looked at me as if I were a royal nitwit. "What?"

"Yes, sir. Fatten them like livestock. Sell them to the Vietnamese. They'll eat anything."

Horan stared blankly at me. That was my one and only effort at humor with him. Other than his lacking a sense of humor, my best read on him was no read at all. He inspired neither loyalty nor confidence nor contempt. Like the stationmaster in *Heart of Darkness*, he inspired unease. Norwood felt much the same. On occasion while on guard, I crumbled a few crackers atop the new team leader's bunker just to make certain he had something to complain about. I don't think I was the only one who did this. He couldn't find any logical explanation for why rats seemed to favor his bunker. The rest of us pretty much agreed that it was a mystery to us as well.

THIRTY-SIX

When Captain Horan pulled me aside from sandbagging walls in the trench, I began cataloging acts or omissions he might question me about. I couldn't imagine fucking up, but what was nothing to Spec. 5 could be a big deal to him, a West Pointer with little else to occupy his time. I was wearing tiger stripes, shower shoes, and no shirt, how I often dressed in camp. Maybe that was it.

He asked, "Is the 57 bore-sighted and ready?"

I figured it was a test. "Always."

"Okay, I want you to get it."

I returned with the weapon. The captain stood waiting with a photographer from some military journal or newspaper who'd flown in. The photographer wanted some authentic shots for his publication, and the captain selected Willy and me.

"These are my best men on the weapons," the captain said.

I was best on the 57 mostly because nobody else wanted to hug it close and pop an eardrum loose. Willy, on the other hand, could put a mortar round in a man's shirt pocket from half a mile away. We set up to fire a round or two while the photographer got his *f*-setting and focus in good order. Willy fired a 60mm handheld mortar. The round exploded in the dead center in the target zone, a spot about fifty feet on the other side of the river, easy as a free throw from under the basket for him. The smiling photographer captured the moment on film.

It seemed pretty artificial, but that was what was called for — artificial authentic. I pointed to a shelf of loose rock at the base of a cliff some four hundred meters across the river.

The day was clear and windless, and the scope wouldn't require adjusting. I sat squarely facing the target as Willy loaded a high explosive in the breach. He tapped my shoulder, signaling it was loaded, then stepped aside. I planted my feet, waited for the wobble to settle, and centered the target in the crosshair of the scope. I took a deep breath, released half of the air, and then steadied the barrel and squeezed the triggering mechanism evenly. Everything was normal.

But then the weapon drove the scope into my eye and snapped my head back. The 57, designed to regulate escaping gases to prevent recoil, recoiled. Not just recoiled, but did so with a force violent enough to pitch me backward and lift my feet off the ground and crack my neck. I heard the whistle and the explosion but never saw the round hit the target.

"Got it," the photographer said.

Numbed by the force of the recoil, I stood and walked around until I recovered my sense of equilibrium. Willy, so unemotional he wouldn't show a reaction to a wasp sting, couldn't hide his surprise, and the look he gave me confirmed what I was thinking. I opened the breach and extracted the hot casing. As we'd surmised, someone had loosened the throat blocks and knocked the sight out of adjustment. Warnings given us by the cadre in premission training had just played out. One or more among the indigenous who had access to our compound had sabotaged the weapon. Had the misplay occurred in the field when the weapon was needed, it would have been too late.

Willy and I readjusted its throat blocks and re-bore-sighted the 57. From then on, except when I took it on an operation, the weapon stayed in my bunker, and I kept a close eye on Ong Dao and his laborers and on any striker who happened to wander inside our compound.

THIRTY-SEVEN

The two weeks of training at Dong Ba Tinh was actually twelve days. Cu and the Yards were on their way to Da Nang. I decided to spend a night in Nha Trang before flying north. I flopped out for a siesta in the billets and woke up as the sun was setting. Hungry for anything but army chow or a hamburger, I hitched a lift to the beach clubs and found a table at the Nautique. The walls of the club were secured by Vietnamese soldiers and one or two Vietnamese diminutive policemen in white uniforms who were called white mice. I figured to have a drink or two but stay sober and walk back to the SFOB on my own.

I was on the veranda, taking in the smell of the ocean, nursing a beer, and enjoying a warm feeling left in my belly from a bowl of bird's-nest soup, when a boy about ten showed up. He carried a box under his arm. Except for his being frail, he was nondescript in dress, size, and haircut. Under normal circumstances nothing about him would spark a memory later on. He stopped at a couple of tables and rattled off something in Vietnamese. Once he got the attention of the soldiers, he pointed to his box and their boots. The soldiers told him to "*di di*" and motioned him away.

A waiter, seeing the commotion, hurried to the table and shooed him off. The boy merely moved to the next table, one adjacent to mine, and solicited the men. He opened his box, took out a brush, and kneeled down. When the waiter came up from behind and tried to lift the boy up, one of the soldiers said that it was okay, that the boy could shine his boots, not just his but all of theirs. I was distracted a moment, then raised the Ba Muy Ba to my lips.

The waiter arrived with my dinner, beef over a concoction

of greens on a bed of rice. I forked a mouthful and began chewing. Before I swallowed it a commotion broke out at the next table. The boy was standing now, clutching a grenade, and trying to pull the pin. One of the soldiers reached out and grabbed for the boy, who panicked and tossed the grenade on the tile floor. I turned my table over, dived to the ground, and in anticipation of the blast buried my head in my arms. Two critical seconds ticked off, but there was no explosion, only the sound of the boy's footfalls as he darted past the Vietnamese policeman at the gate and disappeared into the night, as the police blew their whistles.

I figured the grenade was a dud. Slowly, those of us in the circle of danger drew ourselves up and stood. We stared at the grenade where it lay under a table a few feet away. The pin was halfway out. No one spoke, just exchanged looks that said we were astounded and relieved. By then the boy had disappeared into the darkened street. He'd left behind his box with the shoe polish and brush. A soldier who'd been seated at the table where the grenade landed bent down, picked it up, and pressed the pin back in. He held it up for all to see.

I lifted up my table and chair but didn't sit down. My meal lay scattered on the tile along with the shattered bottle of Ba Muy Ba. I glanced around, alert now for any further sign of a threat. Soldiers nearby did the same. Then a whistle sounded on the other side of the courtyard wall. An instant later three Vietnamese soldiers charged into the veranda. As waiters and the bar girls recapped the sequence of events in shrill voices, one of the Vietnamese troops took custody of the grenade. From beginning to end, no more than five minutes had passed since the boy first appeared. It seemed much longer than that.

I dropped a handful of piasters on the table and left. Later, I lay in the billets, listening to mosquitoes and the growling of my empty stomach. I didn't want to think too much about luck for fear of becoming superstitious. After all, it's unlucky to be superstitious, and any soldier worth his salt knows it.

THIRTY-EIGHT

As soon as Cu and I returned from Dong Ba Tinh, Horan wanted a recon of the southern slopes that ranged to the eastern plateau. To my knowledge, no one had operated in the area before. The idea was to bypass the villages and see if Charlie was using the mountains as a staging area or infiltration route. An hour before dawn Luthy and I departed with a squad of Yards, slipped in and out of the nearby village of Tra Bac 1, and climbed halfway up Hill 753 before sunup.

The back trails were trade routes for villagers. Crossing them, we noted signs of recent human traffic but nothing indicating Charlie had bivouacked anywhere on the route. We'd had a recent rain, the ground was damp and slick, and the undergrowth was some of the thickest I'd ever negotiated. Along the way I'd picked up more than a few passengers.

We topped the first peak and took a break. I dropped my web gear, wiped sweat from my face, and then removed my socks and plucked off leeches from my ankles and calves. The blood-bloated ones I popped between my fingers. Thinner ones I stretched and tied in knots before tossing them aside. I dropped my trousers and removed another batch of bloodsuckers from my inner thighs. Then I slipped into my socks and boots, sprayed insect repellent on the boot tops, and harnessed up.

We stayed in the brush, skirting the ridgeline. Through midafternoon the walk proved unremarkable except for the abundance of flies and leeches. We stopped for breaks repeatedly to shed ourselves of parasites. Then late in the day we hit thicket that descended to a saddle between two peaks where we lost radio contact. We'd left behind some twenty kilometers of hard land and had uncovered no evidence indicating a body of guerrillas of any size had passed through. At the base of the declivity, we crossed a stream. It was nearing dusk, and the jungle was darkening. We were played out by then but couldn't set down in the low ground. We rested for a few minutes, filled canteens, and began the ascent up the next incline.

We climbed the last two or three hundred meters in the dark to the top of a promontory. There the squad leader deployed the men in a defensive perimeter. Without bedding down, we settled in to wait out the dark. I rested my back against a tree trunk and plucked leeches from my legs. I wrapped my poncho liner over my shoulders to ward off the chill and dozed intermittently as my wet boots incubated fungus. The leech bites dripped blood. Mosquitoes fed on me. My crotch itched. Scratching it was the only pleasure I had, so I scratched until it too bled.

In the morning we checked coordinates and got our bearings. We realized we'd brought the squad farther by more than ten kilometers than planned. We decided that we'd come this far, we might as well take the squad all the way to the plateau lands and to Ha Tanh, the next Special Forces camp south of Tra Bong. It was twenty-two miles in a straight line to the southeast, thirty or more over mountains that topped out at thirty-six hundred feet and valleys that dropped to a thousand. We made radio contact with Ha Tanh and told them we were dropping by for coffee.

We reached the camp in another two hours. It occupied the high point on what is largely a flat area of barren clay. Our hosts looked at us as if we were crazy, then swung open the main gate and invited us in for a bite and a beer. They asked what was out there. Nothing, we told them, but a lot of it. What, they wanted to know, possessed our commander to send us through Charlie Land this far? One informed us of intelligence that a VC company was operating somewhere in the mountains we'd just traversed, the same mountains we had to hump again to return to camp.

Within the hour, we filled canteens and began our return journey. Halfway to camp we stumbled on two men who turned to flee. The point man fired a single round above their heads and brought them to a halt. They were father and son and terrified, simple tea gatherers with skin the color of bark. The older man pleaded with Seymore to let him and his son go. Neither was armed and they seemed guiltless on the face of it, but this was Charlie's sandbox. Everyone was considered a hostile. We bound their hands and brought them along.

In camp Fox said we were crazy to take the patrol that far.

"Why single me out? Luthy outranks me."

"You're supposed to be smart enough to know." He asked what I saw.

"Other than the two we brought back, a lot of nothing."

He stared at me with that lazy eye. "Nothing?"

That revelation hatched the plan for the next operation.

Lieutenant Jockims and I left with Trung Sí Cu and the Combat Recon Platoon. We took a line southeasterly into the mountains, our objective a spot where the forest opened up into a hundred-meter apron of elephant grass that terminated above a wooded promontory. At least one sniper was entrenched there beneath boulders that enabled him to survive the bombs and napalm we'd called in on the location. Our mission was to get him or them.

Following roughly the route Luthy and I had previously taken, we slipped through the village and climbed the foothills south of Tra Bac due south of Tra Bong. The lieutenant huffed at first but kept up on the climb through the foothills. I wasn't fond of having him along, and he probably didn't relish being on patrol with the youngest member of the team. He wasn't used to the ways of the Yards, who climbed straight up the slopes and avoided trails. After we hit the mountainside, he soon began to falter. He called for a break a little beyond the halfway point of the climb, plopped down on a boulder, and lit up.

We reached the peak before noon, slightly behind schedule, turned east, and descended the other side about two hundred meters. There we made a com check, set up defenses, and waited out the heat of the day. As before, I hosted a hoard of leeches. When the arc of the sun neared the western slopes, the patrol resumed. By evening we'd covered a dozen kilometers and circled back through the rough brush. We came into position on a ridge four hundred meters above the elephant grass. After securing the perimeter, the Yards ate. Lieutenant Jockims contacted base camp and lit a cigarette, the smell of which hung in the air long after he stubbed it out.

We settled in for the long night. Off and on I catnapped sitting up. Lieutenant Jockims lay on his back and snored occasionally. When I nudged him, he seemed not to notice but stopped snoring, at least for a time. I wondered what was looking at us. Charlie? A tiger? I heard more snoring, looked over, and saw the lieutenant's shadow. Whatever was out there didn't have to see us. It could hear its way to us.

I shook him. "Hey, wake up, sir."

He stirred, didn't open his eyes or speak, but stopped snoring.

I was hungry but had no appetite. Food could neither fill nor satisfy me. That was what the jungle and the sweat and the humping did to a man. Only the blind or those who have experienced a night in it could know the darkness of a moonless rain forest. Everything was damp. The jungle floor, in a constant state of decomposition, smelled of it. Tigers lurked nearby. Snakes slithered through the undergrowth. The air was alive with insect sounds and the ground populated with all manner of crawling things.

You hear. You smell. But you don't see. Darkness rules. All the clichéd metaphors for it seem lame. Darker than a bat cave. Darker than a grave. Darker than evil. Throughout the dark, you're left with your thoughts. Muscles in your thighs twitch involuntarily. You sip from your canteen and listen. In the morning you'll rise, slip into harness, and assault a fixed position. You should be wary. Perhaps you are. Strangely, you like the way apprehension stirs inside your guts.

Tomorrow, I thought as I sat huddled in my poncho liner, can't come soon enough.

An hour or so before daylight Trung Sí Cu brought our Yards to life. They gathered their gear in silence, ate rice balls, and waited. At sun break, we filed quietly down the mountainside. A half hour later the patrol reached the wood line overlooking the elephant grass. It was now a matter of waiting until the rest of the plan was implemented.

To circumvent the rule that not more than three Americans from any single A-Team go jointly on any one operation, the captain determined that it was permissible to use an Aussie. Mr. Green, being an accommodating sort, left camp just before dawn with Norwood and a company of Yards and Vietnamese. To be as obtrusive as possible, they marched up the road to Binh Hoa as if they had an invitation to tea.

A Bird Dog dropped in to keep an eye on the ground operation.

Two hours later Norwood and Mr. Green turned the bend in the road and drew fire from the sniper, the same Charlie who regularly popped caps at us. The BAR, its signature headspace timing slightly askew, pumped off three slow bursts.

We emerged from the shadows of the trees and positioned ourselves to advance. Trung Sí Cu ordered the two squads to spread out in a skirmish line. As we readied to move out, Norwood and Green's strikers exchanged fire with the sniper. That's when we heard the second shooter, this one using an M-1.

The BAR chattered again. I had it located. Below, the volume of shooting increased. Mr. Green called over the radio and asked when in the hell we were going to take action. I told Lieutenant Jockims that I could take a couple of Yards along, sneak up behind the sniper, and take him out. When we fired, he could lead the rest down. He brushed off the idea, said, "Stay with me," and then turned to Henry and told him to have Cu start the advance.

Cu motioned to a Montagnard carrying a grenade launcher. The lieutenant reported over the radio that we were assaulting the sniper position. The Yard stepped forward and raised the weapon. A good plan going bad. It's fucked up now, I thought. If a half-dozen sorties dropping bombs and napalm couldn't get the sniper, a 40mm grenade wasn't likely to. The Yard pulled the trigger. The projectile exploded in the boughs of the trees. The next instant, we came under fire from the wood line south of the elephant grass. A lone machine gun chattered. The Charlie shooting at us was firing uphill from the blind, and the bullets whizzed benignly overhead.

Our position compromised, we had to assault before the snipers had time to disappear. I wasn't waiting for Lieutenant Jockims to get his paddle in the water. I headed down the slope at double time, two strikers at my heels. The elephant grass cut into my arms and hands and neck.

We reached the tree line and slowed as we entered the shade. Straight ahead and below the other side of the near boulder, the sniper fired a burst. The strikers ducked and found cover in the trees. But his shots were directed at the patrol below. The sniper was unaware that a second unit was advancing behind him. Again the machine gun fired at us. Though ineffective against the patrol, it served to alert the sniper.

The clatter of metal echoed as he abandoned his position. I signaled to the Yards that I was going down and inched my way up the boulder. I peered over and caught a fleeting glimpse of one sniper just as his head and shoulders disappeared through the cleave where the huge rocks conjoined. I waved the strikers forward, swung down over the face of the boulder, and landed running. Using the stone for cover, I peered around. A well-worn path ran between the rock formation. It twisted right, then switched back. A waist-high rock blocked the passage where the sniper had retreated.

The Yards circled the boulders and came up behind me. Without the aid of an interpreter, all I could do was hope they understood. I motioned for them to stay and cover me, that I was going forward. They stepped to either side of the passage and provided cover. I cleared the rock and entered the shadow of an overhang. A path in the cleft widened here. A few feet away from the opening where the sniper had disappeared was a hole at the base of the boulder; another, similarly dug, lay a dozen paces beyond it.

I crouched and approached the first hole. I hollered down and waited. Nothing. I scooped up a fistful of dirt and tossed it down. The dirt was answered with a burst of gunfire. The bullets grazed the boulder behind me and ricocheted. I aimed my rifle at the hole.

Metal rattled behind me. Either the Yards hadn't understood or felt obligated to stay with me. I pointed to the hole. Both aimed their weapons toward it. I unhooked an HE grenade from my shoulder strap. My companions backpedaled a few steps and squatted. I pulled the pin, let the handle fly, and counted one before dropping the grenade. Then I hurried in the direction of the second hole. The ground behind me trembled. Smoke and dirt billowed up into the cranny.

A few strikers followed Cu into the passage as others crawled atop the boulder. I gathered up a handful of dirt and tossed it down, as I'd done with the first hole. I got no response. A Yard ran up, stuck the barrel of his rifle in the hole, and shouted down. We heard the slamming of a bolt. The VC answered with a single shot. The Yard responded with a couple of his own and backed off. I pulled the pin on another grenade, tossed it down, and stepped away. The concussion moved through the ground and traveled up my feet and through my bones to my head and plugged my ears.

Lieutenant Jockims shouted as he negotiated the cleft. I couldn't hear him or much of anything, but he was furious about something. Then the strikers accompanying him located two more holes, and the lieutenant blew them. By the time he caught up with me, he'd calmed down and seemed pleased with the results or perhaps himself.

There were no heroes on either side, just a lot of bad shooting, some loud noise, and two or more dead snipers. It was enough to appease the lieutenant, who mentioned nothing about my taking off ahead of him. He contacted base camp to report we were successful and would be coming down from the ridge and for Norwood's patrol to hold their fire.

Norwood waited at the roadside with Mr. Green. He saw us emerge out of the scrub and gave me a sardonic grin, which I returned. We merged the two units into one and marched back to camp. I needed a meal. My feet hurt. My muscles ached. My ears rang. My teeth were coated with grunge. My insect bites itched. My leech bites bled. All in all, I felt great.

THIRTY-NINE

Until he popped in, I had no idea Special Forces had a chaplain, but here he was, a major with a beret and a cross on his collar. He arrived one day before half our Vietnamese were to go on an operation east. Captain Horan decided a company-size force could land in helicopters and assault the VC emplacements on southern foothills between Binh Hoa and Vin Thuy. The chaplain invited himself to accompany the force. He had an Irish name, and the night before the operation he downed a substantial amount of beer and slurred his way through a debate with Luthy, who'd also been drinking. Someone later said the confrontation was over the nature of God and the sin of sloth. Somehow the argument escalated, ending with Luthy challenging him to a fight. I was on guard and didn't witness the dispute, and no one else seemed to know what started it.

Early the next morning the skies were clear all the way to the South China Sea, and the operation was on. At least the weather was favorable. At least that. The whiskey priest woke up, drank some coffee, and then shook off his hangover and set aside his Bible and clerical vows and armed himself with an M-16 and hand grenades. Though his going defied common sense and we had men in camp well prepared for the operation, he was going on it. No one raised the issue that his action might violate some clause in the Geneva Convention governing the dos and don'ts for chaplains, but it seemed logical that his taking up arms had to be on the list of don'ts.

I didn't know whose idea it was but assumed it originated from Captain Horan. Even if he wasn't the author, he owned the plan because he didn't override it. It called for two platoons of strikers to be set down some two kilometers east of Binh Hoa. Someone reasoned that helicopters picking up an armed force in our camp and transporting them straight up the valley might go unnoticed by the VC, which was a little like imagining a fashion model's going nude and unnoticed on the sands of Miami Beach. Someone also assumed that our strikers, though untrained in it, could perform a vertical assault.

The force left in three slicks, each armed with single side-door M-60s and a couple of rockets mounted between the belly and the skids. From below strikers in camp waved as the assault force headed to a ridge that divided Vin Thuy 5 and Phu Thanh, far out of range for our mortars. I shaded my eyes from the sun and watched the craft diminish to the size of wasps.

We in camp went about our daily business. I'd come to believe going out on an operation was easier on the nerves than waiting in camp, particularly when Norwood went out. Inevitably, he seemed to bump into a firefight. At least for this operation, he was in camp. I turned my attention to the walls of the trench leading to the commo bunker that needed repair. I handed two stacks of sandbags to Ong Dao. He put the laborers to shoveling. Save for the sound of their blades sinking into the clay and turning dirt, the camp was silent. As I had since the incident with the 57, I kept close watch on them. I occasionally scanned the horizon but saw nothing.

When the assault force hit the enemy, the only surprise was that the enemy wasn't surprised. The LZ erupted with automatic fire. The strikers were too far east for us to determine the intensity of the battle, but from the expression on his face and way Cam rushed out of his bunker, I figured our side was in trouble. And they were, as they faced a well-armed, well-entrenched foe.

In passing he said, "They took fire going in. Heavy casualties. Called for a medevac."

News turned worse. Claiming the LZ was too hot to land, the Vietnamese helicopter pilots flying refused to land and save the wounded. Then a dispatch came that an American was hit and the entire force was pinned down. Again, I thought. Another well-planned fuckup. One of ours getting shot changed matters. Americans flew slicks in from Quang Ngai and began evacuating out wounded, both American and Vietnamese. Marine jets arrived to bail the force out.

By afternoon those not shot up returned to camp, and the debriefings began. It seemed the first helicopter took no fire, but when the second and third landed, the LZ went hot. The chaplain, hit almost immediately with a burst from a machine gun, was pulled to cover and later lifted to a field hospital. Five Vietnamese took severe wounds. Two died. Charlie faded into the landscape. Mission half accomplished.

On his first (and I'm sure last) combat operation the chaplain earned a Purple Heart and perhaps a Combat Infantry Badge, maybe an artificial limb or a colostomy bag. We never heard how badly he was wounded, but my bet was it brought him closer to God than he cared to be. To me he was just another officer who'd come out looking for a medal or a war story to tell. And he got his. Questions about the operation lingered: Who thought our strikers capable of a vertical assault on a fixed position? Why was a chaplain allowed on a combat operation? Why not someone trained and ready? Who fucked up this time? I wasn't alone with questions. Norwood and Luthy shared similar concerns. If J. V. or Fox did, they never proclaimed them.

Though not naturally superstitious, I was beginning to think the camp was jinxed. Malone, Hunter, Norwood, and Luthy knew the score. Like all of them, I was as familiar with our area of operation and the capabilities of our Vietnamese, but no one who was now in charge was likely to solicit advice from them or me.

FORTY

A Caribou flew in with supplies, some barrels of gasoline, and the 4.2-inch mortar I'd requisitioned months before. It was a huge chunk of metal and required four men to haul it onto the bed of the truck. It was an even greater chore to hoist down when we reached camp.

Fox wanted it ready for use as soon as possible. Willy Hunter was gone to Da Nang or Nha Trang for three days, so the task fell on Malone and me. He, four laborers, and I toted the new gun to the pit atop the camp. The pit had housed an 81mm and was too small to oblige the new mortar. The day was too hot for pick and shovel. Nonetheless, the laborers and I began the work. We stripped out the old sandbags from the walls, and the next day we dug and sand-bagged the walls until the pit was deep and wide enough to accommodate the new beast.

Every once in a while Fox strolled up, eyeballed the hole, and either nodded or shook his head, both an indication of disapproval. He asked how much longer. I offered him a shovel and said he was welcome to take a turn. He told me not to be a flannel mouth. Once the pit was deep enough, Malone suggested we lay a foundation of sandbags and rocks to house the base plate. I argued for digging deeper by several inches and using a truck tire filled with gravel to absorb the shock. Malone insisted the sandbags would do fine.

It took a half-dozen pairs of hands to lower the cumbersome weapon and mount it on the foundation. As soon as the mortar was in place, Malone set about registering it and seating the base plate. His specialty being light weapons, he seemed somewhat at a loss. I asked if he'd fired a 4.2 before. Indignant over the question, he assured me that he had.

Pablo helped fill the magazine with two dozen canisters containing mortar rounds. I opened one and looked at it—big and deadly, but unlike the 81s, these shells lacked fins. Puzzled by the shape of the round, I looked down the tube and saw that it had riflings. Like an artillery piece, the big mortar was configured so the round would spiral out of the tube. Pablo, who was being reassigned to Saigon, was content to let Malone tinker with the gun.

Though it was the least-likely place for Charlie to launch an assault, Malone determined the first registration point to be a hillside east of the village of Tra Bac. He aligned the mortar and cranked the lever until the tube was at a 50-degree angle. He leveled the bubble on the sight and spread a map out on the sandbags. Serious as a priest giving high mass, he looked at the foothills and then returned to the mortar, aimed the scope on a sighting stake, and studied a chart that accompanied the weapon.

Malone asked for a white-phosphorus round, told me how many increments to cut. He seemed assured now with what he was doing. I followed his instructions and handed him the round. He pulled the pin, announced that it was in the tube, and sent it home. I plugged my ears in anticipation of a loud concussion, but when the weapon went off, it sounded like a burp. The round wobbled and climbed about a hundred yards in the air, did a feeble full gainer, and plunged toward the center of the paddy adjacent to the camp. It landed with a sickening splash.

I winced as it hit. Two women standing calf deep in the paddy water stopped and looked at us. Malone, hands on his hips, looked at the rings of rippling water and shook his head.

When I realized that the round wasn't going to go off, I said, "Pretty impressive."

Malone was not one to take blame. "Not enough increments. You cut too many off."

"I cut exactly what you said to."

He grabbed a second round out of the magazine and repeated the earlier procedure but cut the increments himself. He delivered the round in the tube. I plugged my ears.

This one spiraled as it climbed, but as it did, it appeared something again was wrong. A short round, destined for who knew what. I pursed my lips and watched it burst near a stand of palm trees at the edge of the village. A reddish orange flame flashed, followed by a surge of gray smoke. Malone stared as the smoke darkened and rose above the fronds.

"Nice shot," I said.

He circled the mortar, discussing with himself what might have caused the error and then finally asked what I thought went wrong.

"What went wrong is we didn't wait for Willy," I said.

The civil affairs officer, Lieutenant Bussey, drove into the village to assess the damage and prove how democracy works. No one was injured. A hut lay in chars. Another received damage to its roof. The incident was reduced to paperwork, which the civil affairs officer resolved by handing over money to rebuild the hut and a few extra piasters to allay any ill feelings.

The next day after I repaired the mortar's foundation, Malone and I, cautioned by the captain to avoid firing over the village, set about mastering it. Malone adjusted the sight. I, having figured out what caused the mistake, unscrewed the excess extensions as I cut increments. The first round flew over the river and exploded in the foothills short of the target. His confidence up, Malone cranked the handle and readjusted the mortar. I prepped another round and set it atop the sandbag wall. He told me to get a third ready. I bent over and unscrewed an adapter.

Malone pulled the pin on a round and, without warning, sent it down the tube. I felt as if someone had run a spike into my ear. I stepped back, leaned against the parapet for support, and cupped a hand over my ear. I managed to keep hold of the round I was prepping and laid it atop the sandbags. I looked at my hand, sticky with blood. Malone was unaware of what had happened. I shouted his name and held out my hand. He saw the blood and said something. Though his lips moved, all I heard was a terrible ringing in my head.

Norwood, who'd heard the commotion, hustled me down into the med bunker. Blood from my ear dripped on the floor. He cleaned my ear and bandaged it. He was talking, but I couldn't hear. I pointed to my ear, indicating as much.

Days later hearing returned to my right ear but not my left. I experienced headaches. My sense of balance was disrupted. Short of taking a bullet or shrapnel we didn't leave because of injury. I went about my duties until I couldn't because of dizziness. Finally, I reported to Norwood, who sucked some peroxide into a syringe, held a pad up to the ear, and squeezed it into the canal. Almost instantly, the pressure inside the ear dissipated, and a mixture of scab and earwax poured into the basin he held against my neck. I recovered my hearing well enough to be annoyed with the Buck Owens song J. V. loved playing over and over again on the record player.

FORTY-ONE

Six months at Tra Bong, and I'd never gone on an operation with J. V., never been outside the camp with him unless it was a run to the airstrip. Then, out of the blue, Norwood and I were assigned not on an operation in the flats but on a reconnaissance into the greenest part of the map, a planned two-day walk with J. V. Why him, I wondered? If Charlie hit the camp, I'd want him in the mortar pit with me. But he was in no shape for the mountains. He carried enough flesh above his belt to endure a year of famine, smoked a pack of Camels a day, and drank enough beer and Jim Beam to gain honorable mention in *Guinness*. Still, three hours before sunup, he was in harness and drinking a cup of coffee.

If we pressed hard, we could breach the summits before the midmorning sun. We crossed the Song Tra Bong into foothills and skirted the river west. By dawn we were at least a kilometer short of where we planned to ascend, and J. V. was sucking air. The only thing he'd prepared himself for was contact. He totted ammunition for two and four grenades, but the load in his rucksack seemed far too light for a two-day patrol. I figured he'd lightened his load to compensate for his condition. Every fifty or sixty paces, he would slow or pause, but he didn't stop for a break.

We began our ascent, an hour behind schedule. Norwood and I kept J. V. between us. When we hit steep patches, I offered him a hand up. J. V. shook his head, slid and struggled, until finally he relented. Whether guts or pride, he pushed on. Halfway up the foothill, we took a break. He shed his pack and leaned into a boulder. I asked if he was okay. He said he was fine.

When Norwood repeated my question, J. V. snarled, "I'll

do anything you pups can." He slipped into harness and stood. "Let's go."

We nodded. Dating back to the day the team had formed for training at Bragg, we'd known him almost a year, long enough to understand his prideful ways and the futility of arguing with him. This time as we formed the column, he huffed and stepped in front of me, and I let him.

More and more J. V. had been bingeing on Jim Beam and occasionally wobbling down the hall from his realm of maps and colored pins. Drunk sometimes by midafternoon, sometimes red-eyed for two or three days. He was obsessed over trying to get our dead teammates decorated. Too often he sat at the team table recapping his latest efforts to this end along with theories of how the battle actually played out. He'd interviewed dozens of informants, every captured VC, his questions first and always centering around the day of the battle. The accounts were roughly the same, and none included any particular acts of bravery. Then one day a villager brought to camp by a patrol signed a statement about the big American sergeant getting shot while carrying a wounded striker out of the line of fire. This piece of uncorroborated intelligence gave him a burst of hope. Jake could be honored, or so it seemed. The news sobered J. V. for a short time, but when the paperwork bottlenecked elsewhere, he fell into a state of despondence. He struggled for a time to stay sober, but the booze, the curse of too many lifers, had owned him for too long.

He did well for a time, only because he was stubborn. The next leg up proved difficult. We stopped again. J. V. said we were too exposed on the slope. He pointed to the next slope to the west and told Henry to tell the Yards that we were taking an alternate route. If we took that course, we would be delayed and climbing under the oppressive noon sun. Nothing came of arguing with him. We turned west.

There we hit a thicket of elephant grass that grew up the

side of a steep promontory and spread wide a hundred meters or so in both directions. Already the sun beat down on us. Passing through would be slow and arduous. From high ground on the adjacent slopes anyone could see us. Blinded on all sides, we waded into it. A couple of needed rests and an hour later we finally breached the elephant grass and reached the wood line, still no closer to the top.

J. V. sank to the ground in shade below a boulder. The Yards formed a perimeter and waited. While I called our coordinates to base camp, J. V. lit a cigarette and went into a coughing spasm. From his expression, I figured Norwood's thoughts mirrored my own. The longer we were stuck on the mountainside, the greater our risk of being seen. Disheartening as it was, J. V. was a liability. His condition wasn't lost on the Yards, who eyed him warily. No matter how spent J. V. was, we couldn't risk staying where we were.

"J. V., you ready?" I asked.

"I'll tell you when." He stubbed out his smoke and looked at Norwood. "I'm ready."

Neither Norwood nor I said what we were thinking. We moved out. J. V. seemed fine for a few minutes, but when the angle steepened to near vertical, he could manage only two or three steps at a time before stopping and leaning on his rifle to catch his breath. He would start again, take a step up, and slide back. Though more than an hour behind schedule, I halted the patrol.

Their eyes telegraphing concern to one another and me, the Yards spread out. I had to consider aborting the operation. Even if J. V. was senior to me, I owed a duty to the Recon Platoon to do what was best. "J. V., are you up for this?" I asked.

He gazed up at the steep incline. "Climbed worse'n this," he snapped. "I'll be just fine after I get my second wind."

The onus was on me to force the issue. I decided to give

him another chance, but if he became a threat to the security of the patrol, I would do what was necessary. "Okay, Pap."

He shed his backpack, rested his back against a boulder, and lit up a Camel. He lifted the flap to his pack and reached in. I figured, fine, some food might help. Instead of food, he took out a can of Schlitz, slipped an opener out of his pocket, and popped open the top. Norwood and I stared as he sucked foam from the top.

He looked at us. "Water'll just give me the runs." His Adam's apple bobbled as he downed the beer. Finished, J. V. indicated he was ready.

I motioned to the Yards to proceed. A half hour later we neared the final ascent. J. V. reeled forward, bent over, and puked. His face was pale, and he trembled as he leaned into a boulder for support. Norwood eased him down to a sitting position and examined him, taking his pulse and looking at his eyes. He concluded what had been obvious all along, that J. V. was in no condition to go. He looked in J. V.'s backpack but found no food in it, nothing but five cans of beer. He looked to me, his expression one of disgust. I nodded.

"Pap," I said, "I'm telling them we're aborting the patrol."

"No, no, you ain't. I can damn well make it." He popped open another can and said that Norwood and I were quitters. He swallowed a mouthful, then stood ready to ream us out some more. Instead, he turned away and vomited. When he looked up, his face was blanched. He tried to speak, but his lips merely trembled. Norwood helped him to a rock, where he sat looking down at his boots. No one had to convince him any further.

Norwood said that it was over. "You're dehydrated."

J. V. looked up. Norwood had given him an out that made it easier. He lowered his head and nodded.

That wasn't what any of us wanted. Despite his pride,

cantankerousness, and runaway alcoholism, a soldier lived inside J. V.'s weakened body, and seeing him in his current condition saddened me. I pressed the mic button and informed camp we were returning, that one of us was too sick to continue. Captain Horan, sounding displeased, told us to bring it home.

"Don't tell 'em why," J. V. said.

We emptied his backpack of beer, split up his gear between the two of us, and headed down to the river, where we crossed at the Montagnard village. The jeep met us on the other bank and drove J. V. in from there.

Norwood and I never mentioned what happened out there. It was dehydration. Anyone could get dehydrated in heat like that. The others could figure out what happened on their own. I had my own theory behind the incident. That it was intended. That Horan wanted J. V. to fail.

FORTY-TWO

I was in Dong Ba Tinh with Trung Sí Cu and the Combat Recon Platoon when Luthy transferred to A-100, the MIKE Force stationed out of Da Nang. Luthy had filled a lot of space when he was around and now left a big void. He'd been a tonic to the drudgery of routine camp life. We all respected the soldier in him. I remembered a patrol that took place after he'd flown back from a two-day in-country R & R, and, grinning, still half inebriated, he'd spilled out of the side door, bent under the swinging blades, and lurched toward the jeep. He had a black eye that he didn't care to explain. He tossed his pack in the rear. Before he was fully seated, he asked what the hell I was waiting for.

He and I were scheduled to take out a squad of Yards the next morning. That evening, after downing a few beers and playing a few hands of pinochle, he grabbed four hours of snore. At the appointed time about two hours before dawn, he stood in full gear ready to soldier. He grunted through the first stretch of the patrol but kept pace.

By midmorning the patrol had reached the first checkpoint. He'd nearly sweated off his binge. When we stopped to radio base camp, he leaned against a rock, opened his backpack, and whipped out a pair of black women's silk panties. He wiped sweat from his forehead and then ran the panties over his cheeks and the back of his neck. The amused strikers pointed to him and chuckled. Seeing that he was the center of attention, he asked me what was wrong.

"Look," I said, pointing to his hand.

He eyed the panties as if to ask how they got there. He smiled, tucked them back in his pack, and said, "We done here?"

His replacement, whoever he turned out to be, had an impossible act to follow, and I was prepared for the worst. We hadn't fared well with replacements, and when Specialist 4th Class Aaron Gritzmacher stepped down from the craft for his introduction to Tra Bong, I thought my worst expectations were realized. He was as short as the average Vietnamese but stocky. His skin was still Stateside pale, his cheeks round, and his eyes, as he took in his new surroundings, had a kind of Dorothy-landing-in-Oz look to them. He greeted us with a high-pitched drawl, not the slow southern type but the aw-shucks of a cowpuncher. He introduced himself as Gritzmacher, informed us that people called him Gritz, and shook hands.

J. V. pointed out an area on the map several kilometers beyond the western edge of the Tra Bong district. He said a unit of vc was reported operating somewhere in a five-kilometer radius of the village of Ha Nang.

Captain Horan said, "We need to run a patrol there," and added that I'd be taking Gritz along with two squads from the Recon Platoon.

"Sir, one squad would be better. Less chance of being seen."

"You'll take two."

"Yes, sir. What size unit?"

"Could be a company. Could be a battalion," J. V. said.

Could be his imagination at work or booze. That was all? One battalion?

"If you make contact," Captain Horan said, "don't engage them. Call an air strike."

Engagement was a last resort. The best defense invisibility, and the second-best defense swift evacuation. Choppers were two hours away—if radio contact was even possible. The third choice was calling in an air strike, again provided communication was possible. I'd already asked one question too many for the captain's liking, so I didn't ask the obvious question, which was if we made contact, weren't we already engaged?

"Shouldn't I take Norwood?"

The captain said, "I already told Gritz."

Gritz beamed as he came in from whatever detail he'd been on. When excited his voice, high-pitched under normal circumstances, rose an octave. His voice hit a record-high C as he announced, "We're goin' out together, Barnes."

"Yep. Tomorrow."

I didn't want to dampen his spirits by telling him this patrol wasn't one to be overjoyed about. It was serious Indian country. I'd flown over it on aerial recons and taken patrols south of there. Some of Vietnam's higher peaks were there. The terrain was steep, densely canopied, and generally unfavorable to radio contact over five or six miles.

I liked him already. He said what was on his mind. In part

249

because of his enthusiasm, but mostly because of his height, I had the impression he was younger. It turned out he was older and that we shared some coincidental history. He'd once lived in Roswell, New Mexico, where I'd attended South Junior High School for a semester, and we'd both lived in Texas.

"Tomorrow," he said, still smiling.

Tomorrow, I thought, tomorrow the mountains will dampen your enthusiasm soon enough.

Not even the early hour stifled Gritz's spirit. He showed up two hours before dawn packing a poncho and poncho liner, C rations, and enough ammunition to fight his way to Thailand. I was tempted to ask if he was planning a permanent move, but I didn't. He smiled as we marched out. The guard closed the gate as soon as the last man passed through. The Yards spread out. Silence fell over the patrol. I couldn't hear a breath among the Montagnard.

The river was low despite rain two days earlier. I sent two Yards across to secure the far bank. When they signaled the side was clear, we crossed. The current was slow. Near the middle water rose over my hips. I looked back. Gritz chest deep in water reminded me of the Little Locomotive Who Could as he held his rifle overhead and chugged along.

It was essential to reach the wood line before sunup. We proceeded steadily up the steep grade in the dark until we arrived at a rocky passage that narrowed beneath an outcropping. The gap could accommodate only one man at a time, and the dim light made climbing arduous, even for the Yards. The rubber soles of their boots slipped on the loose dirt and rock. I looked back to check on Gritz. The only thing visible under his slouch hat was his can-do smile. He'd kept up this far, but it was obvious he was hindered by the amount of gear he was packing. I balanced myself, offered him a hand up, took his backpack from him, and shouldered it.

At sunrise we'd reached the summit. We'd negotiated the worst part of the climb. I returned his pack to Gritz and made the first com check with base camp, then asked if he was okay. He smiled and nodded.

The Yards set a good pace. Here and there we crossed well-worn trails. The dense woods filtered out sunlight and created optical illusions. Matter became shadow and shadow became matter. The thick undergrowth made it tempting to use the trails. We avoided them unless necessary. We followed one for a short distance and then retreated into the brush.

The climb taxed Gritz, but he kept up. We made the second com check on schedule, then arrived at the next faster than anticipated. By early afternoon we topped a promontory where we stopped and looked out over the vast canopy. The benchland to the north and west extended for miles. To the south about a mile a sheer cliff rose. A waterfall cascaded down its face. Below us, seeming just out of reach, wispy clouds floated by. As we descended into the plateau, we passed through a valley where a B52 strike had unmoored trees and bored craters twenty feet wide. The Yards surveyed the damage with reverence.

At the foot of the slope the ground leveled. Bushes and ferns grew no more than knee high. The flat ground and sparse undergrowth rendered us vulnerable to distant eyes. I sensed a wariness spread among the Yards, and Seymore glued himself to Gritz and me. Then two meters farther the jungle closed around us again.

We stumbled upon a path, punji fields on either side of it. The bamboo spikes were stained from age and decay, planted a foot apart, and set row upon row that ran all the way to the far slope. I pulled one out, broke it in two, and tossed it aside. The field sprawled on both sides a half mile. It was possibly laid to slow Japanese in the Good War or more likely to trap French in the Indochina War. How many hands made it? It spoke of determination; spoke of a footpath between bad choices on ground suited for ambushing, if . . . Despite the condition of the stakes, crossing through them would be risky. Though it went against sound judgment, we took the trail.

Before dusk closed in the point man uncovered a tunnel entrance camouflaged by dead leaves spread over a bamboo grating. The squad secured the perimeter while I checked for mines and booby traps. The entrance led to a bunker furnished with a bamboo cot and two grass mats. On the floor were bandages rotted brown. We lifted mats and baskets, searched for documents, but found nothing other than some tarnished cans used to boil water and dry bloodstains, evidence that wounded had been treated here. Like the punji field, the aid station might have been a relic from a previous war, or it could have been used just months ago. Nothing indicated recent activity.

I marked the point on the map. B52s would pay it a visit sometime soon.

We encountered the first of many streams to come. I sent two Yards across to secure the opposite bank. When they returned we crossed the bubbling water. On the other side I bent down, splashed my face, and then wet my bandanna and wiped my neck. We filled our canteens, plopped in chlorine pills, and shook the contents. The spot would be ideal for weekend camping. Water silvered over moss-covered rocks. The damp ground above the bank was flat. Dead leaves cushioned the ground everywhere. But Charlie wouldn't set down there. Neither could we.

At dusk we laid up on the side of a wooded slope. I radioed the coordinates, plucked off some leeches, changed socks, and sprayed fresh insect repellent on my cuffs. Gritz followed my lead. After a meal of rice balls and crackers, washed down with cool water, we set up for the night. I strung up my makeshift hammock. Gritz watched and took note. For now his night's rest consisted of hard ground and a poncho liner to ward off the coming cold.

We lay and listened to the shrill of darkness in the jungle: bird calls, monkey shrieks, insect buzzes. Tigers, leopards prowled the night. Pythons and deadly vipers crawled the damp floor. My feet and back ached; leeches left my legs bleeding. It was impossible to find a comfortable position for sleep. I couldn't know what might happen, now or at dawn or the next day, but I wanted to be nowhere else. Welcome to the highlands, Gritz, I thought. He'd earned his first day out here. I wondered how much of it he would remember, how much of it I would remember, if any.

We woke an hour before dawn. I made a static-riddled com check with base camp and managed to get across that we had made no contact and were proceeding. A few strikers lit up cigarettes. The smoke could compromise us. I ordered them to snuff them out and get moving. We had to be long gone if Charlie happened upon the campsite.

That morning went as the first. We breached the next crest to the west and descended to where the canopy was so dense that it was like walking in perpetual twilight. Birds and monkeys in the boughs announced themselves. It was impossible to locate where sounds came from, but so long as we heard them, we were comforted. Vines gnarled up at our feet, and tree roots rose knee high out of the earth. We saw no sign of Charlie. The rare but well-traveled foot trails were the sole evidence that humans existed here.

The Yard on point led us to the next ridge and then the next. There were no landmarks. We navigated by compass and by guess. Always farther west. Going up went slow, but once we capped a peak, the undergrowth thinned and for a time we weren't climbing. But descent was hard on the knees and toes and especially the toenails.

We moved uneventfully, measuring steps, pausing only to drink from a canteen, or stopping to make a com check. Where the boughs thinned, the sun struck through and lay iron-hot on our necks. Our effort was quantified by beads of sweat that never flowed in amounts sufficient to cool us, and by the dozens of times we wiped sweat from our foreheads or the backs of our necks. We watched shadows that preceded us and shadows on our flanks and looked back at the shadows we passed through.

The day was punctuated by ever-increasing pain from canvas straps digging into our shoulder wells, numbness in our fingers from gripping weapons, and discomfort in our feet. Gritz eased into the rhythm of the patrol and observed the silence that passed man to man and the careful laying of boot sole and cautious transfer of body weight forward.

At midmorning the patrol left the forest and came to a promontory. I called for a com check, spread the map, and set the compass on the nearest peak to the east. As I did, I realized that we'd crossed into the frayed hem of the world, beyond the western fringe of the map that ended at 108 degrees longitude. On the far side of the next cordillera lay Attapu and the Plateau des Bolovens. Laos. Without a map to identify land features, I couldn't say precisely where we were, but if not in Laos, so close we might encounter a few Hmong at the nearest local pub. At an elevation of more than two thousand meters at 107 degrees, 20 minutes longitude and 15 degrees, 22 minutes latitude, we'd outdistanced any safety net and entered into the gardens of the ancients. Hundreds may have flown over it, but how many round-eyes had ever seen this from the ground?

I tried raising base camp, but we were out of range. The radio produced nothing but static. We had to go east to reach radio range before the captain or xo requested planes to search for us, a sure signal to Charlie that a patrol was in the area. I told Gritz I couldn't raise the camp. He'd guessed that much on his own.

Circling back or going north was impossible. Over the northern mountain range lay the benchland where I'd shot at the three VC from an L-19. I studied the next peak west where the ridge turned south. I suggested we move farther south and circle back. I pointed in that direction.

"Over that ridge." The jungle was seductive and the Yards at ease here, and so far our luck had held up. "Or there." I pointed west and asked Gritz if he was okay with that. He nodded. "Might be in Laos," I said. "I can't be sure. We're off the map here."

He smiled, indicating he was a bit touched. That was good to know because a completely sane man wouldn't serve much purpose out here. A sane man wouldn't even be out here. I pointed west and told Seymore that's where we were heading. He shook his head, said I was dinky dau, and we should go back.

"Get the strikers moving, or I will leave you here."

At first the interpreter seemed to doubt me, but when he saw my face was utterly expressionless, he shook his head and looked at me as if I were a crazy man, which was largely true. Then he turned to the Yards and translated my instructions. I wondered myself if I was just posturing or if I'd actually meant that I'd leave him.

I sent the tallest of the Yards on point. We filed into woods so dense we lost sight of him and had to tighten the gaps between us, which made us vulnerable to higher casualties if ambushed.

Vine knots clogged the floor. Trees towered some seventy and eighty feet above us. Ferns grew as high as our shoulders. The point man pointed out a tree trunk intentionally strung across a footpath. We avoided the path and moved on cautiously, each man following the footsteps of the man in front.

We crossed to the next ridgeline at a point that looked out over the open valley. I signaled for a break, shed my gear, and flopped down. I took out the map. It matched none of the surrounding land features. We headed west and ascended what seemed the highest peak yet. On the downslope the air smelled faintly of cinnamon, a spice that was the gold of commerce of the mountain people. The farther we descended, the more the scent thickened in the air, and when we stepped out of the jungle, we entered a grove of thin-leafed cinnamon trees, one about every five to ten paces. Bark had recently been harvested from the trunks, and the heady smell in the middle of the grove was unearthly.

A hundred meters later, we returned to the jungle, and the spiced air seemed no more than an illusion because we smelled burning wood. We sighted a thin shaft of smoke above trees about a half mile ahead. We headed in that direction, and when we stepped out of the shadowed tree line, we entered a clearing where the mountain flattened into an open shelf and the vegetation was sparse. The noon sky was ablaze in sunlight. A well-worn path turned south and dead-ended at a longhouse. It was built on stilts atop a precipice that overlooked miles of canopied valley.

We were already compromised, so there was no point in retreating into the woods. The village appeared harmless enough. Weapons ready, we walked the trail. Chickens scattered before us as we neared the habitation. An old man, a boy, and a half-dozen shy women and girls awaited us. None had probably ever seen a round-eye. They seemed as surprised at seeing us as we were at stumbling upon them.

Strips of bark were spread out on the ground like shingles drying in the sun. These would be toted across the mountains and traded to Vietnamese, who would then channel the cinnamon to Chinese apothecaries, who in turn would grind the bark into a cinnamon curative. The women and children retreated to the longhouse, but the man stood his ground. He was wrinkled, his hair black with streaks of gray, his goatee long and scraggly, his eyes deep set and kindly. He greeted the Yards. In a three-way translation from me to Seymore to the Vietnamese squad leader to a Yard and finally to the old man, I explained that he would be rewarded for any information about the Vietcong and convinced him to accompany us back to Tra Bong so J. V. could interrogate him. He took to the idea, smilingly. Maybe he knew something helpful. Maybe he didn't. We took him with us anyhow.

On the morning of the fifth day we trudged into base camp with our guest. Gritz was so tired he couldn't smile. We turned the old man over to J. V. and dumped our gear, and then returned and reported what we'd seen, which was nothing important, just the bunker once used as an aid station. I showered in cold water, lathered soap all over myself. Blood trickled from leech bites on my legs. I watched it turn pink and swirl away with the water.

We'd been lucky, had no encounters, had seen no VC units, done nothing to advance the war. What we had done was go farther from Tra Bong and stay out longer than anyone up to then had. I was tired and hungry and mostly glad it was over. At the same time, I already missed being out there in the fringes. There was more to see. Gritz, the Yards, and I could go hump it forever, the only things holding us back—Charlie, the war, and an army-issued map. I dried myself off. Tonight I looked forward to eight hours of sleep. In the morning I would continue construction on the tower above the bunker. Then tomorrow night I would pull a guard shift and remember what the world here looked like above the clouds.

FORTY-THREE

Late July Mr. Whitten left, and the team got a fresh assistant intel man. Brassfield was American, black, my age, and welcomed. He arrived with a rifle, two Supremes records, a miniature chess game, and an irreverent sense of humor. He quickly figured out the situation in camp. I liked him right off, and after he went on one patrol with me and the Yards, I had a pal. Come dark, instead of playing pinochle, I sat across the table from him, moved pieces over the board, and listened to Diana Ross until J. V. bitched or put on some Buck Owens.

Lela's dad, Mark Terrell, had first introduced me to chess when I was a high school junior, and in college I'd wasted untold hours of study time playing chess with Randy Villarreal, who'd wake me up in the morning to finish a game we'd started at five the night before. Brassfield didn't treat the game as life and death, but he was no slouch. His game was a patient, thoughtful one, and while he liked to win, he was a good loser as well. For a few hours in the evening we could make the war disappear.

I didn't miss Mr. Whitten. Nor did anyone else.

Fox unceremoniously transferred somewhere to II Corps. He gave me a final piece of advice before he left, to keep my head down and not hear what I wasn't supposed to. I wasn't sure what that meant, but I thanked him and told him I would. Contentious but levelheaded when sober, Fox never tried to impress anyone. I was accustomed to his ways. All in all, we could have done worse for a team sergeant. He was ready to leave, had spent hard months here, but he seemed sad to go, perhaps because he was departing under the cloud of his teammates' deaths.

J. V. temporarily took Fox's place as operations sergeant and for a few days got what he'd long wanted. He stayed sober, but his sour disposition mellowed only moderately. He had hopes of getting his third rocker and taking on the permanent role of team sergeant. Because we were now among strangers, he took me into his confidence, told me there was another buildup of hard-core regional-force guerrillas in the area east of Binh Hoa and west of Vin Thuy, said that Captain Horan didn't listen to him and probably wouldn't listen to anyone.

"G-2. Don't tell no one," he said.

"Sure. No one." I didn't know whether to believe him. His imagination could be as wild sober as it was when he was on a binge. Or his call could be as accurate as it was on January 21. The last option was to follow Fox's advice and not hear what I wasn't supposed to.

The other original team members, except for J. V. and I, planned on rotating to new assignments. The camp remained short a radio operator. Willy Hunter left August 1, the week after Fox, and the next day the new man arrived.

Master Sgt. Roger T. Holman, six feet tall and well over two hundred pounds, blustered in on the same flight that took Willy away. His prior experience in 'Nam, so I was told, consisted of running a club in Saigon. He was in his early thirties, young for his rank. Climbed fast. "Rear-echelon motherfucker" was imprinted on him. He tossed his gear in his bunker, took a first look at the camp, and then took each of us aside and reminded us that even in the field, this was still the army. Patted a lot of backs.

When my turn came, he said he was glad I was aboard and that the camp needed "shaping up," as if nothing had been accomplished. He added, with emphasis, that things were going to change. What things? Was he going to pacify Charlie?

Negotiate a surrender from Uncle Ho? Change the menu from rice and Spam to Spam and rice? Bring in a troupe of uso entertainers? Control the direction of wind so that the smell of shit from the latrine didn't blow into the team house?

He looked at my blond hair, an inch long or more on top, and said I needed to visit a barber. He made a point of dropping in the conversation that he'd fought in Korea, then added that he'd heard good reports on me. Good reports? From whom? Though young, I was wise enough to see a curtain going up on a bad acting job.

He was too eager, too braggadocian, traits in themselves not so troubling if he took his time to get a fix on the camp and the team. I'd seen the results when deliberation gave way to haste. But by his third day in camp I pretty much had him figured—a bully, or worse, a know-it-all bully with big plans, and I finally knew what a flannel mouth was.

It seemed at times that Captain Horan and Holman sincerely wanted to make the men into a team, but neither knew how to go about it. At other times it seemed they didn't give a whit about the team. It soon became clear that the experience the rest of us had gained over the months was meaningless to the new captain and team sergeant. They didn't seek opinions, and if offered one, they viewed it with skepticism or dismissed it, perhaps even saw it as a form of insubordination. All of us were their inferiors. The message sounded in their do-as-I-say tone, and it showed in the shadows of their critical eyes. Fox was already sorely missed.

FORTY-FOUR

Horan and Holman wasted no time setting up shop. Norwood and Malone were sent out on an operation not unlike the failed one that got the chaplain shot up. Near the same place. Same method. The strategy this time called for a company of strikers to land in a rice paddy on level ground, avoid contact with snipers holding the high ground, and sweep back through Binh Hoa. Though he wouldn't say as much, Norwood didn't want any part of the operation or of Captain Horan or Holman, but he was a good soldier bound by duty. He gave his opinion, saying that the operation was a bad idea. He was ready to go, but he wanted his transfer approved.

At midmorning a fleet of five choppers lifted Malone and Norwood and a company of strikers down the valley. The slicks dropped the entire company in a rice paddy and lifted off without incident. As soon as the choppers lifted off, the hillside erupted with intense automatic and small-arms fire, and the force was pinned down by crossfire. The ambush came off as if the VC had participated in the planning of the assault. A few Vietnamese were wounded in the first burst of gunfire, and Malone took a bullet in the thigh that hit his femur and ruptured an artery. Norwood gave him aid, a shot of morphine, and called for a dust-off. Wounded were scattered around the LZ, a couple in grave condition.

Protocol called for the South Vietnamese to lift their own wounded out, but when the helicopters arrived, the Vietnamese pilots wouldn't land to evacuate the casualties. Gunfire by then had abated to the degree that Norwood could move Malone to cover behind a berm. He'd managed to slow the bleeding in Malone's thigh, but Malone was in severe pain by then and asked for more morphine. Norwood gave him another dose.

The machine-gun fire intensified. The best the strikers could do was hold the berm and return enough fire to discourage an assault on the paddy. The Vietnamese pilots circled safely out of range of the automatic fire. In a short time, just as before, it became obvious they weren't going to put themselves at risk. Norwood called for an air strike and an American chopper. The wait was marked by a decline in fire. Fortunately, the enemy didn't have a mortar to take advantage of the pinned-down defenders.

Finally, after a forty-minute wait, an American helicopter arrived. Norwood tossed out a smoke grenade and readied Malone. The Vietnamese pilots still marked time at a safe distance. The American pilot brought his craft straight into the LZ and hovered over the paddy. Even as machine-gun fire intensified and bullets dinged off the fuselage and struts, the pilot held the stick steady. Norwood lifted Malone and the wounded Vietnamese aboard to the crew chief. All the while the pilot kept the helicopter hanging as close to the ground as possible. When the final casualty was aboard, he looked through his side mirror and gave Norwood a thumbs-up. Norwood returned the gesture. The craft lifted off.

Shortly after, jets peppered the hillside with 40mm's and rockets, dumped some bombs, and flew back to Da Nang in time for lunch. Norwood brought the patrol home. Red-faced but in control, he marched into the team house and requested a signature on his request for transfer.

The captain said, "I'm considering it."

Norwood understood. In Tra Bong indecision was now the only thing more immediate than bad decisions.

FORTY-FIVE

Holman shifted about in his improvised hammock. I lay in mine a few feet away. It seemed the more I tried to avoid him, the more he insisted on being around me. As its builder, I'd been first to see the tower's other potential and the first to string up a hammock and claim it as a place to sleep. It easily accommodated two and was about as close to comfort as it got in Tra Bong. It was peacefully quiet, cool, provided protection from rain, didn't smell of mold, and was too high up for mosquitoes. I didn't mind Gritzmacher racking out on his hammock, but Holman lumbered up the ladder in the calm of night like an invader scaling a castle wall and took Gritz's spot.

He was a horrific snorer. He kept me awake, first with un-important chatter, then some full-blown snoring. Norwood and I were leery of him. His personality clashed with ours, as did his high opinion of himself, his insistence on being right about everything, his quick dismissal of ideas he didn't originate. What troubled us most was that he didn't seem to grasp we were an A-Team or any kind of team.

For the time being I'd given up on sleep because of his snoring in the background. I gazed at the stars. Lately, I'd been thinking of Lela a lot. I had five months left in country and was considering returning to El Paso to see if we might resuscitate what had once sparked between us. I needed a fantasy to hold on to, and mine was her opening the door to her parents' house, her face alight when she saw the bouquet of roses in my hand and realized why I'd come. The image was as unrealistic as it was romantic, but it effectively carried me off to sleep.

I was in the early fog of a dream when a deafening

explosion shook me out of sleep. It rumbled through the ground, and the tower shuddered. A chunk of shrapnel whistled overhead. Another chunk of hot metal rattled off the galvanized cover and clattered down the ladder. I spilled out of the hammock, grabbed my M-16, and lay belly down atop the bunker.

Holman swung his feet onto the deck and shouted, "What the hell?"

Another explosion went off and tore up earth about fifty meters beyond the perimeter. A shock wave came up through the concrete. The tower shook again. The pea-shooter arsenal Charlie had at his disposal couldn't make the entire camp shake. Below in the Vietnamese compound, strikers shouted, "*Bac si! Bac si!*" —their word for "doctor." We'd heard the whistle bang before when artillery from the marine battery at Camp Starlite tore up the mountains to the north.

I said the only thing it was possible to surmise. "One-five-fives. One hit the camp."

An exploding 155 had a potential kill radius of fifty yards and could demolish any bunker we had in camp, and one round had already done so. I laced my boots—two wraps around the top, tied off—and hit the ladder, heading to my station. I quickly figured out what had happened or at least the varied scenarios—some gunner had failed to level a bubble on the sight or mischarted coordinates or smoked too much dope. The big guns, intended to fire harassment and interdiction at Charlie, were hitting us instead. I bumped into Norwood as we rounded a turn in the trench.

"One-five-fives," he said.

"Right."

Whether in a bunker, the trench, or a mortar pit, all of us found cover underground. Cam radioed for a cease-fire. Before the message, relayed up and back through channels, reached the marines, the battery dropped another package outside the camp near the riverbank. We heard the distinct whizbang. A few minutes later Cam shouted to Captain Horan, in a trench somewhere nearby my pit, that the officer in charge at the battery claimed the shelling wasn't coming from marines.

Following a brief lull another round whistled up the valley and passed over the camp. It struck somewhere near the village or the airstrip, close enough to keep us pinned under cover. Captain Horan shouted for Cam to somehow get on the horn directly to the battery.

Three or four minutes passed before Cam reported the battery had shut down the guns. We waited another few seconds, in case, then we converged in the trench outside the team house. A few Vietnamese braved the barrage and carried their wounded to the gate to our compound where they shouted for help.

Norwood rushed to the med bunker and returned packing a medical bag. Gritz trailed him, and along the way they recruited me to help. Norwood handed over the bag and told me to stand by in the team house. That said, he left to get stretchers. Cam, several steps ahead of Horan or Holman, called to the C-Team and requested medevacs.

Norwood, Gritz, and some strikers carried in the casualties, five in all. Two, including one with a bleeding head wound, required only bandaging. The less fortunate three needed surgery as soon as possible. They lay on stretchers on the floor of the team house; no other place provided enough light and space for our medics to work on them. I waited for instructions. The captain and Holman hovered in the background shadows. Cam reported to the captain that dust-offs were en route for the wounded. Accompanying this news was a second message from the marine battery denying that their artillery hit the camp.

Captain Horan said, "Tell them we've got five wounded Vietnamese who say otherwise."

Another kind of patching remained to be done. Americans were responsible. Someone had to explain the unexplainable and somehow fix the unfixable. The captain and Henry headed to the Vietnamese command center. Norwood and Gritz set to work. Gritz administered to one, using scissors to cut away the victim's uniform. Norwood started an iv feed on one who was in shock, then turned his attention to the third, that one writhing in pain.

Norwood asked me to hold the struggling man down. He tapped the feed line until the tube dripped saline. The next one was also in shock. He'd taken a pie-slice piece of shrapnel in his buttocks. Norwood hooked up a drip line, handed it over, and told me to give the patient an iv. I kneeled, took his arm, and tied off his reedy biceps. His buttocks were shredded, his hip rendered to bone and gristle, his arterial flow all but shut down. I couldn't find a vein. He moaned and twisted his head back and forth. Norwood glanced up and told me to tap his arm a few times. I flicked the vein with a finger until enough of it showed to give me a target.

"He's in pain," I said.

Norwood passed a morphine syrette, then another. Told me, "Inject it in the feed line."

Norwood left him in my care and moved on to the next casualty, whose leg was shattered above the knee. He fixed a drip line, administered fluids, and said, "I have to amputate the leg." A statement aimed at no one in particular. He introduced an anesthetic into the tube, then pulled out a scalpel and surgical saw from his aid kit.

Others sat or stood around the room, talking, smoking. My patient's eyes fluttered. He moved his fingers and moaned, then lifted his hand to me. His fingers tightened feebly around mine. His hand was cold. "*Sau lam*," he said just above whisper. Not good.

I gave him another dose of morphine and continued holding

his hand. Nearby, Norwood prepped for surgery. There was no time for niceties. He slipped on gloves, poured alcohol on the site of the wound, and went to work with a scalpel. He clamped off arteries, took a saw in hand, and performed the amputation as if he'd done a dozen. The sound of the saw shaving through bone silenced the room. Afterward, he wrapped the limb in gauze, placed it in a plastic bag, and handed it off to someone to dispose of it. He covered the bloodied stump and moved onto those whose wounds were less serious. He bandaged injuries and administered morphine.

My man's chest rose convulsively, and his eyes opened. He looked up as if to ask what was next. At least that was the question I imagined in his eyes. His hand went limp, but I held it a bit longer, in case.

The helicopter took the wounded to Quang Ngai. Norwood, Gritz, and I returned to the team house. Holman sat at the table, telling his audience how some shrapnel nearly wiped him out. I said it careened off a stud and hit the stairs.

He glared at me and said, "You weren't there. How would you know?"

I said, "I *was* there. My hammock's still up there." It was strung up between the four-by-fours as proof.

"Are you calling me a liar?"

I looked at him, then at the bloodstain on the floor where my patient had died. "Doesn't matter." But it did matter.

And it mattered to the captain as well. He said no one was to sleep outside the bunkers from now on, no exceptions. I went to my bunker, collapsed on the cot, pulled the mosquito net closed. I took in a lungful of air. Despite the mildew, all I smelled was the metallic odor human blood emits. A few minutes later Norwood stuck his head in and asked if he could bunk there for the night. He'd been sleeping on a stretcher in the medical bunker, and now there were none.

"Sure."

It seemed unnecessary to tell him what a good job he'd done, and we were too tired for talk. I thought it odd that as the ranks had dwindled of us who'd come over together, he and I, the youngest two, remained. We'd been through a lot, but I knew little about him, none of his history. Then, too, none of us spoke of that other life, of the history that had shaped us. I knew only that he was more than competent and more than just dependable and had guts. And soon he'd likely be gone, and I'd never get to know him other than as a teammate.

The artillery incident triggered a pissing match, marines denying fault, Special Forces command insisting that marine artillery had caused the calamity. In the morning the marines shuttled in an officer by helicopter, his job to determine if the damage in camp was caused by 155s. After an initial look at the camp, Captain Horan drove the visitor into the village, taking Norwood and Gritz along in case there had been any civilian casualties. Damage was minimal, no humans hit, but one farmer's water buffalo took a piece of shrapnel in the dense wattle hanging from his throat.

Captain Horan told Gritz and Norwood to treat the animal. The medics looked at the big beast, penned and frightened and in no mood to welcome strangers. Boys who herded them could control them, but the buffalo, one step removed from the wild, stood four feet at the shoulder, weighed more than a thousand pounds, and were nearsighted, unpredictable, and dumb. Norwood and Gritz knew this. And this one was wounded.

They said it wouldn't be wise to go into the pen. The captain, more insistent the second time, told them to give it a try, that he could make it an order.

Gritzmacher had no qualms about saying, "In that case, sir, I'd have to refuse."

"Sergeant Norwood?" the captain said.

Norwood shook his head. "Not me, sir."

Captain Horan was faced with two young soldiers as stubborn as a buffalo. It must have been embarrassing for him, and at the same time, he must have realized ordering them into the stall could stir up problems later. He reluctantly dropped the matter.

The captain and his visitor returned and walked to the site of the ruined bunker and surveyed the damage. As the marine circled the crater, a Vietnamese soldier casually strolled up and extended the leg Norwood had amputated as an offering of sorts. It was in the bloody gauze Norwood had used to cover it before discarding it. The officer stood, mouth agape, and stared at the bloody package. Nothing in the military manuals had prepared him for this.

Two days later Gritzmacher flew by helicopter to the Vietnamese hospital in Quang Ngai to check on the wounded strikers. He returned with news that Norwood's patient had died in the hospital in Quang Ngai. The rest lived. How, he couldn't quite fathom, because "the smell of gangrene was everywhere."

FORTY-SIX

In mid-August I went on R & R to Singapore. Seven days. I picked the island because I'd read Kipling and Conrad in high school, and because Singapore had been a port for clipper ships. In my youth I'd imagined nothing could be more romantic than bringing spice from the Orient on a tall ship. And there were historical landmarks from the colonial era—the Raffles Hotel, where British aristocracy slept. Tiger Balm gardens. The House of Jade. I rode a rickshaw through streets that smelled of the Orient I'd read about. Commerce everywhere. Dead chickens and pigs' heads hung from hooks on vendors' carts. Women bartered for mangoes and plums. I checked into the 7 Story Hotel, fully intending to drop off my gear and walk the teeming streets.

Unlike the hero in Erich Maria Remarque's *All Quiet on the Western Front*, I was not returning home to see some ironic interpretation of the war I was fighting. I wasn't even allowed to visit American soil. I was one American, isolated from anyone I knew and left to my own thoughts, which mostly centered on food and rest. I sat down on the bed, smelled the clean sheets, and decided first to shower. Water steamed out. My first hot shower in six months. The scabs on my legs broke open, and the leech bites bled as if fresh wounds. By then I was used to it. The luxury of hot water made a smattering of blood all the more piddling. I toweled off, brushed my teeth, and pulled back the bedcover to test the sheets. Twelve hours later a shaft of sunlight in the window woke me.

After breakfast I went out to see the sights. The streets of Singapore were so narrow they barely accommodated the flood of foot traffic. I hired a rickshaw, pedaled by a man older probably than my father, and paid him for a full day. He asked what I wanted to see. I told him the few things I'd decided on, then asked what else was interesting. He drove me to a café, where I ate a huge lunch and he waited for me. After we plowed through the usual places visitors were interested in seeing, he asked if I'd ever had my fortune read, seemed sincerely interested in my having it done. I said I wasn't interested in knowing what might lie ahead and that I didn't believe in fortune-telling.

Near the end of the day, I saw a snake charmer play his recorder in front of a basket. The rickshaw driver asked if I wanted to see the snake. For two dollars I got to watch a cobra emerge and spread its hood. It seemed to have no interest in the charmer or me or my driver. It tasted the air with its tongue and bobbed its head back and forth, and when the music ended, it sank into its coils and the charmer closed the lid. The driver asked if I found the snake frightening. Only in the dark. Only in the wild.

The next to the last day in Singapore my driver took me to the fortune-teller, an elderly Chinese man who held my open palm and studied it with the intensity of an astronomer studying a distant galaxy. He held and traced the lines with a long fingernail for several minutes, nodding, grunting, then told me I would live to be a hundred and have many sons. I gave him five Singapore dollars for his comforting lie.

Over the week I saw all I'd come for. I ate slow meals in restaurants. I showered until my skin wrinkled. I slept on a clean, dry bed. Slept and slept. Wherever I went, I had the sense that I didn't belong there, that I was seeing someone else pretending to be me. And then I took a plane back to where I belonged. When the airplane returning me turned northeast, I watched the island coastline disappear, then tilted my seat back and slept.

When I returned to camp, Norwood and Cam Gamble said they were transferring to A-100, the newly designated MIKE Force team in Da Nang, Luthy's current team. Luthy had recommended Norwood especially and Norwood had filled out a formal request, but Horan resisted approving transfers and refused Norwood outright, perhaps out of vindication or indecision or because too many transfers over a short period might make him look bad. Nonetheless, Norwood had packed his gear and indicated he was intent on leaving.

Norwood may have been prepared to leave for a new assignment, but the captain had other plans for him—another venture up the valley to the Binh Hoa area. Norwood would lead the operation and go it alone—no other round-eye. It was an unprecedented command decision and highly suspect. Even worse, Norwood would be assaulting a vc stronghold with four squads of Vietnamese strikers. Whatever the captain's motivation, the operation was another in a string of blunders he'd made.

Though he realized the risk he would be taking, Norwood said, "Fine, I'll go again, but when it's over I want my transfer signed." He wanted out. He'd had it with being asked to perform surgery on water buffalo and sent out on harebrained operations. Horan agreed. The question in Norwood's mind was whether the captain would honor his word.

The patrol left at midnight and crossed the north side of the Song Tra Bong about a kilometer east of the camp, Norwood the lone American with a platoon, some of whom were recent replacements and had no combat experience. Norwood was left with no Vietnamese Special Forces counterpart to lead the patrol. The striker in charge was a young sergeant, and when the men balked at entering the river, he turned to Norwood to prod them across. They were unusually noisy in crossing it and seemed intent on subverting the operation. Compounding the problem was the interpreter, who was too scared himself to cross. Finally, after Norwood nudged man after man into the water, they breached the river.

They gathered on the north bank and set up a defensive perimeter. The leery strikers imagined enemy lurking in every shadow. "Beaucoup vc," they said, an old saw to Norwood. Concerned that one of them might fire a weapon and compromise the patrol, he calmed them as best he could, assuring them there were no Vietcong near the bank. Before dawn they advanced on roughly the same path Mr. Whitten and I had used months before.

Taking advantage of the last bit of darkness for cover, .

Norwood ordered the strikers to recross the river and form up for an assault on the village. Again the strikers made considerable noise. Still, they reached the south bank about a half kilometer from the village edge. Norwood directed them to spread out in a line to assault.

As soon as the patrol neared the rice paddy, it received small-arms fire from snipers on the hillside south of Binh Hoa. The strikers set up a machine gun behind the berm and returned fire. The sniper retreated. It was clear the operation was already a failure; nonetheless, Norwood ordered the CIDG to advance. As they approached the edge of Binh Hoa, the strikers took more small-arms fire from the rubble of what was once a Buddhist shrine. The Vietnamese returned fire as they usually did, from behind cover, lifting weapons overhead and firing blindly. The VC, fortunately, had little more gumption than the strikers and retreated—a ploy.

Norwood led the patrol over the dike and into the village. The strikers moved hooch to hooch, searching for VC or weapons, villagers even. They found nothing but chickens and pigs. The animals scurried about underfoot. The patrol came out on the south side of the village near the road, and patrol again took enemy fire. The CIDG formed a skirmish line and returned fire as Norwood called in air support. The exchange of small-arms fire was ineffective on both sides and went on for fifteen minutes before air force jets arrived.

Norwood directed the planes to the target. He couldn't measure the results from where the patrol was positioned, but when the air strike ended, he sighted a scattering of VC in black as they retreated toward the far tree line. The patrol opened fire, but by then the enemy was too far away to do any damage.

Norwood, his patience exhausted, reported what happened to Horan, said that a deal was a deal, and that he was "outta here on the next chopper." He toted his already packed gear to the landing pad and flew out that afternoon. In addition to combat gear, he carried the unshakable belief that Captain Horan had intentionally sent him out to die on that last mission.

We got a replacement for the radio operator, when Cam left shortly before Norwood. Then after his months of interviewing villagers and VC and typing recommendations, J. V.'s worth to the camp came to an end. The SFOB ordered him transferred to a B-Team in III Corps. I was on a water run the day he left. As the helicopter circled, I waved along with the Vietnamese who were with me. I doubted that J. V. noticed. He was pretty hungover that morning.

I was left among newcomers and, with the exception of Brassfield and Gritz, a group of men whose names I didn't want to know. I was the last of team A7/03. I became cynical and even scornful of the newcomers. I rarely sat in their card games.

I'd landed in country naive and eager and, at a solid 185 pounds, fit. Now I weighed less than 170, my bowels were constantly inflamed, and I had fungus on my crotch and feet and cavities in my teeth. I was otherwise hard as flint, inside and out. I spent my days doing labor like a good inmate; evenings, I tossed Mr. Whitten's darts at a pockmarked dartboard that was now half cork, half holes. I played the random hand of pinochle or hearts, talked infrequently. Even if it were a team, which it never could be under Horan, I didn't feel I belonged.

The night J. V. left I sat as Jake once had, a Montagnard crossbow on my lap, cocked and ready with a bamboo bolt. The cards were on the table.

"What's with the crossbow?" someone asked.

"You'll see," I said to Mr. No Name.

I never announced it, but I'd come to believe I was charmed

and others were unlucky or potentially unlucky—and dangerous by virtue of being unlucky. My charm began at the C-Team when I didn't go to A Shau and gained strength the morning of January 22 when the god of Numbers and Probabilities thought he'd claimed me but the captain told me that Brownie was taking my place. Since then, I'd survived a half-dozen firefights without a scratch and the act of a scared kid who couldn't manage to pull a pin out of a grenade. Illogical, of course, but it made as much sense as most of what I'd witnessed.

Few in camp could keep up or move as silently in the brush as well, or endure the daytime heat or the cold and mosquitoes at night. I tackled the mountains as the Yards did, straight up the sides, half climb, half walk. When others seemed ready to quit, I motioned to the Yards to pick up the pace. I was convinced they and I could climb the mountains and go north across the DMZ into North Vietnam and on into China.

On two occasions I was a tour guide for green lieutenants assigned to headquarters in Nha Trang. They'd come to Tra Bong to earn Combat Infantry Badges. They came soft from their hard labor shuffling papers and carrying briefcases. As we geared up to go out, I looked at their pale faces, their sweating brows, and thought, Welcome to fucking Disneyland with risk. Come on, paleface. I'm your guide. Let's make tracks. You don't have to worry about paper cuts out here.

When one of the lieutenants faltered, I took his pack, gave him a scornful smile, hoisted his gear over my shoulder, and winked. At the end of each patrol I erased their faces from all memory. All I could recall was their nervous eagerness.

Someone told me to pick up my hand, but as I did I heard a rat crossing the rafters. I watched for its shadow. Usually they scurried so fast that I didn't have a prayer. This one took his sweet fucking time—tiptoe, tiptoe—and looked right at me. I raised the bow to my shoulder, leveled it, and pulled the primitive trigger. The rat ran halfway across the beam and fell, the bamboo shaft protruding from its neck at the base of its head. It was a winning shot, one every basketball player dreams of, traveling the length of the court and touching nothing but skirt at the other end.

"Lucky shot," Brassfield said.

I nodded.

It was one for Jake. I walked over and crushed its skull. Some Mr. No Name complained that it would spread disease. Disease? What fucking country did he think he was in? Vietnam is a disease.

"Someone play my hand," I said and left.

FORTY-SEVEN

I adjusted the radio to the assigned frequency, lifted it on the Yard's shoulders, and nodded to him. He smiled. They often smiled before a patrol, but their faces turned severe as soon as the gate was thrown open. By then I'd lost count of the patrols I'd been on with them. More than a dozen but fewer than twenty. Today Cu was staying behind, which bode poorly for us, considering this would be Holman's first walk in the mountains. Why he chose to go with me and why west into the higher ranges were mysteries.

He was loaded up for war: thirty pounds of ammunition, rifle, two canteens, a backpack with more food than he needed, poncho, poncho liner, rope hammock. After crossing the river, his wet boots would add a pound to his load, his wet trousers another. By midmorning when we reached the steepest inclines, his load would feel as if it had increased another ten pounds. Leeches and other parasites awaited him. He would sweat off a pound halfway up the hill, two pounds before noon, and when he sat to eat, he wouldn't have an appetite. By midafternoon the patrol would have crossed two streams where he could refill his canteen. These things I knew. I also knew that if we made contact with Charlie and had to *di di mau* into the brush, Holman was in deep shit, unless he shed half of what he was toting.

His features barely distinguishable in the predawn, he motioned Seymore over and said it was time to hit it. He postured as if the cameras were rolling. The gate opened. We marched out with a squad of strikers, three of them and Seymore between us. We'd had no rain for a few days. The ground was hard, and the squad, the best of the Recon Platoon, treaded lightly over it. We waded into the river, our backs covered for the next two kilometers by a teammate manning the mortar.

The climb taxed Holman pretty much as I'd expected. He made a lot of racket but kept up. I credited that to stubbornness. An hour and a half later the patrol broke out of the foothills. The canopy remained thick overhead, but the ground cover thinned. Our first objective was Hill 1152 north of Suoi Tra Co. We were on reconnaissance, looking for signs of infiltrators in the valley due west. Two days and back, unless we happened upon a vc unit, in which case we'd call for an air strike.

Holman halted the patrol. He said that we'd made good progress and were ahead of schedule. He took a drink, wiped sweat from his face, and spread open his map.

I looked to the east at the terrain we'd crossed, saw landmarks—the southern edge of Tra Bong and the village of Tra Bac. "We're still about two hours from our checkpoint," I said.

He waved me off, pulled out a compass, and studied the landscape to the west.

"I can see Tra Bong."

"I don't need you telling me how to read a map." He jotted down numbers on the acetate with a grease pencil, called for the radio, and reported that we'd reached our first objective, which lay two kilometers to the west. When he signed off the radio, I told him he was wrong. He didn't say a word, but his eyes said, "Insubordinate."

He looked at Seymore and said, "Tell 'em to move out."

He pointed to the west, which would take us down to low ground again; going due west would put us south of Hill 1152. I suggested skirting the ridgeline and taking a route through the forest. Holman chose due west. The patrol proceeded in that direction and soon encountered a steep downslope. We could no longer see the peaks. Without mountains as landmarks, we had to rely on the compass. An hour, then another, passed before we reached the next incline and encountered a stretch of elephant grass. In the open now, we could see the peaks again and orient ourselves. Holman halted the patrol and asked if there was a way to the left around the tall grass. If we veered off to avoid the field of grass, we would end up in the foothills and be forced to climb up again.

"We'll just have to go back up," I said.

He studied it a moment. "It'll provide cover for the patrol."

I knew what awaited if we entered. The blades sliced fine cuts in any exposed skin. Sweat burned in the cuts like acid. If Cu were along, he'd refuse to go in.

"Top," I said, "anyone on the ridge will see movement in the grass."

"We'll go straight," he said and charged in.

He soon slowed, then stopped every ten or twelve paces for a drink or to shift the load on his back. He looked up at the peak to our right, the one we would have breached had he listened and skirted the ridge. It took a painful hour to traverse the elephant grass and reach the trees on the other side, where the point man motioned to a ravine leading to the top. We paused to assess options. The ravine to the top was the shortest route up but risky. Either side was thick with undergrowth and boulders ideal for concealing an ambush, and below its apex the squad would face a climb of more than fifty feet up a steep wall of rock.

The tromp through the grass, the load he bore, and his weight had taken a toll. "Is there a better way up?"

"The Yards know what they're doing. They've done this before."

Next time, I thought, he'd listen. I led out, two behind the point man, who headed straight into the underbrush and up the side of the slope. The climb was steep, as difficult as I'd ever encountered. Here and there, Holman slipped on loose dirt. I reached back, smiled, and gave him a hand a couple of times, said that he'd get used to it. He didn't smile. He was having a hard-enough time just breathing. When we breached the top, he collapsed, shed his web gear, and gulped water from his canteen. After a rest, he called for the radio, took out map and compass, and again called in the wrong coordinates.

Even if he realized he was wrong, he had to call in the wrong location, because now we *were* on an outcropping near the top of Hill 1152. The Vietnamese squad leader also called in our location. I hoped if we needed air support that someone in camp would catch the discrepancy. Below us clouds that seemed spun from silk flowed over the emerald valley. I sat back, took a sip, and weighed my options.

We crossed a stream just before dark, filled our canteens, and set up for the night on a densely wooded slope about a hundred feet below a mountain peak. After I checked perimeter security, I spread my poncho and sat on it. Holman asked how I thought it went. Knowing he wanted affirmation, I looked for something positive in it all. We'd seen no signs of Charlie and hadn't been ambushed. I used those two affirmatives as benchmarks and said, "Fine."

I didn't ask how the hell he earned three chevrons and three rockers without knowing how to read a map. Nor did I tell him what he needed to hear — that so far we'd been lucky and that Charlie cut blundering fools like him no slack. I ate a rice ball and watched the jungle go dark.

The next day was uneventful until just before noon, when the patrol crossed a tributary to the Song Tra Bong. Beside a trail that intersected the stream, the Yards found sandal prints. Could have been Montagnard. Could have been vc. We checked the area further and turned up some dead coals. A few feet into the thicket a Yard uncovered a shallow hole in the side of a cut bank, then another. Charlie had holed up here but not recently. Still, this was a route he used. I marked the coordinates on my map. I pointed them out and said that we hadn't gone far enough west the previous day and were closer to camp than he thought.

"You got a crystal ball?" he said.

I shook my head.

"We're headed back. We saw what we needed to. I'm cuttin' the patrol off so we can call in an air strike."

Now he wanted to blow up empty holes. Uncle Sam wasted a million a day dropping bombs all over the country, much of them landing where Charlie wasn't. What the hell, I thought, back a day early, a cooked meal, a full night's sleep.

"We'll follow the stream down."

The stream ran down to the valley and merged with the Song Tra Bong somewhere west of the Montagnard village where we drew water. To the right the ground was covered with brush. On the left even thicker vegetation banked upward sharply into a ridge. If we were hit from that side, we couldn't possibly break through the ambush.

"I'd go that way," I said, pointing to the east, "below the ridgeline."

"We'll go this way."

We followed the stream. Holman stepped out and trudged across a stretch of dead leaves and twigs, making no effort to avoid them. I waited and followed several paces behind, keeping Seymore and the squad leader between Holman and me. Two Yards brought up the rear.

About a mile downstream I heard a clicking sound in the brush to the rear. I looked at the Yards trailing. They too had stopped. I paused and listened but heard nothing. We couldn't be certain of what we'd heard, but I didn't want to take a chance on getting hit from behind. I jogged forward and told Seymore to have the squad leader hold up the squad. Seymore nodded. The two trailing strikers came up. I motioned them to follow. The ground was loose; I used branches to pull myself up into the undergrowth. I climbed a rock-strewn ledge from where I could see down over the stream. I looked up at the treetops, listened.

When I looked back where the water flowed, I realized that I was alone. The strikers hadn't followed. I couldn't see or hear the patrol, not even Holman's size 11s crunching twigs underfoot. I'd acted impulsively. Or perhaps I'd done it subconsciously. Either way, I'd used poor judgment. I knew better. I should have insisted Seymore repeat what I'd told him. I should have grabbed the last striker by his harness straps and dragged him along. Mostly, I never should have assumed Holman would see that I was missing from the column.

Surely, Seymore would inform Holman if not the squad leader. Someone had to notice I wasn't in the column. I wasn't about to follow the stream down to catch up. I'd been foolhardy enough for one day. I assumed Charlie was nearby. Thinking in any other terms was stupid. The undergrowth on the ledge was thick and would provide concealment. I crawled under a blind and waited for the patrol to circle back. The wait turned into minutes. Then a half hour. I stayed put.

Something moved in the vegetation beside the ledge. I watched warily. A moment passed, then a snake slithered through some brush just below me. I had no idea what kind it was. I saw only its tail. That was enough to make the rest of my time in the bushes uncomfortable.

An hour clicked off, and I began feeling relieved to be on my own. I decided to wait another hour or so before heading toward Tra Bong. I figured to go due east across the foothills, where concealment was best. A few minutes later I buried those plans. Small-arms fire came from downstream more. I estimated the sound came from a kilometer away, a single shot. That was followed a few seconds later by two shots, then another. Holman was trying to guide me to them — good intention, bad idea. If Charlie had missed us before, he knew where the patrol was now. A suppressed contempt festered up in me, but there was nothing I could do about Holman or his bad decision. Garbage thinking balls up the brain; the situation is always clear if the head remains clear, a sergeant in Branch Training had said. I needed a clear head.

I'd created my circumstances and took the blame for it, but going downstream to meet up with the patrol was the worst-possible choice. The best course the patrol could take now was to head straight to camp. My best choice was to take any other route. I knew the tenets of escape and evasion. Avoid open and populated areas, follow no trails, conserve food, stay in the brush, and move at night whenever possible.

No doubt I'd been reported as missing. That was sure to draw Captain Horan's ire. Someone would send up a spotter plane to search for me, perhaps more than one, and draw Charlie's curiosity. I crawled to the top of the embankment, lay down, and studied the terrain. To the east lay successive humps of foothills that led to the far ridge. I recalled a small stream there. Barely a trickle, it ran south down a narrow ravine and fed into the Song Tra Bong. If I crossed the foothills to the ridge, I could descend from that point and reach camp before dark. I headed in that direction.

I hadn't yet reached the ridge when a plane flew over and circled the area I'd left. I listened to the hum of its engine but stayed out of sight in the undergrowth. I progressed quietly and steadily and reached the stream by midafternoon. A second search plane came up the valley, and the first one left. This pilot widened his search to an area due west of me as I navigated the steep ravine; by then it was dusk, and the second plane flew off.

I found a thicket on a bank above the stream and scarfed down crackers and a rice ball. Then I curled up, my weapon at the ready, and waited out the night.

I reached the Montagnard village west of Tra Bong by early morning. As I passed though Tra Bong, the villagers stopped whatever they were doing and watched. In camp I told what had happened and took full responsibility for it. No one could fault my explanation. I avoided saying anything that reflected on Holman's competence — or lack of it. As expected, Captain Horan was upset.

"The MIKE Force was on alert to fly in and search for you."

What I saw was his concern that a missing man might reflect badly on him . . . and Holman. Their careers. I saw no point in speaking up. Holman asked why I hadn't tossed a smoke grenade to alert the planes of my location.

"Guess I was at least that smart," I said.

He looked at the captain. Neither of them liked my answer, but it was the only one I had.

As I was playing chess with Brassfield that evening, he leaned over the board and asked me what really happened out there, said that he knew me well enough to know my separation from the patrol wasn't a mistake.

"There are mistakes," I said. "And there are mistakes."

He nodded and studied the pieces.

FORTY-EIGHT

Every combat soldier has his last patrol. For some, as in the case of my teammates in January, a last patrol meant a last heartbeat. My patrol came weeks after that initial walk with Holman. It was late October. In three weeks I'd be pulled out of camp to begin the discharge process unless I opted to re-up, an unlikely option given the leadership I'd served under since Captain Gregory had left. Still, short-timer or not, a soldier's duty was to obey orders up to the time of his discharge. The captain said Gritz would be going along and that Holman would lead the patrol. I stiffened at hearing this. Words such as *concern* and *anger* didn't adequately describe my feelings at hearing it. *Disgust* came closest. I didn't protest, just nodded and said, "Yes, sir." I'd kept a clean slate and wanted a smooth landing into civilian life.

So the morning of my final walk, another that began long before sunrise, I loaded my ammo pouches, put on my web gear, and stood ready in the ranks of my Yards. Holman was his usual blustery self as he readied to go. Recently, he'd made some effort to be friendly, mostly directed at enticing me to reenlist. He'd talked about my value to the team, bonus money Uncle Sam would put up, and hinted that a promotion to staff sergeant awaited me. He'd dangled an award, said he was recommending me for a Bronze Star. I thanked him but wondered what for. For being here? For humping mountains? For building a concrete bunker with a tower? He wanted me to "think seriously about re-upping."

Reenlisting was the last thing on my mind as I slammed a loaded magazine in my M-16 and snugged another grenade on my straps. I was seasoned enough that I'd given up any ideas that I or even an army of men like me could avenge Jake's, Brownie's, and Captain Fewell's deaths, but this one last crack at taking out a few VC had some appeal. I thought, what the hell. At worst we'd make contact, and at best we'd see some virgin jungle from atop a high peak or two. I kept my thoughts and reservations private and lined up. The Combat Recon Platoon was still my responsibility, and I was obligated to see them safely through this walk, them, Gritz, and my soon-to-be civilian self. If Holman blundered, I had to fix it. If he got himself killed, I'd send him and his dog tags home in a zip-up coffin.

Though he wouldn't be going, Trung Sí Cu was at the gate as we formed to leave. He helped me check the Yards' weapons. Finished, he gave me a thumbs-up.

I said, "Cam on, Ong," meaning, "Thank you."

Something in the way he lingered told me he wanted to go out with us. Perhaps because he too was leery of Holman's competence? Old Cu was wise.

"Can than," he said and repeated it. "Be careful." Twice.

Then we were out of the gate and across the river, as always in dark.

The patrol started no differently than the last. Holman struggled. I followed close at his insistence because he didn't want us to "separate again." I watched him bull his way through the scrub, and after catching a few whiplashes from branches, I backed up and let a striker trail him. The Yard was displeased with the move, but he was short enough to duck under the branches.

Even as my guts rumbled, I held my tongue as we climbed

higher into the rain forest. It played on my mind that I'd been remiss. I should have requested a trip to the C-Team, gone over the captain's head, and told the sergeant major about the degeneration of morale at Tra Bong and the cause. But I hadn't, mostly because I'd seen enough to understand the futility of speaking out.

Soon after reaching the top we crossed a well-worn trail and descended a few meters below a ridge. We moved slowly, skirting the ridgeline. The going was rough in the thick brush and loose soil, but it was safer traveling. Holman halted the patrol and ordered us to the top. I complained that it wasn't a good idea. He said he thought we were moving too slowly. When we reached the top again, we followed a trail along the ridge. The Yards' normally stoic faces filled with apprehension as we crossed over the peak. Seymore asked if the Trung Sí was *diên cà dàu*. Gritz and I exchanged glances.

I had to speak up. "Top, it might be better if we don't use the trail."

"Are you in charge?"

"No."

"And I know what I'm doing. Less noise."

Less noise from you, I thought, and again kept my tongue.

We continued on the path down and up the next peak. We stopped twice for com checks. We followed more trails into the early afternoon, moving in and out of the shadows of the trees, moving at a fast pace while disregarding caution. It seemed Holman was trying to impress someone with our progress from check-in point to check-in point, a fact not lost on the Yards. Nor was it lost on them that Charlie could be lying in shadows beside any of the trails. It appeared as if Holman was doing his best to get us killed in the shortest time possible.

I told Gritz to stick close. "If we're hit, we charge in. You with me?"

"Right."

When Holman called for the next break, I told him we had to slow down.

"Settin' too hard a pace for you?"

"We won't see much moving this fast."

He glared at me and then drank from his canteen and studied his map. I picked off a couple of leeches and sprayed repellent on my boot tops. We had a day and a half to go. I didn't expect to see the end of it.

When we saddled up to go, he said, "Remember who makes the decisions."

I nodded. The day had heated up, but something like a cold fist gripped my chest. I tried but couldn't shed the thought that out of stubbornness and pride, Holman was going to get us all killed. I thought that in case we were hit because of Holman's blundering and Charlie missed shooting him, I just might.

As the afternoon wore on, I further distorted matters and strangely came to hope we would get ambushed. But we didn't. Luck.

Near dusk we left the trail for a time and came out of the undergrowth into a clearing on the mountainside where the brush had been burned and hacked out by Montagnard for planting rice. The area, surrounded on four sides by jungle, was no place to set down for the night. Holman, however, had his own opinion on that. He said it would provide good fields of fire.

"We'll lay up here for the night."

I mentioned that the trees would provide an easy approach and good cover for vc.

He looked around. "We'll set out guards." As if giving it some thought, he pointed uphill and said to the interpreter, "Tell them to secure the perimeter."

The strikers spread out in a circle. We made a final com check, ate a couple of rice balls, and then Holman said one of us should take first watch, that he'd take third. He bedded down by some rocks. At least he had sense enough to grab the safest spot for himself. Gritz and I bedded down some fifteen yards away on higher ground. Using bayonets, we hacked out shallow holes and ringed them with some rocks.

The jungle and its sounds took over. Soon after, Holman began snoring. Probably for the first time ever while on patrol I lay staring up at the stars as I weighed our situation, our vulnerability to attack. We should have bedded down in the wood line. That was where Luthy and Hunter and Malone would have holed up for the night. That's what Norwood and I would have chosen. That's where Jockims would have insisted we wait out the dark. That's probably where Charlie's set up.

The Yards stirred about, shifting positions and tightening their circle. Holman's snoring stopped for a time, then started up again and went on intermittently. I kept thinking that Holman was as big a liability asleep as he was awake. Finally, I went down and shook his shoulder. He awoke instantly and brought the barrel of his rifle up.

"It's me, Top."

"What? What's goin' on? Is it my watch already?"

"No. You were snoring."

"No, I wasn't. Go on back. I'm gettin' some sleep."

Soon enough, the snoring began. When I could take it no longer, I rolled over and faced Gritz. "You awake?" I whispered.

"Yeah."

"You hear that?"

"For the last hour."

I couldn't be certain what I'd do if he agreed to it, but the notion had been playing out in the back of my mind for hours. I said, "I'm thinking I should roll a hand grenade down there. He's going to get us killed."

He looked in Holman's direction as if considering it.

Though I wasn't sure to what degree I meant it, I decided to push it. "We could blame it on the vc," I said. "Who would know?"

"You serious?"

"Yeah." And suddenly I was.

"That's crazy."

Crazy? Perhaps. Maybe I'd lost sight of reality, lost all sense of perspective. Or perhaps this was the reality of the moment. Under the circumstances our fragging Holman began to seem justified. "Come on, think about it."

He thought a moment as if seriously considering it, then said, "No. We can't."

"You're sure?"

"Yeah. It wouldn't be right. I can't."

I nodded.

But who *would* know? Gritz didn't have to say it. I figured it out on my own. That question had an easy answer, and it brought me back into reality, the other reality that measures morality and responsibility. We would have known, and it would have haunted us for as long as we lived. For a while longer I looked up at the stars, pondering how far I'd come from everything I'd once been. Had I lost my moral compass? If I had, Gritz gave it back to me.

We completed the patrol without incident and a day later returned to camp with nothing to report. But it wasn't over between Holman and me.

Shortly after my last patrol, Holman cornered me and pointed to the elephant grass I'd defoliated on the river side of the camp. "That dead grass over there, burn it. This is still the military, and our camp should look like one. That looks like shit."

Nuts, I thought. What would be the point? The grass

would grow back after the first good rain. Charlie could use the cover to crawl to the wire and breach it with a bangalore.

"That's not a good idea."

"I want it done. Get to it right away."

"Top, if you burn it out, it'll just regrow next time it rains. The flat layer of dead grass keeps it from doing that."

He stared at it a moment. "Yeah."

"Yeah. It'll grow high enough to conceal a company of VC."

"I don't care," he said. "It looks like shit."

"It runs up into the minefield. A fire could set off the mines."

He locked eyes with me. "I'm telling you to do it."

I considered it a moment. Sometime later someone else would have to defoliate it again. That same someone might have to replant the minefield. I owed it to him to refuse. I owed it to myself as well. The contempt I'd sheathed for months rose up and took hold of me. I squared up with him and said, "I won't."

"You're refusing an order."

"I guess."

He outweighed me by forty pounds and was used to intimidating others with his size. I didn't care. I'd confronted enough bullies when I was kid moving around to know they'll back down if they can't intimidate you. Besides, I was confident I could take him. I was prepared to face any consequences. I matched his glare with my own. "If you want a piece of me, come on."

We faced off in silence for perhaps another two seconds. His eyes shifted away. He wasn't going to make a move. Finally, he turned away. I figured he'd use his rank in some manner to get revenge, most likely recommend an Article 15. I was prepared for that. I'd soldiered here for nearly a year and had done whatever was asked of me. What I'd accomplished wasn't much, but I'd done my duty and a hundred Holmans couldn't take that away.

I didn't burn the dead grass, and it was never again mentioned. My days in camp were shortened by three. They wanted me gone. I wanted me gone. The camp belonged to new guys now. I hoped that they would somehow become a team and survive Holman and Horan.

In the evening when Captain Horan cornered me and told me to pack and be ready to leave on the next chopper out, I felt saddened. This wasn't how I wanted to end my tour at Tra Bong or in Vietnam. I'd expected more, maybe a little appreciation. I'd volunteered and followed my conscience to come so that I could earn a full right to say I served and fought with the best men in the military. In the end, I'd lost more than teammates.

FORTY-NINE

I packed the last of my gear in my duffel bag, looked around the bunker to see if I was forgetting anything. I took a whiff of the mold for the last time, gathered up my gear, and, rifle in hand, walked through the trench. No one came out of the team house to bid me good-bye. The sun was low and to my back. I followed my shadow down the road to the gate from which my dead teammates had marched more than ten months before. A smattering of strikers stood outside their bunkers and tracked my progress. The guard unlocked the chain and spread open the gate.

The day would come when I'd realize the many things I was leaving behind and the many things I forgot. My youth. My friends. I couldn't know it at the time; it was the last thing on my mind as I walked to the helipad. Now, I wanted to be as good a civilian as I had been a soldier. No, better.

I had to be better for Brownie, who had filled a grave that easily could have been mine. For him and for my friend Jake. Norwood and Pablo would understand that, but they were gone, and so was I.

One day I would come to wish I'd recorded every detail. I would realize also what had nipped at my tail for so long had been a longing to be in a place I'd never seen and have a life I'd never experienced, one of promise. Owing to fate and Brownie and Captain Fewell's decisions, I had that possibility.

The helicopter sent to ferry me away chugged up the center of the valley, taking its time, like a dutiful tugboat. I carried my own smoke canister, anchored by its handle to a shirt pocket of my fatigues. The craft was several minutes away. I stood at the helipad where Norwood and I had lifted Jake's body for his flight home, just yesterday, it seemed. I set the smoke grenade atop my gear and waited.

Then I caught sight of Trung Sí Cu, a lone figure leaving the Vietnamese compound. I couldn't miss his unmistakable stride. He was unarmed, a rarity, not even a holstered .45 on his hip. He waved. I waved back, pulled the pin on the smoke grenade, and tossed it.

He arrived as the helicopter neared its final approach. He offered a hand for me to shake. His was small in mine, but the grip was surprisingly firm. He pumped my arm vigorously. Every one of his gold crowns showed as his hand dropped to his side. In his other hand he held a folded cloth. He extended it and let the cloth unfurl. I glanced at the flagpole above the Vietnamese compound. It was bare. He placed the flag in my hand and cupped his hand over mine.

"*Chau Ong*, Trung Sí Barnes."

Good-bye, Sergeant Barnes. He'd never before spoken my name, had never even attempted it. I was amazed he knew it at all. He'd led at least half the patrols and operations I went on. Now he'd said my name and given me their flag to take home. I felt a knot grow in my throat.

"*Chau Ong*, Trung Sí Cu. *Cam on*," I said.

Had I known Vietnamese better, I would have wished him good luck. I was going, and he was staying to continue the fight, lost though it was. Of course, neither of us knew this as we stood waiting for the helicopter. He said something else, but the engine of the chopper drowned out his words. He saluted. I did likewise. He turned and left. I would never know what fate befell him but would always recall him as a good soldier, as I wished to be remembered by him.

The crew chief helped with my duffel bag and gave me a hand up. I snapped the seat belt as the chief signaled the pilot with a thumbs-up. Standing on bunkers were the little soldiers I'd humped mountains with. They waved. Of course, they waved at everything flying in or out. Perhaps they were waving at their own dream of flying out someday.

The helicopter rose above the valley. All below was a tiny world—neatly laid-out plots of glistening paddies and stands of trees, ribbons of red clay that marked the roads, and squat men in tiger stripes and black pajamas waving, waving, waving. As the sun reflected off the mirrored surface of the rice paddies, the thought of going home suddenly saddened me. I clutched the flag to my chest and watched the valley get smaller and smaller, until it was as if I were leaving a world I'd never before seen.

You consider 130 grains of lead spiraling across a hundred-meter expanse at twelve hundred feet per second—toward you. You consider a mortar round bursting mere yards away, its concussion slamming a man to the ground, steel fragments slicing into another's shoulder and shielding you from damage. You consider an unpinned grenade, a boy, and how he dropped it in panic and ran. You consider those who fell to such events, the wounds weapons of war inflict—sinew and viscera exposed, dark-red blood pouring life from a wound as a man's story gurgles away in his throat. You consider your teammates' unplanned departures, zipped up in nylon coffins and tagged. You consider yourself—your sole injury an eardrum damaged in a mortar pit. You consider the fire-fights, the close misses and nearby hits. You once wrote in a book that survival was a matter of spitting in one direction and not another. You consider the truth of that and how lucky you were, how lucky you are. Then you see the beetle, your foot smashing it, and you think of them, the ones left behind, the slanting rain, the waiting and not knowing.

Bennie Adkins received the Distinguished Service Cross for his actions at A Shau. Though nominated for and deserving of the Medal of Honor, he was awarded the second-highest medal, a sad commentary on how the bravery of those who manned Special Forces camps at all costs was overlooked by those high up in the chain of command. Adkins's current status and whereabouts are unknown.

Andrew Brassfield, whose tour at Tra Bong was brief, remains missing in action, one of more than a thousand Americans still left unaccounted for from the Vietnam War.

Earl Brown, killed in action near Binh Hoa, received the Purple Heart. His daughter maintains a Web memorial to his and his teammates' memory on the Internet.

Donald Cameron served his tour and returned to Australia. He is retired there.

J. V. Carroll retired from the U.S. Army with the rank of sergeant major. He died in 2000.

Neil Davidson transferred out of Tra Bong. Current status unknown.

Capt. F. Fazekas was awarded the Military Cross for his efforts in trying to relieve Warrant Officer Swanton and Warrant Officer Wheatley. He served his tour and returned to Australia. Current status unknown.

John P. Fewell, killed in action in the area of Binh Hoa, received the Purple Heart.

Douglas Fox retired from the U.S. Army and died in 2005.

Cam Gamble left the army following two tours of duty, worked as an electrician, and after suffering post-traumatic stress disorder for an extended period retired in Georgia on a Veterans Administration pension.

Bill Green served his tour and returned to Australia. He died in 1999.

Richard Gregory transferred out of Tra Bong. Current status unknown.

Aaron Gritzmacher completed his tour and returned to civilian life. He retired from the airline industry in Texas. After the author's departure from Tra Bong, Gritz had a confrontation with Roger Holman, who threatened him. Gritz, carrying a shotgun at the time, jabbed the barrel in Holman's abdomen and told him to proceed. He was transported out of Tra Bong the next day, reassigned to Ha Tanh and later A-100, where he earned the Purple Heart and was twice awarded the Bronze Star with a *V* for valor.

Harmon Hodge served out his tour and returned Stateside. Current status unknown.

Roger Holman retired from the U.S. Army and reportedly became a police officer in Fayetteville, North Carolina. Current status unknown.

Earl Horan retired from the U.S. Army as a lieutenant colonel and currently sells real estate in Fayetteville, North Carolina.

Willy Hunter went to officer candidate school and became an officer. He served two more tours in Vietnam, the second as a company commander with the 101st Airborne. He receive the Bronze Star with a *V* for valor and retired as a captain. At last report he tours the country in an RV.

Donald "Jake" Jacobsen, killed in action west of Binh Hoa, received the Purple Heart.

Henry D. Luthy advanced to the post of command sergeant major of Special Forces and has since retired to civilian life. He serves as a consultant to security firms and the government.

Douglas Malone, wounded in action east of Binh Hoa, received the Purple Heart. Current status unknown.

Raymond C. Morris, lieutenant and assistant team leader

of team A7/03, left Ba To and transferred to A-100, where he served with both Henry Luthy and Richard Norwood. He received the Bronze Star with a *V* and an oak leaf. He retired from the army a lieutenant colonel and now resides in Florida with his wife. He has published three books, one being about Project Delta teams.

Richard Norwood served his tour, was discharged into civilian life, and earned a degree in literature. While serving with A-100 he received the Bronze Star. He lives in Orange County, California, where he worked as a consultant in the private sector. He is now retired.

Pablo Olivarez retired from the U.S. Army with the rank of master sergeant. He served a second tour in Vietnam with the MIKE Force and earned a Bronze Star for his service. He moved to Las Vegas, Nevada, in 1999, where he worked in the construction-equipment rental business. He died of liver failure on April 10, 2009. The author was at his side during Pablo's final days and read a eulogy at his funeral. More than two hundred attended, a testimony to his character.

Elmer J. Reifschneider, killed in action near Binh Hoa, received the Purple Heart. His children stay in touch with Earl Brown's daughter.

Paul Sheppard retired from the U.S. Army as a sergeant major and lives in the countryside in northwestern North Carolina.

Robert J. Swanton was killed in action near Binh Hoa along with Kevin Wheatley, who was attempting to save him.

John H. Truesdale was reported as killed in action. Information remains unconfirmed.

Kevin A. Wheatley, killed in action in Binh Hoa east of Tra Bong, posthumously received the Victoria Cross, the highest award for valor in the British Commonwealth.

Ralph Whitten served out his tour in Vietnam and returned to Australia.

The name of the chaplain, who was wounded on the operation, remains unknown to the author, as does the name of the radio operator accidentally wounded.

There is no knowing the fates of Cu or the Montagnard who served in Tra Bong. However, in return for their unwavering loyalty, the Special Forces Association has sponsored the safe emigration to the United States, raised money, and bought land for many Yards.

The author resides in Las Vegas, Nevada, where he teaches as a professor of English at the College of Southern Nevada. After his discharge, he worked as a deputy sheriff, a private investigator, a narcotics agent, a construction worker, a martial arts instructor, and a casino dealer. Like others on this list of men who served, he would trade the last four decades of life to return to that tour in Vietnam and again share hardship, heartbreak, and the rare, wonderful moments of laughter with his teammates.

This book was a search for truth and assembled mostly from the memories of the author and those who served with him. The contributions of former teammates were invaluable. Official documentation supporting the events was scant, so actions and time lines were reconstructed as accurately as possible from memory. Whatever small inaccuracies may exist in the text, they are unintentional and a direct result of the weakness of recall after the eclipse of four decades. The author did take liberties reconstructing conversations. The intention of the dialogue is to re-create some truthful representation of the moment. If the story fails to meet the expectation of those wishing to read about heroics, it's because it is a truthful examination, blemishes and all, of the author's experience. Soft-pedaling of any matter contained herein was never a consideration. Perhaps also, because we live in a time when courage and heroism are ill-defined, a reader may have the wrong impression of what constitutes heroism.

When we consider the number of notable battles that took place in Vietnam, the firefights and operations in and around Tra Bong may seem insignificant under the microscope of history, but they are deeply meaningful to those who served there. The casualty figures, six KIA and two WIA among advisers at the camp in a three-month period, speak of the high cost of war. However, these do not reflect the full measure in terms of the cost of human life. A modest estimate of allied casualties in Tra Bong would be more than a hundred. The VC did not leave their dead to be counted, so fixing a number to enemy KIAs would be a guess, but their losses had to have approximated those of our Vietnamese allies.

The actions of those who died in January 1966 were never recognized by the U.S. Army because no credible witnesses survived to offer accounts. Those of us who knew them have no doubt how they represented themselves that January day. They died honorably.

We answered the call to duty and soldiered as good men must. We were not honored in parades; no one shook our hands and thanked us when we returned. We built lives after the fact in much the way we answered the call to duty. We who survived tours at Tra Bong value those we served with by remembering that the finest honor is not to receive medals or accolades but to be honored by those whom you most honor. Two days before his death, surrounded by family and friends, Pablo introduced me as his brother, his "true brother," to all who came and went. What greater recognition can a man receive?

Gunning for Ho

Dummy Up and Deal: Inside the Culture of Casino Dealing

Talk to Me, James Dean

The Lucky

Minimal Damage